NICK FAWCETT
A Calendar of Classic Prayer

**kevin
mayhew**

First published in 2007 by
KEVIN MAYHEW LTD
Buxhall, Stowmarket, Suffolk, IP14 3BW
info@kevinmayhewltd.com
www.kevinmayhew.com

9 8 7 6 5 4 3 2 1 0

Paperback
ISBN-13: 978 184417 725 7
Catalogue No. 1500977

Presentation
ISBN-13: 978 184417 739 4
Catalogue No. 1500989

Cover design by Sara-Jane Came
Edited by Katherine Laidler
Typeset by Richard Weaver

Printed and bound in China

Contents

*In loving memory of Julie Aldridge
who faced life and death
with such courage, cheerfulness and dignity*

Introduction

One of the first pieces of advice I received during my training for the ministry was to compile a resource of classic prayers for use in personal devotion and public worship. Foolishly, I ignored that suggestion for many years. Yes, I had a handful of excellent devotional books such as John Baillie's *A Diary of Private Prayer*, Leslie Weatherhead's *A Private House of Prayer* and George Appleton's *Daily Prayers and Praise*, supplemented by a couple of second-hand anthologies, but I used them as the exception rather than the rule, preferring on the whole to extemporise in my prayers. Once in pastorate, however, I was soon struck by the beauty of many historic prayers such as those found in the ancient Order of Compline, the *Book of Common Prayer*, or those of spiritual giants like Augustine of Hippo, Thomas Aquinas, Francis of Assisi and Ignatius Loyola. Their lyricism was matched by profound spiritual insight, speaking for me in a way I couldn't achieve alone and, more than that, speaking *to* me. Time and again I felt God challenging, inspiring, comforting and teaching through their words.

I'm not suggesting for a moment that other people's prayers can be a substitute for our own, however eloquent they may be. That would risk settling for a borrowed faith rather than personal relationship with Christ. But classic prayers can be a wonderful complement to our own, not only helping to articulate our thoughts when words don't come easily, but also opening up new horizons, expressing our deepest needs and drawing us into a deeper awareness of God's presence.

Of course, there are no accepted criteria by which a prayer can be judged a classic. What appeals to one may leave another cold, comparisons being arbitrary if not odious. For me, though, what matters above all is that the prayer combines sincerity with insight, expressing deep faith coupled with genuine wisdom. Thousands of prayers do just that, but those I've selected for this book touched me personally, leaving a sense that I've been in touch with God. Some were found online, others in compilations of prayers, and others again in service books, while many are simply so well known they've become integral to the rich heritage of the Church.

A particular aim in my selection has been to emphasise that prayer is wider than it's sometimes painted. As well as silent contemplation, which cannot easily be reproduced in the written word, it includes poetry, which most certainly *can*. So here you will find prayers drawn from some surprising sources: the poetry of Gerard Manley Hopkins and Anne Brontë, for example, not to mention some of our most celebrated hymns. God can also speak through the insights of other faiths, so although most of the prayers here are drawn from the Christian tradition, you'll find examples of Muslim, Hindu, Buddhist, Jewish and Baha'i spirituality, among others, often in words of great beauty. Nor are great prayers reserved for the outwardly pious: there are a couple here from Sir Francis Drake – hero to some but bloodthirsty pirate to others – and several more written by people whose lifestyles were questionable, to say the least. All this gives just a taste of the stunning variety of sources, concerns and styles of prayer repre-sented in these pages.

I chose the format of a calendar of prayer for two simple reasons. One was to encourage a daily discipline of prayer. In our frenetic modern-day world it can be hard sometimes to find as much time and space for prayer as we'd like, and the few moments we snatch can be unsatisfying simply because we scarcely have time to gather our thoughts. A devotional resource at such times can be invaluable, often leading to prayers of our own. My second aim was to encourage reflection. The temptation when reading a compilation of prayers is to rush through it without fully taking in what's being said. Taking the prayers day by day gives time to consider them more carefully, making their words our own or at least being challenged by them. With that in mind I've given a brief introduction to each one, giving a little biographical information about the author and some thoughts on their theme.

We are privileged to have a rich legacy of prayers that has been handed down across the centuries. They have stood the test of time simply because they've spoken so powerfully to so many people. If I would add one prayer in the context of this book it would be that they speak as powerfully to *you* each day.

Nick Fawcett

JANUARY

1 January

Another day, another month, another year. Today, perhaps more than any other, inspires thoughts of past, present and future. What words could be more apposite, then, than the memorable lines of Isaac Watts (1674–1748), taken from one his hymns but, at heart, a prayer of faith and trust.

Our God, our help in ages past,
our hope for years to come,
our shelter from the stormy blast,
and our eternal home!

Beneath the shadow of thy throne
still may we dwell secure;
sufficient is thine arm alone,
and our defence is sure.

Before the hills in order stood,
or earth received her frame,
from everlasting thou art God,
to endless years the same.

A thousand ages in thy sight
are like an evening gone;
short as the watch that ends the night
before the rising sun.

Time, like an ever rolling stream,
bears all its sons away;
they fly forgotten as a dream
dies at the opening day.

Our God our help in ages past,
our hope for years to come,
be thou our guard while life shall last,
and our eternal home.

2 January

Although described as an old English prayer, I'm not sure
that the following is really a prayer. In the traditional
sense, it's probably not, but there's actually far more to
prayer than addressing God in religious language, or
indeed even addressing God at all. Meditation and
reflection can play as much a part, and without doubt
these words are worth reflecting upon. Who wrote them
is not known, but they can speak to us as surely as God
must have spoken to their author.

Take time to work,
    it is the price of success.
Take time to think,
    it is the source of power.
Take time to play,
    it is the secret of perpetual youth.
Take time to read,
    it is the foundation of wisdom.
Take time to be friendly,
    it is the road to happiness.
Take time to dream,
    it is hitching your wagon to a star.
Take time to love and be loved,
    it is the privilege of the gods.
Take time to look around,
    it is too short a day to be selfish.
Take time to laugh,
    it is the music of the soul.

3 January

One of the most prolific early writers of prayers was St Augustine of Hippo (354–430). Raised as a Christian by his devout mother, it looked for a time as though his pagan father's influence would win over, for the young Augustine turned away from his faith and for a time lived a dissolute life, details of which were later recounted in what is probably his most celebrated work, *Confessions*. Perhaps it was memories of these misspent years that inspired his longing to know and love God better. The following is but one example: a plea for help and guidance in life now, so that we may be the more ready for life to come.

My God, let me know and love you,
    so that I may find my happiness in you.
Since I cannot fully achieve this on earth,
    help me to improve daily until I may do so
        to the full.
Enable me to know you ever more on earth,
    so that I may know you perfectly in heaven.
Enable me to love you ever more on earth,
    so that I may love you perfectly in heaven.
In that way my joy may be great on earth,
    and perfect with you in heaven.
Amen.

4 January

One of the most celebrated prayers of all time is that of St Patrick (sometimes known as St Patrick's Breastplate). A simple and all-embracing expression of trust, it has inspired countless generations of believers, speaking powerfully for them in turn. We'll come to the best-known part later in this book, but here are the opening stanzas – a memorable prayer in themselves.

I arise today
    through a mighty strength, the invocation of the
        Trinity,
    through the belief in the threeness,
    through confession of the oneness of the Creator
        of Creation.

I arise today
    through the strength of Christ's birth with his
        baptism,
    through the strength of his crucifixion with his burial,
    through the strength of his resurrection with his
        ascension,
    through the strength of his descent for the
        judgement of Doom.

I arise today
    through the strength of the love of Cherubim,
    in obedience of angels,
    in the service of archangels,
    in hope of resurrection to meet with reward,
    in prayers of patriarchs,
    in predictions of prophets,
    in preaching of apostles,
    in faith of confessors,
    in innocence of holy virgins,
    in deeds of righteous men.

CALENDAR OF CLASSIC PRAYER

I arise today
    through the strength of heaven:
    light of sun,
    radiance of moon,
    splendour of fire,
    speed of lightning,
    swiftness of wind,
    depth of sea,
    stability of earth,
    firmness of rock.

5 January

If you're looking for classic prayers then there's no better place to start than the Bible, yet strangely we often overlook this wonderful source. The Psalms in particular brim over with expressions of praise, confession and thanksgiving, countless passages able to speak both to and for us. Below I've linked together words from Psalms 139:23, 24; 69:5; 119:176a and 51:10 to create a powerful prayer of confession.

Search me, O God, and know my heart.
Test me and know my thoughts.
Look to see if there is any wickedness within me,
    and lead me in your everlasting way.
You know my folly, O God;
    there can be no hiding my wrongs from you.
I have wandered astray like a lost sheep.
Fashion a new and unblemished heart within me,
    O God; imbue me with a true and faithful spirit.

6 January

Our prayer today comes from Thomas Ken (1637–1711), Anglican bishop, poet and celebrated hymn-writer. Ordained in 1662, he served parishes in Essex, the Isle of Wight and Hampshire before later being appointed by Charles II as chaplain to Princess Mary. Subsequently made Bishop of Bath and Wells, one of his first duties in that office was to minister to King Charles as he lay on his deathbed. Later, during the reign of James II, he was imprisoned in the Tower of London for refusing to accept the Declaration of Indulgence, also known as the Declaration for the Liberty of Conscience, which suspended laws punishing Catholics and Protestant dissenters, but he was acquitted in the same year. He died at Longleat House, the home of his friend, Lord Weymouth.

The following prayer, one of several you'll find in this book written by Ken, celebrates the forgiveness and new life won for us through Christ's suffering and death.

To God the Father who first loved us,
    and made us accepted in the beloved Son;
    to God the Son, who loved us
    and washed us from our sins in his own blood;
    to God the Holy Spirit,
    who sheds abroad the love of God in our hearts;
    to the one true God
    be all love and all glory for time and eternity.
Amen.

7 January

I'm not altogether sure who wrote the following prayer, though it may have been the American theologian Reinhold Niebuhr (1892–1971). Incredibly simple, it is equally profound, consecrating the past, present and future into God's sure keeping.

Lord,
  forgive what I have been,
  bless what I am,
  and direct what I shall be.
Amen.

8 January

Our words today come from Richard of Chichester (1197–1253). After a time as chancellor of Oxford University and then of the Diocese of Canterbury, he went on to become Bishop of Chichester in 1244, earning widespread acclaim for his devout life and faithful ministry. He's remembered above all for the following prayer – a joyful outpouring of thanksgiving coupled with a plea for growth in grace. Its closing sentence was popularised in the Christian musical production *Godspell*.

Thanks be to you, my Lord Jesus Christ,
    for all the benefits you have won for me;
    for all the pains and insults you have borne for me,
    O most merciful redeemer, friend and brother.
May I know you more clearly,
    love you more dearly
    and follow you more nearly,
    day by day.
Amen.

9 January

A number of historical prayers are known as the 'Universal Prayer', including the following. It is one of many memorable prayers written by popes, and this one is the work of Clement XI (1649–1721). As well as being spiritually profound it is also incredibly long, so much so that I've chosen to reproduce it in excerpts during the course of this book. Today's section asks for wisdom and guidance in daily life.

Make me prudent in planning,
    courageous in taking risks.
Make me patient in suffering,
    unassuming in prosperity.
Keep me, Lord, attentive in prayer,
    temperate in food and drink,
    diligent in my work,
    firm in my good intentions.
Let my conscience be clear,
    my conduct without fault,
    my speech blameless,
    my life well-ordered.
Put me on guard against my human weaknesses.
Let me cherish your love for me,
    keep your law,
    and come at last to your salvation.
Amen.

10 January

One of the most influential Christian writers of the early twentieth century was the Anglican novelist, poet and mystic Evelyn Underhill (1875–1941). Raised by parents with little interest in spirituality, she was an atheist in her youth, but later became a committed Anglo-Catholic. One of her chief aims was to earth the gospel in daily life, many of her writings (including several written under the pseudonym John Cordelier) developing a practical Christianity, accessible to all. The following, taken from her book *Meditations and Prayers* (1949), is an example of that concern, and offers a perfect way to commit the routine of each day into God's care.

Lord, help me to think of my small, formless,
    imperfect soul
    as constantly subject to your loving, creative action,
    here and now, in all the bustle of my daily life,
    its ups and downs,
    its anxieties and tensions
    and its dreary, unspiritual stretches –
    and gradually giving it, through these things,
    its ordained form and significance.
So that in all the events of my life,
    even the most trivial,
    I experience your pressure,
    Creative Artist.
Amen.

11 January

I've spoken already of the Bible as an excellent source of prayer, and nowhere is that more so than when it comes to praise. Passage after passage bubbles over with joyful acclamation of God's greatness and goodness. Below, for example, is a selection of verses from the Psalms and book of Isaiah (Psalm 40:5; Isaiah 25:1; Psalm 89:1, 2a).

Lord God,
    you have piled high your marvellous deeds
    and your thoughtfulness towards us;
    none can begin to compare with you!
I will make known what you have done to all,
    speaking of your blessings beyond number.
You, O Lord, are my God.
I will acclaim you and praise your name,
    for you have done marvellous things,
    fulfilling your age-old purpose,
    dependable and certain.
I will sing unceasingly of your unfailing love, O Lord;
    I will declare your faithfulness to all generations.
Your constant love is unchanged from the beginning
    of time, and your faithfulness is as permanent
    as the heavens.

12 January

Today we have another prayer written originally as a hymn. Penned by the Scottish Congregational minister John Hunter (1848–1917), it simply but eloquently sums up the frustration we can feel at failing to live up to our faith. Despite our best intentions, time and again we fail to produce the goods, obedience in discipleship coming far less easily than we'd like to think. As with learning anything, we have to work at it if we are to achieve our goal. Practice, as they say, makes perfect.

Dear Master, in whose life I see
all that I long, but fail to be,
let thy clear light for ever shine,
to shame and guide this life of mine.

Though what I dream and what I do
in my poor days are always two,
help me, oppressed by things undone,
O thou, whose deeds and dreams were one.

13 January

On 13 January Catholics remember St Hilary of Poitiers (315–367), bishop and doctor of the Church, so it seems appropriate to include one of his prayers here. Hilary (Latin name 'Hilarius') is noted especially for his defence of Christianity against the so-called Arian heresy, which downplayed the status of Christ in relation to God and thus undermined the doctrine of the Trinity. Labelled 'the illustrious doctor of the churches' by none other than Augustine of Hippo, his name lives on in 'Hilary term', a name given to the second academic semester in certain universities. In this prayer, his concern for true faith takes centre stage.

Father, keep us from vain strife of words.
Grant to us constant profession of the truth!
Preserve us in a true and undefiled faith
　　so that we may hold fast to that which we professed
　　when we were baptised in the Name of the Father,
　　Son and Holy Spirit –
　　that we may have thee for our Father,
　　that we may abide in thy Son
　　and in the fellowship of the Holy Spirit,
　　through Jesus Christ our Lord.
Amen.

14 January

God has different ways of answering prayer when we find ourselves up against it. Sometimes he removes the problem, but at other times, as a prayer of the sixteenth-century bishop Miles Coverdale indicates, he may simply give us the strength we need to face it.

O give us patience and steadfastness in adversity,
   strengthen our weakness,
   comfort us in trouble and distress,
   help us to fight;
   grant unto us that in true obedience and
      contentment of mind
   we may give over our own wills unto thee,
   our Father in all things,
   according to the example of thy beloved Son;
   that in adversity we grudge not,
   but offer up ourselves unto thee without
      contradiction.
O give us a willing and cheerful mind,
   that we may gladly suffer and bear all things
      for thy sake.
Amen.

15 January

Our prayer for today was written as a hymn by Thomas Curtis Clark (1877–1953). It reminds us that nowhere is outside Christ's love and purpose. That doesn't mean, though, that we can leave everything to him. For too many, life is a constant and demanding struggle, the plight of millions calling for a response. Use these words, then, not simply to remind yourself of God's concern for all but to commit yourself to responding to others in whatever way you can.

Where restless crowds are thronging along the city ways,
where pride and greed and turmoil consume the
     fevered days,
where vain ambitions banish all thoughts of praise
     and prayer,
the people's spirits waver: but thou, O Christ, art there.

In scenes of want and sorrow and haunts of flagrant
     wrong,
in homes where kindness falters, and strife and fear
     are strong,
in busy street of barter, in lonely thoroughfare,
the people's spirits languish: but thou, O Christ,
     art there.

O Christ, behold thy people – they press on every hand!
Bring light to all the cities of our beloved land.
May all our bitter striving give way to visions fair
of righteousness and justice: for thou, O Christ,
     art there.

16 January

Today a prayer of the third-century theologian, Origen of Alexandria (185–254). Origen's father was martyred for his faith in 202, a fate Origen was to share just over 50 years later. During his lifetime, however, he achieved fame as a teacher, preacher and scholar, his reputation continuing today as one of the most eminent of the early Church Fathers. His books include a massive commentary on the Bible, together with various other exegetical works. When renewed persecution of the Church erupted in the middle of the third century, Origen was brutally tortured, his death almost certainly resulting from the horrific treatment he endured, but through it all his faith held firm. The following words help to explain the secret of his courage and commitment.

Lord, put your hands on our eyes,
  that we shall be able to see not only that which is
    visible
  but also that which is invisible.
Let our eyes be focused
  not only on that which is present
  but also on things that are yet to come.
Unveil our heart's visions,
  that in spirit we may gaze on your glory.
Amen.

17 January

What should we pray for when things are so difficult we barely feel like praying? Many feel that due reverence before God precludes them from opening up and expressing their true feelings. Surely he'll be shocked by our presumption, perhaps even angered to the point of punishing us? If you think that, then you haven't read the Psalms recently, for time and again there we find blunt outpourings of dismay and frustration. The following, for example, comes from Psalm 55 (verses 1, 2a, 4 and 5).

O God,
    listen to my prayer,
    and do not keep your distance when I appeal for
      your mercy.
Attend to me, and answer me;
    I am agitated, whingeing and grumbling.
My heart is tormented,
    crushed by the fear of death,
    all manner of anxiety and dread having come over
      me
    to the point that terror overwhelms me.

18 January

Another prayer today from the pen – or should it be quill! – of St Augustine of Hippo (354–430). If yesterday's prayer articulated a sense of despair at God failing to answer when we call, here is a perfect counter-balance, Augustine gratefully acknowledging God's presence in every moment of life. We may not always see it, but he is there nonetheless, and sometimes it's good simply to thank him for that assurance he gives.

O my God,
   light of the blind and strength of the weak;
   yes, also light of those that see and strength of the
      strong:
   we turn and seek you,
   for we know you are here in our hearts when we
      converse with you;
   when we cast ourselves upon you;
   when we weep, and you do gently wipe away our
      tears,
   and also when we weep for joy
   because you who made us does remake and
      comfort us.
Grant that we may entirely love you,
   even unto the end.
Amen.

19 January

One of the most respected theologians and churchmen of the fourth century was St Ambrose, Bishop of Milan (c. 340–397). Renowned for his ascetic lifestyle and generosity to the poor as much as for his theological achievements, he is designated by historians as one of the four Western Doctors of the Church, the others being St Augustine of Hippo, St Jerome and St Gregory. An example of his faith and courage is seen in the reply he reputedly gave to a general council of the Church called by the emperor Gratian to discuss the issue of Arianism: 'If you demand my person, I am ready to submit: carry me to prison or to death, I will not resist; but I will never betray the Church of Christ. I will not call upon the people to succour me; I will die at the foot of the altar rather than desert it.' Alongside his many writings, characterised by an emphasis on divine grace, Ambrose composed several hymns, both tunes and words, of which the following is an example. His lovely words remind us that God touches every part of life, anything and everything able to speak of his love and presence.

O splendour of God's glory bright,
who bringest forth the light from Light;
O Light, of light the fountain-spring;
O Day, our days illumining;
come, very Sun of truth and love,
come in thy radiance from above,
and shed the Holy Spirit's ray
on all we think or do today.

20 January

Of all the early Church Fathers and Doctors, none was more learned than St Jerome (c. 347–420). Best known for translating the Bible from Hebrew and Greek into Latin in what's known as the Vulgate, he lived much of his life as a hermit, continuing this ascetic existence even after he was ordained as a bishop. His extensive writings and letters are largely concerned with fighting what he saw as threats to the orthodoxy of the Church, but if that sounds a little arid, the following prayer is remarkably warm and human in contrast.

O Lord,
   show your mercy to me and gladden my heart.
I am like the man on the way to Jericho
   who was overtaken by robbers,
     wounded and left for dead.
O Good Samaritan, come to my aid,
   I am like the sheep that went astray.
O Good Shepherd, seek me out
   and bring me home in accord with your will.
Let me dwell in your house all the days of my life
   and praise you for ever and ever
     with those who are there.
Amen.

21 January

I've already mentioned the power of the Psalms to express praise and worship, and here today is another classic example. The words come from Psalm 89:5 and 86:8-10, and between them they celebrate God's awesome power and faithfulness, beyond comparing to anyone or anything else. Use these words to acknowledge his greatness and declare your faith in his eternal purpose.

The heavens acknowledge your mighty deeds, O Lord;
    and the congregation of the holy ones proclaims
       your constancy.
No one among the gods is like you, O Lord,
    nor are any deeds like yours.
All people that you have made will come and bow
    in homage before you, O Lord,
    and give glory to your name,
       for you are great and do breathtaking things.
You alone are God.

22 January

It's not known who wrote the following prayer or when exactly it was written; the most that can be said is that it was found on a papyrus dated to between the second and fourth century. Whoever wrote it, though, its plea for mercy and trust in God's ability to wipe the slate clean and help us start again is one that speaks as powerfully today as ever.

Helper of all who turn to you,
    light of all who are in the dark,
    creator of all that grows from seed,
    promoter of all spiritual growth,
    have mercy on me, Lord,
    and make me a temple fit for you.
Do not look too closely at my sins,
    for if you are quick to notice my faults
    I shall not dare to appear before you.
In your great mercy,
    in your boundless love,
    wash away my sins by the hand of Jesus Christ,
    your only child,
    the chief healer of souls.
Amen.

23 January

Of all the prayers expressing a response to God's love, few can be more powerful than the following, written by St Francis de Sales (1567–1662). Highly regarded for his abilities as a spiritual counsellor and preacher, he emphasised that growth in Christian maturity is open to all rather than reserved for the religious elite. As Bishop of Geneva he was to become one of the leading lights in the Counter-Reformation, the movement of missionary activity and reform in the Catholic Church beginning in the mid-sixteenth century in the wake of the Protestant Reformation. Francis is perhaps best remembered, however, for his classic books, his literary talents causing Pope Pius XI in 1923 to declare him the patron of writers and journalists. The prayer below gives us a flavour of his way with words. Make it your own.

Lord, I am yours,
    and I must belong to no one but you.
My soul is yours,
    and must live only by you.
My will is yours,
    and must love only for you.
I must love you as my first cause,
    since I am from you.
I must love you as my end and rest,
    since I am for you.
I must love you more than my own being,
    since my being subsists by you.
I must love you more than myself,
    since I am all yours and all in you.
Amen.

24 January

Confession, they say, is good for the soul. One person who wouldn't have argued with that is King David, the writer of the thirty-second psalm. His words there (verses 1-5) exude thanksgiving to God for the forgiveness he so willingly offers and for the inner health of body, mind and spirit that comes from getting mistakes off our chest and putting them for ever behind us.

How happy are those whose sins are forgiven,
    covered over once and for all.
How happy are those who God regards as blameless,
    and who have found purity of spirit.
While I remained silent,
    my body grew weary with my constant groaning,
    for day and night your hand weighed heavily upon
       me;
    my strength dried up like sap in the heat of
       summer.
Then I acknowledged my sin and did not conceal my
    guilt from you.
I said, 'I will confess my disobedience to the Lord',
    and you absolved me from my guilt and sin.
Hallelujah!
Amen.

25 January

Few times have seen such religious and political ferment in Britain as the years of the English Civil War (1642–1648) – a conflict that ended, of course, with the triumph of Oliver Cromwell and his Puritan supporters. Not that the victory was long-lived, the austere and sometimes bigoted religious views subsequently foisted upon the common people provoking swift hostility, and, in time, the return of the English monarchy. One man who opposed the excesses of Puritanism from the start was churchman William Laud (1573–1645), who, under the patronage of Charles I became Bishop of Bath and Wells, and then of London, and finally Archbishop of Canterbury. His zeal for the Anglican liturgy, however, was his undoing, his attempt to impose this in Scotland leading to his arrest, imprisonment and subsequent beheading on Tower Hill. Few of us today will feel anywhere near as strongly about Church order and practice, but I'm sure we'd all happily share in this beautiful prayer for the Church.

Gracious Father, I pray for your holy Christian
    Church.
Fill it with all truth, in all truth with all peace.
Where it is corrupt, cleanse it.
Where it is in error, direct it.
Where it is superstitious, rectify it.
Where anything is amiss, reform it.
Where it is right, strengthen and confirm it.
Where it is in want, supply its need.
Where it is divided and torn apart, heal the divisions,
    O Holy One of Israel.
Amen.

26 January

An adaptation today of a prayer by the twelfth-century Cistercian monk, philosopher and theologian Isaac of Stella (*c.* 1100–1169). In contrast to many theologians of his time, he strongly believed that, with God's help, the human mind can gain deep insight into eternal spiritual truths, even though full understanding will always be beyond us. His memorable words here fully bear out that conviction.

You yourself are my contemplation,
  my delight.
I seek you, for your own sake, above all else.
From you yourself I feed within.
You are the field in which I labour,
  the food for which I labour.
You are my cause,
  my goal,
  my beginning,
  and my end without end.
You, for me, are eternity.
Amen.

27 January

Of those revered in some circles as saints, probably few capture the public imagination as much as St Francis of Assisi (1182–1226). Partly, I suspect, that's down to his fabled love of animals, and partly also it reflects the power of his celebrated prayer for peace, which we will come to later in this book. Francis, of course, also founded the Franciscan Order of monks, devoting much of his life to the service of lepers and the poor. He was to write many prayers, including the following, which moves from acknowledgement of sin to a heartfelt plea for renewal.

Almighty, eternal, just and merciful God,
    give us miserable ones the grace to do for you alone
    what we know you want us to do
    and always to desire what pleases you.
Inwardly cleansed,
    interiorly enlightened and inflamed by the fire of
        the Holy Spirit,
    may we be able to follow in the footprints of your
        beloved Son,
    our Lord Jesus Christ,
    and, by your grace alone,
    may we make our way to you, Most High,
    who live and rule in perfect Trinity and simple
        Unity,
    and are glorified,
    God almighty,
    for ever and ever.
Amen.

28 January

Our prayer today comes from St Claude de la Colombiere (1641–1682), a French priest who, during the reign of Charles II, served as chaplain to Mary of Modena, the Duchess of York. Claude's example of holiness captured the imagination of Protestants and Catholics alike, but when he was accused of being part of the Titus Oates plot to overthrow the king he was imprisoned and subsequently banished from England. His time in prison took a heavy toll on his health and he died just two years afterwards. Here, in his so-called Despair Prayer, we catch a glimpse of the inner turmoil he must have experienced but also, and above all, of the faith that sustained him throughout his all-too-short life.

Lord,
    I am in this world to show your mercy to others.
Other people will glorify you by making visible the
    power of your grace
    by their fidelity and constancy to you.
For my part I will glorify you
    by making known how good you are to sinners,
    that your mercy is boundless
    and that no sinner,
    no matter how great his offences,
    should have reason to despair of pardon.
If I have grievously offended you, my Redeemer,
    let me not offend you even more
    by thinking that you are not kind enough to
        pardon me.
Amen.

29 January

Most readers will, I'm sure, immediately recognise today's 'prayer'. The words, of course, come from the great hymn by Thomas O. Chisholm (1866–1960), a favourite of countless Christians across the years, and understandably so given the beauty of the words and depth of faith they express. Raised on a farm in Kentucky, Chisholm went on to become a schoolteacher and finally a Methodist minister. Although he was to write close on a thousand hymns, it's for this one that he will always be remembered.

Great is thy faithfulness, O God my Father,
there is no shadow of turning with thee;
thou changest not, thy compassions they fail not;
as thou hast been thou for ever wilt be.
Great is thy faithfulness! Great is thy faithfulness!
Morning by morning new mercies I see;
all I have needed thy hand hath provided,
great is thy faithfulness, Lord, unto me.

Summer and winter, and springtime and harvest,
sea, moon and stars in their courses above,
join with all nature in manifold witness
to thy great faithfulness, mercy and love.
Great is thy faithfulness! Great is thy faithfulness!
Morning by morning new mercies I see;
all I have needed thy hand hath provided,
great is thy faithfulness, Lord, unto me.

Pardon for sin and a peace that endureth,
thine own dear presence to cheer and to guide;
strength for today and bright hope for tomorrow,
blessing all mine, with ten thousand beside!

Great is thy faithfulness! Great is thy faithfulness!
Morning by morning new mercies I see;
all I have needed thy hand hath provided,
great is thy faithfulness, Lord, unto me.

30 January

Some prayers are so short that they can hardly be called prayers at all, yet their words are truly profound. Today I've chosen two such prayers, both offering much to reflect on. The first comes from the Tudor statesman, scholar, lawyer and martyr St Thomas More (1478–1535), whose faith was so strong he was ready to die for it. Refusing to acknowledge the supremacy of Henry VIII as Supreme Head of the Church of England, he was found guilty of treason and beheaded on Tower Hill, London. It's easy enough to pray the following prayer, much harder to be like More and truly mean it.

The things that we pray for, good Lord,
    give us your grace to work for.
Amen.

The author of our next prayer needs no introduction. It was Mother Teresa (1910–1997), another person who translated prayer into action – in her case among the poor and destitute of India. We rightly marvel at her faith, yet Teresa recognised that, like everything, it depended solely on God.

Lord, increase my faith,
    bless my efforts and work,
    now and for evermore.
Amen.

31 January

We've well-loved words today of the great hymn-writer Charles Wesley (1707–1788). They express a sense of wonder, almost disbelief, that God can have time for flawed and faithless people like you and me. Yet that, of course, is the message at the heart of the gospel: that God, despite all our unworthiness, values us so much that he was willing to give his Son so that we might know his love and share his life. Join now in celebrating that awesome truth.

And can it be that I should gain
an interest in the Saviour's blood?
Died he for me, who caused his pain?
For me, who him to death pursued?
Amazing love! How can it be
that thou, my God, shouldst die for me?

He left his Father's throne above –
so free, so infinite his grace –
emptied himself of all but love,
and bled for Adam's helpless race.
'Tis mercy all, immense and free;
for, O my God, it found out me!

Long my imprisoned spirit lay
fast bound in sin and nature's night;
thine eye diffused a quick'ning ray,
I woke, the dungeon flamed with light;
my chains fell off, my heart was free;
I rose, went forth, and followed thee.

No condemnation now I dread;
Jesus, and all in him, is mine!
Alive in him, my living Head,
and clothed in righteousness divine,
bold I approach the eternal throne,
and claim the crown, through Christ my own.

FEBRUARY

1 February

Undeserved mercy – if one thing sums up the Christian message, it is surely this. However much we fail him, God is ready to show forgiveness, not because we deserve it but because his nature is constantly to show love. That wonderful truth is taken up in the well-loved words of the Scottish hymn-writer Elizabeth Clephane (1830–1869) – a woman who, though dogged by ill health throughout her life, was widely noted for her sunny disposition, being affectionately known in her hometown of Melrose by the delightful sobriquet 'Sunbeam'.

Beneath the cross of Jesus
I fain would take my stand,
the shadow of a mighty rock
within a weary land;
a home within a wilderness,
a rest upon the way,
from the burning heat at noontide
and the burden of the day.

Upon that cross of Jesus
mine eyes at times can see
the very dying form of One
who suffered there for me;
and from my stricken heart, with tears,
two wonders I confess –
the wonders of redeeming love,
and my unworthiness.

2 February

Today we have words of the clergyman and scholar
Lancelot Andrewes (1555–1626). Given high office
during the reigns of Elizabeth I and James I, he served
as the Bishop of Chichester in the time of the latter and
played an important part in overseeing the translation
of the Authorised Version of the Bible. A prolific writer
and preacher, many of his prayers are still used today,
including the following, in which Andrewes gives
thanks for God's constant grace and goodness.

For all these, and also for all other mercies,
    known and unknown,
    open and secret,
    remembered by us or now forgotten,
    kindnesses received by us willingly or even against
      our will,
    we praise you,
    we bless you,
    we thank you,
    and will praise and bless and thank you all the days
      of our life,
    through Jesus Christ our Lord.
Amen.

3 February

Our prayer today is an ancient one, coming from the fourth-century Divine Liturgy of St Basil – the Eucharistic service followed during Lent and Christmas within the Orthodox and other Byzantine traditions. Its author was Basil the Great (c. 330–379), bishop of Caesarea and revered within many traditions as a saint and Doctor of the Church. Somewhat akin to St Nicholas or his Westernised caricature, Father Christmas, within Eastern traditions Basil is believed to give gifts to children every 1 January. An ascetic monk and respected writer, he was especially revered for his work among the poor and disadvantaged, as reflected in his words here.

Lord,
    the help of the helpless,
    the hope of those past hope,
    the rescuer of the storm-tossed,
    the harbour of the voyagers,
    the healer of the sick:
    I ask you to become all things to all people,
    for you know the needs of each one.
Accept us all into your kingdom,
    making us children of light;
    and give us your peace and love,
    Lord our God.
Amen.

4 February

God can speak to us in unusual ways and through unexpected sources, including other religious traditions. The following, for example, is a Baha'i prayer, but it's one, I think, that every Christian would be happy to use. Simply and sincerely it asks God to grant his people help, guidance, unity and strength in all they do – a plea each one of us would echo.

O my God! O my God!
Unite the hearts of your servants,
    and reveal to them your great purpose.
May they follow your commandments
    and abide in your law.
Help them, O God, in their endeavour,
    and grant them strength to serve you, O God.
Leave them not to themselves
    but guide their steps by the light of your
        knowledge,
    and cheer their hearts by your love.
Truly, you are their helper and Lord.
Amen.

5 February

The words of the following prayer will ring a bell with many, but its very familiarity can lead us to forget it's actually taken from Scripture and, what's more, from one of the most unsung books of the New Testament: that of Jude. It's found at the close of the book (verses 24 and 25), and few ascriptions of praise and worship have ever surpassed it.

To him, our only Saviour,
  who is able to keep our feet from slipping
  and to present us faultless and brimming over with
    joy
  into the glorious presence of God –
  to him be glory and majesty,
  dominion and power,
  now and for evermore.
Amen.

6 February

Some words have a special ring to them, don't they, and for me, the following passage, taken from Psalm 51 (verses 1 to 4, 7, and 9 to 12), is a case in point. If ever I'm struggling to express remorse before God, or find myself doubting his mercy, I turn to these words, for they are not only able to speak to me but succeed perfectly in expressing my innermost feelings. Use them in turn to confess your faults and find forgiveness.

Be merciful to me, O God.
Through your constant love and overflowing mercy,
    obliterate my transgressions.
Wash away my faults and purify me from my sins,
    for I am all too aware of my mistakes
    and my weakness daily stares me in the face.
I've sinned ultimately against you and you alone,
    doing what is evil in your sight,
    so your words are justified
    and your verdict is beyond reproach.
Sprinkle me with hyssop,
    and I will be clean;
    wash me,
    and I will become whiter than snow.
Hide your face from my wrongdoings,
    and expunge from the record all my faults.
Create in me a clean heart, O God,
    and renew a right spirit within me.
Cast me not away from your presence,
    and take not your Holy Spirit from me.
Restore to me the joy of your salvation,
and uphold me with a willing spirit.
Amen.

7 February

Sometimes we consciously evade God's presence, unwilling to meet his searching challenge. More often though, we simply fail to see, God's greatness and goodness being almost too much to comprehend. The following words – a lovely poem-cum-prayer written by the country parson, poet and philosopher John Norris (1657–1711) – remind us of that greatness and seek God's help in discerning more clearly his presence in every moment and aspect of life.

In vain, great God, in vain I try
to escape thy quick all-searching eye:
thou with one undivided view
dost look the whole creation through.

My private walks to thee are known;
in solitude I'm not alone:
thou round my bed a guard dost keep;
thine eyes are open while mine sleep.

Thou art the light by which I see;
be it my joy to live in thee:
beset me, Lord, behind, before;
and draw my heart to love thee more.

8 February

Our prayer today comes from the Welsh author, poet, theologian and clergyman Isaac Williams (1802–1865) – a leading figure alongside John Henry Newman and John Keble in the High Anglican reformist group known as the Oxford Movement. He wrote numerous poetic prayers, including the following, asking for God's help and guidance in walking the way of Christ. As each of us will be all too aware, we can so easily slip up, despite our best intentions.

Be thou my guardian and my guide,
and hear me when I call;
let not my slippery footsteps slide,
and hold me lest I fall.

And if I tempted am to sin,
and outward things are strong,
do thou, O Lord, keep watch within,
and save my soul from wrong.

9 February

Our prayer today comes from the Revd Dr J. H. Jowett
(1864–1923), one-time minister of Westminster Chapel.
Its brevity reinforces its theme: namely that the little
things can be as important as the big and that Christian
commitment involves consecrating the small affairs of
life just as much as the large.

My Father in heaven,
   teach me the value of little things.
Show me how to consecrate what seems insignificant,
   and to recognise the light of your presence in every
      moment.
May I glory the day by offering each minute to be
   redeemed by your love.
I offer you all my moments.
Amen.

10 February

Today's prayer, on the face of it, is rather a sombre one. It was written by the Egyptian hermit, mystic and one-time Bishop of Jerusalem, St Macarius (300-390), towards the end of his life, and thus takes the theme of approaching death. Not only this, but it focuses on the writer's unworthiness, his realisation that nothing he might do can atone for his sins. Yet there is nothing mournful or defeatist about his words – on the contrary, he is able to look forward with anticipation, confident that what he cannot do himself God will achieve through his great mercy. Even if we have many years of life still to look forward to, the sentiments of his prayer can speak for us in turn.

Lord,
> be merciful now that my life is approaching its end
> and the evening awaits me.
There is not enough time for me to cleanse myself
> of my sins,
> for they are so many.
Heal me while I am still on earth,
> and I shall be truly healthy.
In your mercy, move me to repent
> so that I shall not be ashamed when I meet you
> > in heaven.
Amen.

11 February

I've chosen for today a prayer by Giovanni Montini (1897–1978), more commonly known as Pope Paul VI. One of the most influential popes in recent history, he presided over the latter stages of the Second Vatican Council, which brought so many reforms to the Catholic Church. His words here reflect the compassionate spirit and global horizons that marked his papacy.

Make us worthy, Lord,
    to serve our brothers and sisters throughout
        the world
    who live and die in poverty and hunger.
Give them by our hands this day their daily bread,
    and by our understanding love give peace and joy.
Amen.

12 February

Today's prayer is ancient indeed, the words going back to the philosopher, mathematician and astronomer Synesius of Cyrene – the Bishop of Ptolemais – (c. 375–c. 414), translated poetically into English by Allen W. Chatfield (1808–1896). Synesius wrote many epistles and hymns, of which the following is an example. It seeks God's guidance and blessing, even in the darkest moments of life.

Lord Jesus, think on me,
nor let me go astray;
through darkness and perplexity
point thou the heavenly way.

Lord Jesus, think on me,
when flows the tempest high:
when on doth rush the enemy,
O Saviour, be thou nigh.

13 February

As Christians we talk of the peace of God that passes all understanding, but too often we fail to make that our own, rushing around instead from one thing to the next and failing to make time for what really matters. If we fail fully to make God's peace our own, we know the fault lies with us rather than him, and so we seek it all the more, not through our own efforts but through his grace. We may think of that as symptomatic of our modern stress-filled world, but probably it's always been the case. It certainly seems to have been so way back in the second century, as evidenced by the following prayer attributed to the Greek theologian and philosopher Titus Flavius Clemens, more commonly known as Clement of Alexandria (c. 150–c. 215). It's taken from the Syrian liturgy that bears his name.

O God, you are the unsearchable abyss of peace,
    the ineffable sea of love,
    and the fountain of blessings.
Water us with plenteous streams,
    from the riches of your grace;
    and from the most sweet springs of your kindness,
    make us children of quietness and heirs of peace.
Amen.

14 February

Today we have another prayer drawn from the 1948 book *Meditations and Prayers*, written by the Anglican theologian Evelyn Underhill (1875–1941). Underhill was the first woman to give lectures to Anglican clergy and first also to conduct retreats in the Anglican Church. The depth of wisdom in words such as her prayer here helps us to understand not only the respect she so evidently commanded but also how she was able to open the minds of Christians from all traditions to the breadth of spirituality within the medieval and early Catholic Church.

Jesus,
    show me what the attachments and cravings are
    which hold me down below your level of total self-
        surrender,
    real love.
Show me the things that lumber up my heart,
    so that it cannot be filled with your life and power.
What are they?
People?
Ambitions?
Interests?
Comforts?
Anxieties?
Self-chosen aims?
Take from me all that hinders my work for you!
Amen.

15 February

If you're looking for words to express praise and adoration, then, as well as the Psalms, there's one other book of the Bible that yields some unforgettable passages. I'm referring, of course, to the book of Revelation. Ruthlessly plundered by sects obsessed with end times and the like, much in its pages is obscure and puzzling, but words like the following, drawn from chapters 4 (v. 11) and 5 (vv. 9, 10, 12, 13b), express the wonder and majesty of God in Christ as few others even begin to. Such worship sets the tone not just for the book of Revelation, or simply the New Testament, but for all who profess the name of Christ.

You are worthy, O Lord our God,
to receive glory, honour and power,
for all things were made by you,
their creation and existence down to your will.
You are worthy, Lord, to take the scroll and unseal it,
since you were slaughtered,
ransoming people for God from every culture,
language, race and continent,
and transforming them into a kingdom and priests
to our God,
who will reign on the earth.
Worthy is the Lamb that was slain
to receive dominion, riches, wisdom, power,
veneration, glory and praise!
To the one who sits on the throne and to the Lamb
be blessing, homage, glory and might,
now and always!
Amen.

16 February

I've not been able to discover anything about today's prayer except that it was written by A. G. Bullivant. Who he was, what he did, or even when he lived I've no idea, but I warm towards him, for his words reflect a joyful and human faith, far removed from the picture of the Church people sometimes have. He reminds us of the important place humour has in life and of the place it should have equally in Christian discipleship.

Give me a sense of humour, Lord,
    and also things to laugh about.
Give me grace to take a joke against myself
    and see the funny side of the things I do.
Save me from annoyance,
    bad temper,
    resentment against my friends.
Help me to laugh even in the face of trouble.
Fill my mind with the love of Jesus,
    for his name's sake.
Amen.

17 February

One of the best-known hymns of thanksgiving must surely be that written by the German poet, dramatist, musician and pastor Martin Rinckart (1586–1649). Drawing upon Ecclesiastes 1:22-24 for its opening lines, he joyfully celebrates what God has done and continues to do. We owe our English version of this wonderful hymn to the acclaimed translator Catherine Winkworth (1827–1878), her text having helped generations of Christians to express their gratitude for God's goodness. The first and last verses in particular positively brim over with appreciation for his many gifts.

Now thank we all our God,
with heart and hands and voices,
who wondrous things hath done,
in whom his world rejoices;
who, from our mother's arms,
hath blessed us on our way
with countless gifts of love,
and still is ours today.

All praise and thanks to God
the Father now be given,
the Son, and him who reigns
with them in highest heaven;
the one eternal God,
whom earth and heaven adore;
for thus it was, is now,
and shall be, evermore.

18 February

As I mentioned earlier in this book, hymn texts can provide wonderful prayers, and today offers a perfect case in point. There can surely be few words that more beautifully express faith and trust at the close of the day than those of the clergyman and hymn-writer John Ellerton (1826–1893). Written in 1870, it was selected by Queen Victoria for use at her Diamond Jubilee service in 1897, and since then it has inspired innumerable generations across the years, reminding us not just of the God we serve but the worldwide fellowship of which we're a part.

The day thou gavest, Lord, is ended,
the darkness falls at thy behest;
to thee our morning hymns ascended,
thy praise shall hallow now our rest.

We thank thee that thy Church unsleeping,
while earth rolls onward into light,
through all the world her watch is keeping
and rests not now by day or night.

As o'er each continent and island
the dawn leads on another day,
the voice of prayer is never silent,
nor dies the strain of praise away.

The sun, that bids us rest, is waking
our brethren 'neath the western sky.
And hour by hour fresh lips are making
thy wondrous doings heard on high.

So be it, Lord; thy throne shall never,
like earth's proud empires, pass away;
thy kingdom stands, and grow for ever,
till all thy creatures own thy sway.

19 February

We looked earlier at how prayers from other traditions can speak for Christians in a new context, helping both to articulate their faith and communicate something of God. That's certainly true of our prayer today, taken from the Vedas, the sacred texts of the Hindus and possibly the oldest religious writings in the world. In its yearning for peace, and its recognition that this comes from God alone, lies a real point of contact for interfaith dialogue.

May there be peace in the higher regions;
    may there be peace in the firmament;
    may there be peace on earth.
May the waters flow peacefully;
    may the herbs and plants grow peacefully;
    may all the divine powers bring unto us peace.
The supreme Lord is peace.
May we all be in peace, peace, and only peace;
    and may that peace come unto each of us.

20 February

Few prayers articulate the sheer wonder of God more powerfully than that of St Gregory of Nazianzus (*c.* 330–390), poet, writer and Bishop of Constantinople. His words of calm assurance belie the inner turmoil he experienced for much of his life. Not only did he feel unworthy to take on the responsibilities of the priesthood, let alone a bishopric, but his attempts to restore harmony to the Church during troubled times led to slanderous and violent attacks upon him, to the point that he finally retired from public life to end his days as a hermit. Through it all, however, he was sustained by the vibrant faith that shines from the following prayer.

O all-transcendent God –
    and what other name could describe you?
    what words can hymn your praises?
No word does you justice.
What mind can probe your secrets?
No mind can encompass you.
You are alone beyond the power of speech,
    yet all that we speak stems from you.
You are alone beyond the power of thought,
    yet all that we can conceive springs from you.
All things proclaim you,
    those endowed with reason and those bereft of it.
All the expectation and pain of the world coalesce
    in you.
All things utter a prayer to you,
    a silent hymn composed by you.
You sustain everything that exists,
    and all things move together to your orders.

You are the goal of all that exists.
You are one and you are all,
 yet you are none of the things that exist,
 neither a part nor the whole.
You can avail yourself of any name;
 how shall I call you,
 the only unnameable?
All-transcendent God!
Amen.

21 February

Today we have the so-called prayer of abandonment, written by Charles de Foucauld (1858–1916). The prayer is remarkable in that De Foucauld followed a debauched lifestyle for many years, only to experience a complete turnaround following distinguished years of military service. He felt called to live 'the hidden life of the poor and humble worker of Nazareth' and entered a Trappist monastery, believing that the austere nature of that order (officially known as the 'Cistercians of the Strict Observance') would suit him. He was later released from the order so that he could devote his life to working among tribal Muslims in the Sahara, where his life was prematurely ended by a fanatical assassin.

Father, I abandon myself into your hands;
    do with me what you will.
Whatever you may do, I thank you:
    I am ready for all, I accept all.
Let only your will be done in me,
    and in all your creatures –
    I wish no more than this, O Lord.
Into your hands I commend my soul;
    I offer it to you with all the love of my heart,
    for I love you Lord,
    and so need to give myself,
    to surrender myself into your hands,
    without reserve,
    and with boundless confidence,
    for you are my Father.
Amen.

22 February

If you're looking for classic prayers there's nowhere better to turn than the *Book of Common Prayer*. Yes, its language may be old-fashioned, harking back to a bygone age, but it's beautiful nonetheless – poetic in a way few modern prayers can even begin to emulate. More important, the depth of spirituality in its pages is second to none, hence its continued use in many churches even today. The following Collect perfectly commits a new day into God's hands.

We give thee hearty thanks, O heavenly Father,
    for the rest of the past night
    and for the gift of a new day,
    with its opportunities of pleasing you.
Grant that we may so pass its hours in the perfect
    freedom of thy service,
    that at eventide we may again give thanks unto
      thee,
    through Jesus Christ our Lord.
Amen.

23 February

A recurring theme in the great prayers of history is our
need of God, and that's precisely the thrust of our
words today. They come from the seventeenth-century
Russian saint Dimitrii of Rostov, and in a few poetic
lines they wonderfully articulate our need of God. He
alone can lead us from darkness to light and death to
life, cleansing, renewing and transforming us through
the touch of Christ's hand. Make these unforgettable
words your own.

Come, my Light,
    and illumine my darkness.
Come, my Life,
    and revive me from death.
Come, my Physician,
    and heal my wounds.
Come, Flame of divine love,
    and burn up the thorns of my sins,
    kindling my heart with the flame of thy love.
Come, my King,
    sit upon the throne of my heart
    and reign there.
For thou alone art my King and my Lord.
Amen.

24 February

Today's prayer comes from the medieval philosopher and theologian St Anselm (1033–1109). Born in Burgundy, he entered the Abbey of Bec aged 27, subsequently becoming prior and then abbot. His monastic duties entailed frequent visits to England, and such was the impression he made there that, in 1093, he was appointed Archbishop of Canterbury. A deeply scholarly man, he emphasised the relationship of faith to reason, producing the so-called ontological argument for the existence of God, which runs roughly as follows: God is a being nothing greater than which can be conceived. If God did not exist, something greater than God could be conceived. Therefore God must exist. If all that seems somewhat highbrow there is nothing at all remote about the following prayer, in which Anselm entrusts the oppressed and disadvantaged of this world into God's loving care.

I bring before you, O Lord,
    the troubles and perils of people and nations,
    the pain of prisoners and captives,
    the sorrows of the bereaved,
    the needs of strangers,
    the vulnerability of the weak,
    the downheartedness of the weary,
    the diminishing powers of the aged.
O Lord, draw near to each,
    for the sake of Jesus Christ our Lord.
Amen.

25 February

We've already encountered some of the prayers of St Augustine of Hippo (354–430), and we'll do so many times again during the course of this book, so much of what he wrote having stood the test of time. Today's prayer is no exception: it bubbles over with a sense of God's life-giving love and a longing to show a similar quality of devotion in return.

O Fire that always burns, and never goes out,
    kindle me!
O Light which ever shines, illuminate me!
Lord, let the flame of your love set on fire my whole
    heart.
May I wholly burn towards you,
    wholly love you,
    set aflame by you.
Amen.

26 February

Many of the prayers in this collection are ancient or at least old, having come to be seen as classics through standing the test of time. Today though, we turn to a comparatively recent prayer, that of the eminent scholar and Catholic theologian Karl Rahner (1904–1984). One of the most respected and influential thinkers in recent Church history, he emphasised in particular the transcendence yet grace of God, most fully revealed in Christ. Both themes are evident in the following words, taken from a much larger prayer that appears, in sections, during the course of this book.

I know that there is only one thing that I can say to
    you: have mercy on me.
I need your mercy, because I am a sinner.
I am unworthy of your mercy, because I am a sinner.
But I humbly desire your unfailing mercy,
    for I am a being of this world, not yet lost;
    one who still longs for the heavens of your
        goodness,
    who willingly and with tears of joy
    receives the inexhaustible gift of your mercy.
Amen.

27 February

Our prayer today comes from the medieval classic *The Imitation of Christ*, written by the monk and scholar Thomas à Kempis (1380–1471). One of the most influential Christian books ever written, it has not only been widely discussed and referred to in scholarship but has also, through its practical guidelines concerning daily discipleship, inspired the devotional life of many. Reading his words, it's hard to believe they were written centuries ago, for they are still as fresh and relevant as ever. Let them speak for you, as you seek to follow Christ in turn.

Lord, you know what is best;
    let this be done or that be done as you please.
Give what you will,
    as much as you will,
    when you will.
Do with me as you know best,
    as will most please you,
    and will be for your greater honour.
Place me where you will
    and deal with me freely in all things.
I am in your hands;
    turn me about whichever way you will.
Behold, I am your servant, ready to obey in all things.
Not for myself do I desire to live, but for you –
    would that I could do this worthily and perfectly!
Amen.

28 February

Another hymn today, this one written by the scholar and clergyman J. H. B. Masterman (1867–1933). In his time a lecturer at Birmingham and Cambridge universities, Rector of St Mary-le-Bow, Cheapside, and Bishop of Plymouth, his language may at times be a little dated but the needs he identifies apply as much to today's world as yesterday's. A good deal may have changed but sadly human nature has not.

Grant us thy peace; for thou alone canst bend
our faltering purpose to a nobler end;
thy love alone can teach our hearts to see
the fellowship that binds all lives in thee.

Grant us thy peace; for men have filled the years
with greed and envy and with foolish fears,
with squandered treasures and ignoble gain,
and fruitless harvests that we reap in vain.

Grant us thy peace; till all our strife shall seem
the hateful memory of some evil dream;
till that new song ring out that shall not cease,
'In heaven thy glory and on earth thy peace!'

MARCH

1 March

The following, written by English poet and artist William Blake (1757–1827), asks the all-important question of whether we can be aware of need and not in some way respond. Called 'On Another's Sorrow', it's not strictly a prayer as traditionally understood, but to me God speaks powerfully through the poet's words, reminding us that, just as he shares the pain of others, so we too are called to respond wherever we are confronted by human need. A committed Christian, Blake leaves us in no doubt where he stood concerning the question he poses. Ironically, he himself lived and died in poverty.

Can I see another's woe,
and not be in sorrow too?
Can I see another's grief,
and not seek for kind relief?

Can I see a falling tear,
and not feel my sorrow's share?
Can a father see his child
weep, nor be with sorrow filled?

Can a mother sit and hear
an infant groan, an infant fear?
No, no! never can it be!
Never, never can it be!

And can He who smiles on all
hear the wren with sorrows small,
hear the small bird's grief and care,
hear the woes that infants bear –

And not sit beside the next,
pouring pity in their breast,
and not sit the cradle near,
weeping tear on infant's tear?

And not sit both night and day,
wiping all our tears away?
Oh no! never can it be!
Never, never can it be!

He doth give his joy to all:
he becomes an infant small,
he becomes a man of woe,
he doth feel the sorrow too.

Think not thou canst sigh a sigh,
and thy Maker is not by:
Think not thou canst weep a tear,
and thy Maker is not near.

2 March

The love and respect of St Francis of Assisi (1182–
1226). for the natural world is well known and finds
expression in many of his prayers. In the following
adapted version of what's known as 'The Canticle of
Brother Sun' or 'The Canticle of Creation', the beauty
of creation acts as a springboard for praise. Use it to
remind yourself of the wonder of our universe and the
way, to the eye of faith, it so eloquently speaks of God.

Praise belongs to you, O Lord, for everything you have
    made.
I praise you first for Brother Sun,
    through whom you bring the day and give us light –
How beautiful he is, how radiant in all his splendour!
He bears, Most High, your likeness.
All praise be yours, my Lord, through Sister Moon and
    Stars;
    you have set them in the heavens,
    bright, precious and fair.
All praise be yours, my Lord, through Sister Water,
    so useful and lowly yet so precious and pure.
All praise be yours, my Lord, through Brother Fire,
    through whom you brighten up the night.
What beauty and brightness he possesses, full of
    power and strength.
All praise be yours, my Lord, through Sister Earth,
    our mother,
    who in her sovereignty feeds us,
    producing diverse fruits and multicoloured herbs,
        flowers and vegetables.
All praise be yours, my Lord, through Sister Death,
    from whose embrace no mortal can escape.

Happy are those she finds doing your will –
    the second death can do no harm to them.
I praise and bless you, Lord, and give you thanks,
    resolved to serve you with great humility.
Amen.

3 March

For our prayer today we turn to the Franciscan theologian, philosopher and, later, cardinal-bishop, St Bonaventure (1221–1274). Reading his words, it's easy to see why he made such an impression on the medieval Church, his spirituality in particular striking a chord with many. He piles up one description on another in his attempt to express what Christ means to him and to gain a yet deeper understanding of his love.

Pierce, O most sweet Lord Jesus, my inmost soul
    with the most joyous and healthful wound of your
      love,
    and with true, calm and most holy apostolic
      charity,
    that my soul may ever languish and melt with
      entire love
    and longing for you,
    may yearn for you and your courts,
    may long to be dissolved and to be with you.
Grant that my soul may hunger after you,
    the Bread of Angels,
    the refreshment of holy souls,
    our daily and super-substantial bread,
    having all sweetness and savour and every
      delightful taste.
May my heart ever hunger after and feed upon you,
    whom the angels desire to look upon,
    and may my inmost soul be filled with the
      sweetness of your savour;
    may it ever thirst for you,
    the fountain of life, wisdom, knowledge
      and eternal light,

the torrent of pleasure,
the fullness of the house of God;
may it ever compass you,
seek you,
find you,
run to you,
come up to you,
meditate on you,
speak of you,
and do all for the praise and glory of your name,
with humility and discretion,
with love and delight,
with ease and affection,
with perseverance to the end;
and be thou alone ever my hope,
   my entire confidence,
my riches,
my delight,
my pleasure,
my joy,
my rest and tranquillity,
my peace,
my sweetness,
my food,
my refreshment,
my refuge,
my help,
my wisdom,
my portion,
my possession,
my treasure;
in whom may my mind and my heart be ever fixed
   and firm
and rooted immovably.
Amen.

4 March

The following is the so-called Gorsedd prayer, written by Edward Williams (1747–1826), a Welsh Druid otherwise known as Iolo Morganwg (meaning 'Ned of Glamorgan'). Strongly influenced by Christianity, despite his Druid affiliation, Williams used this prayer at a ceremony at Primrose Hill, London, to mark the 1792 summer solstice:

Grant, O God, thy protection,
    and in protection, strength,
    and in strength, understanding,
    and in understanding, knowledge,
    and in knowledge, the knowledge of justice,
    and in the knowledge of justice, the love of it,
    and in that love, the love of all existences,
    and in the love of all existences, the love of God,
    God and all goodness.
Amen.

5 March

If I was to ask who is the patron saint of Ireland you'd almost certainly come up with St Patrick, and of course you'd be right, but alongside him stand two others: St Brigid and St Columba (521–597). Also known as St Colme Cille or Columcille (meaning 'dove of the Church'), Columba was one of the Gaelic monk priests who brought the Christian faith back to Scotland, spending most of his life on the island of Iona, from where he conducted a long-running and hugely successful evangelising ministry among the Picts. Here is one of his classic prayers, unmistakably reflecting his Gaelic origins.

Be thou a bright flame before me,
   be thou a guiding star above me,
   be thou a smooth path below me,
   be thou a kindly shepherd behind me,
     today, tonight, and for ever.
Amen.

6 March

In preparing this book the one kind of prayer I struggled to find was intercessions. Praise and confession are available in abundance and when it comes to prayers seeking help in life or faith we're positively spoilt for choice, but it's a different matter when it comes to praying for others. There *is* material, of course, and it includes some of the most memorable prayers ever written, but by comparison they're few and far between. Happily we can turn once again to the *Book of Common Prayer* as a tried and trusted source. The language may be un-PC, but look past that to the underlying senti-ments, and you'll find a perfect way to consecrate the Church and world into God's care.

O God, the Creator and Preserver of all mankind,
    we humbly beseech thee for all sorts and
        conditions of men;
    that you would be pleased to make thy ways known
        unto them,
    thy saving health unto all nations.
More especially we pray for the good estate of the
    Catholic Church;
    that it may be so guided and governed by thy good
        Spirit,
    that all who profess and call themselves Christians
    may be led into the way of truth,
    and hold the faith in unity of spirit,
    in the bond of peace,
    and in righteousness of life.
Finally we commend to thy fatherly goodness
    all those, who are in any way afflicted or distressed
    in mind, body, or estate;
    [especially those for whom our prayers are desired;]

that it may please thee to comfort and relieve them,
according to their several necessities,
giving them patience under their sufferings,
and a happy issue out of all their afflictions.
And this we beg for Jesus Christ's sake.
Amen.

7 March

You don't have to be a Methodist to have heard of the Wesley brothers. They are probably two of the most famous names in Church history, and certainly few have made such an impact on its unfolding story than they did. Both Anglican priests, John (1703–1791), of course, was in time to become the founder of Methodism – a break with the Church of England that Charles Wesley (1707-1788) strongly resisted. Yet, through the countless hymns he wrote, Charles was arguably to have the greatest long-term impact of the two, these having been sung by generations of believers from all kinds of denominations ever since. Not everything he wrote was of the same quality, but much is truly memorable and will probably continue to feature in hymn books for years to come. Its personal and direct language comes unmistakably from the heart, and has touched the hearts of countless others in consequence.

Love divine, all loves excelling,
joy of heaven, to earth come down,
fix in us thy humble dwelling,
all thy faithful mercies crown.
Jesus, thou art all compassion,
pure unbounded love thou art;
visit us with thy salvation,
enter every trembling heart.

Breathe, O breathe thy loving Spirit
into every troubled breast;
let us all in thee inherit,
let us find thy promised rest.
Take away the love of sinning,

Alpha and Omega be;
end of faith, as its beginning,
set our hearts at liberty.

Come, almighty to deliver,
let us all thy grace receive;
suddenly return, and never,
never more thy temples leave.
Thee we would be always blessing,
serve thee as thy hosts above;
pray, and praise thee without ceasing,
glory in thy perfect love.

Finish then thy new creation,
pure and spotless let us be;
let us see thy great salvation
perfectly restored in thee.
Changed from glory into glory,
till in heaven we take our place,
till we cast our crowns before thee,
lost in wonder, love, and praise.

8 March

You may recall from earlier in this book an intercessory prayer of St Basil the Great (*c.* 330–379). Today we've another of his prayers, this one a joyful acknowledgement of God's mercy and goodness. It asks for help in making a fitting response through more committed discipleship – a desire that you, like me, will no doubt share.

O God and Lord of the Powers,
  and Maker of all creation,
  who, because of thy clemency and incomparable
    mercy,
  didst send your only-begotten Son and our Lord
    Jesus Christ
  for the salvation of mankind,
  and with his venerable cross didst tear asunder
    the record of our sins,
  and thereby didst conquer the rulers and powers
    of darkness;
  receive from us sinful people, O merciful Master,
  these prayers of gratitude and supplication,
  and deliver us from every destructive and gloomy
    transgression,
  and from all visible and invisible enemies who seek
    to injure us.
Nail down our flesh with fear of you,
  and let not our hearts be inclined to words
    or thoughts of evil,
  but pierce our souls with thy love,
  that ever contemplating you,
  being enlightened by you,
  and discerning you, the unapproachable
    and everlasting Light,

we may unceasingly render confession
and gratitude to you:
the eternal Father,
with your only-begotten Son,
and with your all-holy, gracious, and life-giving
Spirit,
now and ever, and unto ages of ages.
Amen.

9 March

Today we return to St Augustine of Hippo (354–430). Many of his prayers are instantly recognisable, others less so, such is the volume of his output. In the following, he looks forward to God's eternal kingdom, but this is no taking refuge in some ivory tower, getting through the present by focusing on blessing yet to come. Rather it's a recognition that faith should mean joy here and now, every moment enriched by the touch of God's hand.

O God of truth,
  grant me the happiness of heaven
  so that my joy may be full in accord with your
    promise.
In the meantime let my mind dwell on that
  happiness,
  my tongue speak of it,
  my heart pine for it,
  my mouth pronounce it,
  my soul hunger for it,
  my flesh thirst for it,
  and my entire being desire it
  until I enter through death in the joy of my Lord
    for ever.
Amen.

10 March

Our prayer today is another Collect from the *Book of Common Prayer*. Still, in law, the primary liturgical prayer book of the Church of England, though typically replaced by more modern prayer books, it was written in a time when persecution for one's faith was all too common, hence the reference to 'many and great dangers'. The dangers we face may be different but are no less real. Some are physical, in the shape of violence, terrorism and the like. Others are spiritual: subtle temptations to compromise our faith and succumb to the way of the world. Situations may change but our need of God's guidance and protection stays the same.

O God,
> who knows us to be set in the midst of so many
>   and great dangers
> that by reason of the frailty of our nature
>   we cannot always stand upright:
> grant us such strength and protection,
> as may support us in all dangers
> and carry us through all temptations;
> through Jesus Christ our Lord.
Amen.

11 March

I've chosen two prayers for today, both of them tiny –
so small, in fact, that even put together they are shorter
than most in this book. Who wrote the first is not
known: it's simply called the prayer of a Breton fisher-
man. No doubt it was originally prayed out on the open
water, perhaps in a coracle tossed around on stormy
seas. We may not experience anything like that, but the
storms of life can be just as real, and our resources to
meet them can seem inadequate in the extreme. *Ours*
may well be, but thankfully *God's* are not.

Lord,
    the sea is wide
    and my boat is small.
Be with me.

For our second prayer we turn to words of St Teresa of
Avila (1515–1582), expressing quiet trust in God's
constant presence deep within.

Lord,
    you are closer to me than my own breathing,
    nearer than my hands and feet.
Amen.

12 March

Today a prayer dating back to the ninth century and attributed to Alfred the Great (849– 899), a Saxon king of Wessex who rescued England from a savage onslaught by the Danes. A deeply religious man as well as an erudite scholar, he founded several monasteries and translated a number of sacred writings. The following prayer, in which I've slightly updated the language, is an outpouring of praise and worship.

You, Lord, are the supreme Truth,
    for from you comes all truth,
    and so I pray to you.
You are the highest Wisdom,
    for the wise depend on you for their knowledge,
    and so I bow before you.
You are the supreme Joy,
    all happiness finally owed to you.
You are the Light of minds,
    the giver of all understanding.
I love you above all.
I seek and follow you, and am ready to serve you.
I desire to dwell under your power
    for you are the King of all.
Amen.

13 March

For today's prayer we turn once again to St Anselm (1033–1109) for a mixture of thanksgiving and petition. He acknowledges on the one hand God's faithful provision, on the other his dependence on divine grace if he's to lead anything like the kind of life God desires. The prayer may at first sight seem terse, even presumptuous, but it reflects a quiet confidence in God's transforming touch.

Your patience has hitherto borne with me,
    fed me,
    waited for me.
You wait, good Lord, for my amendment;
    my soul waits for the inbreathing of your grace
    in order to be sufficiently penitent to lead a better
       life.
Amen.

14 March

There's more to wisdom than anything we might learn in books or at college and university, God often speaking through 'ordinary' things in the world around us. The Christian should never despise the insights of academic study and scientific research, for to these we owe so many of the advances we take for granted, but they cannot answer every question relating to life, let alone eternity. On some matters, we need a different kind of guidance that we believe God alone can offer. It's this that the nineteenth-century journalist, poet and reformer William Henry Burleigh (1812–1871) speaks of in the following prayer-cum-hymn.

Lead us, O Father, in the paths of peace:
without thy guiding hand we go astray,
and doubts appal, and sorrows still increase;
lead us through Christ, the true and living way.

Lead us, O Father, in the paths of truth:
unhelped by thee, in error's maze we grope,
while passion stains and folly dims our youth,
and age comes on uncheered by faith and hope.

Lead us, O Father, in the paths of right:
blindly we stumble when we walk alone,
involved in shadows of a darkening night;
only with thee we journey safely on.

Lead us, O Father, to thy heavenly rest,
however rough and steep the path may be,
through joy or sorrow, as thou deemest best,
until our lives are perfected in thee.

15 March

We have another hymn today, this time coming from the university lecturer and theologian Edwin Hatch (1835–1889). An accomplished scholar who held academic posts both in the UK and abroad, he was respected equally for the quality of his commitment and the way his life backed up the claims of the faith he taught. His words here express a longing that has probably inspired more prayers than any other: the desire to know and love God better.

Breathe on me, Breath of God,
fill me with life anew,
that as you love, so may I love,
and do what you would do.

Breathe on me, Breath of God,
until my heart is pure:
until my will is one with yours
to do and to endure.

Breathe on me, Breath of God,
fulfil my heart's desire,
until this earthly part of me
glows with your heavenly fire.

Breathe on me, Breath of God,
so shall I never die,
but live with you the perfect life
of your eternity.

16 March

Our prayer today comes from the Sarum *Book of Hours*, dating back to Tudor times. There would have been many such books in circulation at the time, used both in public worship and for personal devotion. Many took the form of richly illuminated manuscripts, while towards the end of the fifteenth century some included woodcut illustrations. Each contained devotional texts, prayers and psalms for liturgical hours of the day. Sarum is an abbreviation for Salisbury, where a particularly elaborate and beautiful form of the liturgy was developed, of which the following is perhaps the most famous example.

God be in my head,
    and in my understanding.
God be in my eyes,
    and in my looking.
God be in my mouth,
    and in my speaking.
God be in my heart,
    and in my thinking.
God be at my end,
    and at my departing.
Amen.

17 March

Today's prayer is from the eighth-century poet, writer and teacher Alcuin of York (*c.* 735–804). A distinguished scholar, he founded a centre for education in Aachen, Germany, at the invitation of Charlemagne the Great, and went on to establish this as one of the leading centres of learning in Europe. His lovely words here combine an acknowledgement of God's greatness with a request for guidance and mercy.

Eternal Light, shine into my heart.
Eternal Goodness, deliver me from evil.
Eternal Power, be my support.
Eternal Wisdom, scatter the darkness of my ignorance.
Eternal Pity, have mercy upon me,
    that with all my heart and mind,
    and soul and strength
    I may seek your face
    and be brought by your infinite mercy
    to your holy presence,
        through Jesus Christ my Lord.
Amen.

18 March

The author of our prayer today, St Jerome (347–420), spent much of his life in the Holy Land, becoming leader in 386 of a monastery in Bethlehem where he was to spend the rest of his days. Perhaps it was being so close to the places where Jesus ministered to the multitude that inspired the following prayer, in which he thanks God for his word and asks for help through it to walk more fully in the light and love of Christ, the Word made flesh.

O Lord,
    you have given us your word for a light to shine
        upon our path;
    inspire us to meditate on that word
    and to follow its teaching,
    that we may find in it the light that shines more
        and more
    until the perfect day,
    through Jesus Christ our Lord.
Amen.

19 March

Amongst Christian poets I was intrigued to find some of the greatest names in literary history, including the celebrated Brontë sisters. Anne (1820–1849), in particular, wrote several poetic prayers during her tragically short life. The following, a prayer of confession, is titled simply 'A prayer'. It reflects something of the trials she and her family so stoically faced, but also the strong faith that bound them together.

My God (oh, let me call thee mine,
weak, wretched sinner though I be),
my trembling soul would fain be thine;
my feeble faith still clings to thee.

Not only for the past I grieve,
the future fills me with dismay;
unless thou hasten to relieve,
thy suppliant is a castaway.

I cannot say my faith is strong,
I dare not hope my love is great;
but strength and love to thee belong;
oh, do not leave me desolate!

I know I owe my all to thee;
oh, take the heart I cannot give!
Do thou my strength – my Saviour be,
and make me to thy glory live.

20 March

Today we turn to the English scholar and theologian Charles John Vaughan (1816–1897). Having spent three years as a vicar in Leicester, he became headmaster of Harrow School, and though he was later appointed to the bishopric of Rochester, he resigned the post before taking office, preferring to continue his teaching duties. A gifted preacher and writer, he went on to become Dean of Llandaff and President of University College, Cardiff, which he had helped to found. He was clearly determined, however, that high office wouldn't go to his head, as the following prayer to emulate the humility of Christ clearly illustrates.

Take away from our hearts, O Christ,
    all over-confidence and boasting,
    all high and vain thoughts,
    all desire to excuse ourselves for our sins,
    or to compare ourselves proudly with others;
    and grant us rather to take as Master and King
    you who chose to be crowned with thorns
    and to die in shame for us all,
    Jesus Christ our Lord.
Amen.

21 March

The source of today's prayer is an ancient one, namely the sixth-century Gelasian Sacramentary – the second oldest surviving Catholic liturgy in existence, second only to the Verona Sacramentary. It contains prayers, rites and blessings for use by a priest in various celebrations of the Eucharist, and its content is traditionally linked with Pope Gelasius I. The words here express simple thanks and trust at the close of the day.

I thank you, Lord, that you have kept me
　　through this day.
I thank you, Lord, that you will keep me
　　through the night.
Bring me, in safety, Lord, to the morning hours,
　　that you may receive my praise at all times,
　　through Jesus Christ my Lord.
Amen.

22 March

We've another prayer today of the sixteenth-century mystic and ascetic Teresa of Avila (1515–1582), and once more her words reveal the depth of her spirituality and commitment. They offer a classic expression of praise and thanksgiving, acknowledging among other things the faithful outpouring of God's patience, love, blessing and mercy.

May you be blessed for ever, Lord,
    for not abandoning me when I abandoned you.
May you be blessed for ever, Lord,
    for offering your hand of love in my darkest,
        most lonely moments.
May you be blessed for ever, Lord,
    for putting up with such a stubborn soul as mine.
May you be blessed for ever, Lord,
    for loving me more than I love myself.
May you be blessed for ever, Lord,
    for continuing to pour out your blessings upon me,
    even though I respond so poorly.
May you be blessed for ever, Lord,
    for drawing out the goodness in all people,
        even including me.
May you be blessed for ever, Lord,
    for repaying my sin with your love.
May you be blessed for ever, Lord,
    for being constant and unchanging amidst all the
        changes of this world.
May you be blessed for ever, Lord,
    for your countless blessings on me and on all your
        creatures.
Amen.

23 March

Although most famous for *A Dictionary of the English Language*, written between 1747 and 1755, Samuel Johnson (1709–1784) wrote many other works, including a succession of essays on moral and religious topics. The breadth of his learning was unquestionable, yet he always recognised that knowledge is not the same as wisdom, the latter coming from a higher source. Here he asks for help to use wisely whatever gifts God has given him; a prayer we can make our own.

Almighty God,
    Giver of Wisdom,
    without whose help resolutions are in vain,
    without whose blessing study is ineffectual,
    if it be thy will to attain such knowledge
    as may qualify me to direct the doubtful,
    and instruct the ignorant,
    to prevent wrongs,
    and terminate contentions;
    grant that I may use that knowledge,
    which I shall attain,
    to thy glory and my own salvation,
    for Jesus Christ's sake.
Amen.

24 March

Our prayer today is adapted from beautiful words of the Danish theologian Søren Kierkegaard (1813–1855). He reminds us succinctly but unforgettably that our relationship with God should be based not on fear but on childlike trust. Ours is a Father who delights to bless rather than punish, to forgive rather than condemn. Lose sight of that and, quite simply, we have lost sight of God as well.

God our heavenly Father,
    when the thought of you wakens our hearts,
    let its awakening not be like a startled bird
    that flies around in fear.
Instead, let it be like a child waking from sleep
    with a heavenly smile.
Amen.

25 March

One of the most celebrated prayers in history is that of the Benedictine monk and evangelist St Boniface (*c.* 672–754). Born in Devon, England, he spent most of his life as a missionary bishop, taking the message of the gospel into what is now Germany, where he eventually became Archbishop of Mainz around 747. His faith was ultimately to cost him his life as he was martyred by a pagan tribe on Pentecost Sunday. The joy and trust that mark his words here help us to glimpse more fully the God he was ready to die for.

O God the Eternal,
   the refuge and help of all your children,
   in our weakness you are our strength,
   in our darkness you are our light,
   in our sorrow you are comfort and peace.
We cannot number your blessings.
We cannot declare your love.
For all your goodness we bless you.
May we ever live in your presence,
   and love the things you love,
   and serve you with the service of our daily lives,
   through Jesus Christ our Lord.
Amen.

26 March

Today's prayer comes from John Henry Newman (1801–1890), a prominent figure in the Anglican Church of the nineteenth century and later of the Catholic Church following his conversion to Rome in 1845. A leading light of the Tractarian or so-called Oxford Movement, his reservations concerning the Church of England finally led to that decisive break. Thirty-four years later, in 1879, Newman was elevated to the rank of cardinal by Pope Leo XIII. His words here emphasise our dependence on divine grace not simply in doing God's will but in discerning that will in the first place.

I need thee to teach me day by day,
    according to each day's opportunities and needs.
Give me, O my Lord, that purity of conscience
    which alone can receive thy inspirations.
My ears are dull,
    so that I cannot hear thy voice.
My eyes are dim,
    so that I cannot see thy tokens.
Thou alone canst quicken my hearing,
    and purge my sight,
    and cleanse and renew my heart.
Teach me to sit at thy feet,
    and to hear thy word.
Amen.

27 March

The name of the Venerable Bede (673–735) will always be associated with Jarrow, and rightly so, for having been orphaned at the age of seven he was placed in the monastery at Jarrow and, apart from a visit to Lindisfarne and York, remained there for the rest of his days. He went on to distinguish himself as a writer, scholar and teacher, his *Ecclesiastical History* in particular being a valuable resource for researchers to this day. Clearly he also had a deep and vibrant faith, as the following prayer of praise and supplication makes clear. We'd do well today to catch something of his vision.

O Christ, our Morning Star,
  Splendour of Light Eternal,
  shining with the glory of the rainbow,
  come and waken us from the greyness
      of our apathy,
  and renew in us your gift of hope.
Amen.

28 March

Today we turn again to the writings of Evelyn Underhill (1875–1941) and her classic book *Meditations and Prayers* (1949). Once more her emphasis on glimpsing and serving God in daily life shines out from her words. Hers was no faith dusted down on Sunday and then put away for the rest of the week. It shaped each moment of every day, as can be the same for us too if we truly share her prayer.

Lord,
    teach me to accept all that you accepted:
    the ceaseless demands, needs, conflicts, pressures,
      misunderstandings
    even of those who loved you most.
Help me to discern the particular price you asked
    and help me to pay that price whatever it may be.
And oh! Cleanse my vision
    that I may see your pressure in my daily life,
    the ceaseless, purifying action of your generous,
      patient love.
Amen.

29 March

God's strength in our weakness – it's one of the great themes explored by the Apostle Paul in his New Testament letters as, time and again, he reminds us that what *we can't* do, *God can*. We find the same idea in our prayer today, attributed to St Anselm (1033–1109). Use it to commit to God all those things that seem beyond you, remembering that nothing is beyond him!

Hope of my heart,
    strength of my soul,
    help of my weakness,
    by your powerful kindness complete
    what in my powerless weakness I attempt.
Amen.

30 March

How do we get to know God? No doubt you could receive many answers to such a question, but to me one of the best is given by St Benedict of Nursia (c. 480–547) in the following prayer. Spiritual discernment, he reminds us, comes not from ourselves but from God, he alone being able to give us the qualities we need to know him better. Knowledge of God, in other words, is not reserved for the special few but is open to all who are ready to admit their need and open their hearts to his love. As Jesus put it, 'Seek and you will find', to which Benedict would have said a loud 'Amen'.

Gracious and holy Father,
  give me wisdom to recognise you,
  intelligence to understand you,
  diligence to seek you,
  patience to wait for you,
  eyes to see you,
  a heart to meditate on you,
  and life to proclaim you,
  through the power of the Spirit of Jesus Christ
    my Lord.
Amen.

31 March

Today's prayer was written by the Anglican bishop and hymn-writer Jeremy Taylor (1613–1667). Chaplain to the Royalist army during the English Civil War, he was imprisoned for a time by the victorious Puritans, but on the restoration of the monarchy in 1660, which saw the accession of King Charles II to the throne, he was appointed Bishop of Down and Connor. The writer of many devotional books, several of his prayers are still used today, including the following, which entrusts friends and loved ones into God's keeping.

Be pleased, O Lord, to remember my friends,
  all who have prayed for me,
  and all who have been good to me.
Do good to them,
  and return all their kindness twofold,
  rewarding them with blessings,
  sanctifying them with your grace,
  and bringing them to glory.
Amen.

APRIL

1 April

Our prayer today is an ancient one indeed, dating back to St John Chrysostom (347–407), one-time Bishop of Constantinople. Noted for his eloquent preaching and deep understanding of Scripture, Chrysostom also campaigned tirelessly for the poor, speaking out against exploitation and corruption. His words here are an outpouring of praise, joyfully acknowledging the sovereignty of God. Use them to offer your worship in turn.

Blessed are you, Lord God of our fathers,
    to be praised and exalted above all for ever –
    blessed be your glorious and holy name.
Yours, Lord, is the greatness and the power,
    the glory, victory and majesty,
    for everything in heaven and on earth is yours.
Yours is the kingdom,
    and you, Lord, are exalted as the head over all.
We will sing a new song to you Lord.
Amen.

2 April

One of the greatest names associated with religious poetry is Gerard Manley Hopkins (1844–1889), his work having touched a chord for many. Amazingly it was only after his death that his poems came into the public eye, none being published until his friend Robert Bridges produced a collection in 1918. A Jesuit priest, Hopkins' deeply mystical faith shines out from the following poem – a mixture of praise, confession and petition. For me there are shades here of Matthew 5:7 – 'How fortunate are those who show mercy, for they will receive mercy in turn' – and Luke 11:4 – 'Forgive us our sins, as we forgive those who sin against us' – Hopkins moving from a celebration of God's forgiveness to realising we should show similar mercy in turn.

Thee, God, I come from, to thee go,
all day long I like fountain flow
from thy hand out, swayed about
mote-like in thy mighty glow.

What I know of thee I bless,
as acknowledging thy stress
on my being and as seeing
something of thy holiness.

Once I turned from thee and hid,
bound on what thou hadst forbid;
sow the wind I would; I sinned:
I repent of what I did.

Bad I am, but yet thy child.
Father, be thou reconciled.
Spare thou me, since I see
with thy might that thou art mild.

I have life before me still
and thy purpose to fulfil;
yea a debt to pay thee yet:
help me, sir, and so I will.

But thou bidst, and just thou art,
me shew mercy from my heart
towards my brother, every other
man my mate and counterpart.

3 April

We've another prayer today from the Venerable Bede (673–735). It celebrates the joy of knowing Christ but recognises also that our knowledge of him is as yet partial, this life a staging post on the way to the next. Use these words, then, to pray for a continued growth in grace, learning more of Christ each day until that moment when we finally see him face to face and live always in the radiance of his love.

I pray you, noble Jesus,
    that as you have graciously granted me
        joyfully to imbibe the words of your knowledge,
    so you will also of your bounty grant me
        to come at length to yourself,
    the Fount of all wisdom,
        and to dwell in your presence for ever.
Amen.

4 April

We turn today to another of the great names in Christian history – that of the philosopher, monk and scholar St Thomas Aquinas (*c*. 1225–1274). Reckoned by some to be the greatest theologian ever, he unquestionably had a massive impact on the Church both in his own time and ever since, in particular through his monumental work *The Summa Theologiae*. His commitment to the study of Scripture and search for truth is evident in the following prayer. Pray with similar devotion for faith and understanding, and you will not be disappointed.

Creator of all things,
 true source of light and wisdom,
 lofty origin of all being,
 graciously let a ray of your brilliance penetrate
 into the darkness of my understanding
 and take from me the double darkness
  in which I have been born,
 an obscurity of both sin and ignorance.
Give me a sharp sense of understanding,
 a retentive memory,
 and the ability to grasp things correctly
  and fundamentally.
Grant me the talent of being exact in my explanations,
 and the ability to express myself with thoroughness
  and charm.
Point out the beginning,
 direct the progress,
 and help in completion;
 through Christ our Lord.
Amen.

5 April

When it comes to expressing commitment, few prayers have caught the public imagination as much as the Grail Prayer. A memorable outpouring of love and loyalty, it consecrates every aspect of life to God in a yearning to know and serve him better. Repeating the words is easy enough; *meaning* them is altogether more challenging, but that's the aim of the Grail Society, its members being committed to working out faith in daily life. They emphasise the importance of community, respect for others, stewardship of creation and personal spiritual growth, faith involving a personal response rather than mere intellectual assent. Join, then, in these lovely words, reproduced here with the Society's permission – and commit yourself in turn to deeper service of Christ.

Lord Jesus,
    I give you my hands to do your work,
    I give you my feet to go your way,
    I give you my eyes to see as you do,
    I give you my tongue to speak your words,
    I give you my mind that you may think in me,
    I give you my spirit that you may pray in me.
Above all,
    I give you my heart that you may love in me your
        Father and all humanity.
I give you my whole self that you may grow in me,
    so that it is you, Lord Jesus,
    who live and work and pray in me.
Amen.

6 April

I return for inspiration today to the Bible – not the Psalms this time but words of the Apostle Paul at the end of his letter to the Romans (16:25-27). They celebrate the revelation of God's love and purpose in Christ, culminating in a jubilant expression of worship. Did Paul have any idea that Christians would read and repeat his words for centuries to come? I doubt it. But had he done so his only thought would have been to rejoice that God is honoured rather than himself. Let that be *our* aim as we repeat now his words.

Now to the One who,
    in line with the gospel I preach and Lord Jesus
        Christ I proclaim,
    is able to build you up through the unfolding of
        the mystery –
    obscured for so long, but now,
    at God's command and in order to secure obedient
        faith,
    divulged and made known through prophetic
        words to all people –
    to that God, the only source of true wisdom,
    be glory now and always,
    through Jesus Christ!
Amen.

7 April

Some prayers, as we've already seen, are written in the form of poetry, and today we have another example of that genre. It comes from the Jacobean poet, hymn-writer and clergyman John Donne (1572–1631), most famous of course for his immortal lines: 'No man is an island, entire of itself . . . any man's death diminishes me, because I am involved in mankind; and therefore never send to know for whom the bell tolls; it tolls for thee.' Unforgettable though those words may be, Donne wrote much else besides, including the following, titled 'A Hymn to God the Father'. It's partly a lament at his repeated wrongdoing but above all it's a heartfelt celebration of God's unfailing grace.

Wilt thou forgive that sin where I begun,
which was my sin, though it were done before?
Wilt thou forgive that sin through which I run,
and do run still, though still I do deplore?
When thou hast done, thou hast not done;
 for I have more.

Wilt thou forgive that sin which I have won
others to sin, and made my sins their door?
Wilt thou forgive that sin which I did shun
a year or two, but wallow'd in a score?
When thou hast done, thou hast not done;
 for I have more.

I have a sin of fear, that when I've spun
my last thread, I shall perish on the shore;
but swear by thyself that at my death thy Son
shall shine as he shines now and heretofore:
and having done that, thou hast done;
 I fear no more.

8 April

Today we have two very short prayers, both written by the Anglican priest and poet George Herbert (1593–1633). Many of his poems are still sung today as hymns, and others are remarkable for their beauty, fully supporting Herbert's reputation as one of the greatest ever poets in the Church of England. Today, though, we have two very brief prayers, one poetic, the other not. Simple they may be, but they are profound nonetheless. The first sums up what true gratitude is all about – not simply empty talk but emanating from deep within. The second, just a few words, commits all of life into God's care.

You, Lord, have given so much to me;
    give me one thing more,
    a grateful heart.
Amen.

Enrich my heart, mouth, hands in me,
    with faith, with hope, with charity,
    that I may run, rise, rest with thee.

9 April

Some hymns are eminently forgettable, others anything but, and among the latter we must certainly include the ancient Irish hymn 'Be thou my vision'. It would, I suspect, make the top ten of many, and with good reason, for as well as a hymn it's also a perfect expression of consecration and commitment. The version best known to many is this lovely translation by Mary Byrne and Eleanor Hull.

Be thou my vision, O Lord of my heart,
be all else but naught to me, save that thou art;
thou my best thought in the day and the night,
both waking and sleeping, thy presence my light.

Be thou my wisdom, be thou my true word,
be thou ever with me, and I with thee, Lord;
be thou my great Father, and I thy true son;
be thou in me dwelling, and I with thee one.

Be thou my breastplate, my sword for the fight,
be thou my whole armour, be thou my true might,
be thou my soul's shelter, be thou my strong tower,
O raise thou me heavenward, great power of my
    power.

Riches I heed not, nor man's empty praise,
be thou mine inheritance now and always;
be thou and thou only the first in my heart,
O sovereign of heaven, my treasure thou art.

High King of heaven, thou heaven's bright sun,
O grant me its joys, after victory is won;
Great heart of my own heart, whatever befall,
still be thou my vision, O Ruler of all.

10 April

Our prayer today comes from St Edmund of Abingdon
(*c.* 1175–1240), or Edmund Rich as he was first known.
Initially a lecturer in dialectics and mathematics, he
turned subsequently to theology, seeking ordination and
winning renown as a brilliant preacher and scholar.
Treasurer of Salisbury Cathedral while also vicar of
Calne, in Wiltshire, he was appointed Archbishop of
Canterbury in 1233 by Pope Gregory IX, but his
rebukes of King Henry III incurred royal displeasure
and led Edmund finally to seek voluntary exile in France.
Deeply ascetic, he won wide respect for his sacrificial
and saintly lifestyle, repeatedly putting others before
himself. That pastoral concern is reflected in his words
here in a simple prayer of intercession.

Into your hands, O Father and Lord,
   I commend my soul and body,
   my parents and home,
   my family, friends and neighbours,
   all people of faith and love,
   and all who stand in special need.
Lighten our lives with your holy grace,
   and the knowledge of your constant presence,
   O Lord in Trinity, God everlasting.
Amen.

11 April

Today we have another of the many prayers of St Augustine of Hippo (354–430). It may be short, but it's a classic nonetheless, Augustine once again managing to say so much in just a few words and, moreover, doing so in an unforgettable way. Join with him in celebrating God's strength, faithfulness and blessing.

O God, the deathless hope of all,
    we rejoice that you support us both when little
      and even to grey hairs.
When our strength is of you, it is strength indeed;
    but when our own only, it is feebleness.
With you are refreshment and true strength.
Amen.

12 April

The following prayer was written by Charles Henry Brent (1862–1929), a minister of the Episcopal Church. Sent as a missionary bishop to the Philippines, he campaigned there courageously against the narcotics trade, before serving later as Bishop of Western New York. In that capacity he was to be instrumental in helping to organise the first World Conference on Faith and Order, held in Lausanne, Switzerland, in 1927. This prayer of intercession exemplifies that wide-ranging concern for others.

Lord Jesus Christ,
　　you stretched out your arms of love on the hard
　　　　wood of the cross
　　that everyone might come within the reach of your
　　　　saving embrace.
So clothe us with your Spirit that we,
　　reaching forth our hands in love,
　　may bring those who do not know you
　　　　to the knowledge and love of you;
　　for the honour of your name.
Amen.

13 April

I've chosen two prayers today on the theme of personal relationships. The first comes from the French priest, palaeontologist and philosopher Pierre Teilhard de Chardin (1881–1955). A hugely influential thinker, he was a man ahead of his times, exploring, for example, ecological issues that few have fully woken up to today. His writings could at times be complex, but there's nothing difficult to understand in the following.

Grant me to recognise in others, Lord God,
    the radiance of your own face.
Amen.

The second prayer comes from the celebrated Quaker reformer, writer, and statesman William Penn (1644–1718), whose visionary principles of democracy were to prove so influential in the drafting of the US Constitution. Remorselessly persecuted in England on account of his Quaker beliefs, Penn joined the stream of émigrés to America seeking religious, social and political freedom. His short prayer reflects painful personal experience of prejudice and persecution.

Lord,
    help me not to despise or oppose what I do not
      understand.
Amen.

14 April

If we are to boast in anything, said the Apostle Paul, it should be in the cross of Christ. Clearly those words made an impression on the Congregationalist minister and theologian Isaac Watts (1674–1748). Considered by some the father of English hymnody, he undoubtedly penned some memorable works, including such classics as 'Our God, our help in ages past', 'Jesus shall reign where'er the sun', 'Joy to the world!' and the great hymn below. I say 'hymn' but, of course, it's equally a prayer, and what a special one at that. Many, I suspect, could recite it word for word such is the impact it has made upon them. Reflect on it quietly, verse by verse, and make this prayer your own.

When I survey the wondrous cross
on which the Prince of Glory died,
my richest gain I count but loss,
and pour contempt on all my pride.

Forbid it, Lord, that I should boast,
save in the death of Christ, my God;
all the vain things that charm me most,
I sacrifice them to his blood.

See from his head, his hands, his feet,
sorrow and love flow mingling down!
Did e'er such love and sorrow meet,
or thorns compose so rich a crown?

Were the whole realm of nature mine,
that were a present far too small;
love so amazing, so divine,
demands my soul, my life, my all.

15 April

Once more today we've a prayer of St Anselm (1033–
1109), this one a general intercession for those in
need. For many, myself included, intercession isn't
their strongest point, prayers for others tending to take
second place after prayers for oneself. That's understandable, for personal concerns and needs will
inevitably figure large in our minds, but it can lead to
an unhealthy inward-looking faith that has little if anything in common with the pastoral concern characteristic of the life and ministry of Christ – the archetypal
man for others. Make use, then, of prayers like this to
redress the balance and broaden your horizons.

O Lord,
    we bring before you the distress and dangers
        of peoples and nations,
    the pleas of the imprisoned and the captive,
    the sorrows of the grief-stricken,
    the needs of the refugee,
    the impotence of the weak,
    the weariness of the despondent,
    and the diminishments of the ageing.
O Lord, stay close to all of them.
Amen.

16 April

We've made use of words written by Thomas Ken
(1637–1711) earlier in this book, but those I've chosen
for today may be more familiar, still being frequently
sung to the tune 'Tallis' Canon'. Ideal as a closing act of
public worship, this poem-cum-hymn is equally suited
to committing each night into God's safe keeping.

Glory to thee, my God, this night
for all the blessings of the light;
keep me, O keep me, King of kings,
beneath thine own almighty wings.

Forgive me, Lord, for thy dear Son,
the ill that I this day have done,
that with the world, myself, and thee,
I, ere I sleep, at peace may be.

Teach me to live, that I may dread
the grave as little as my bed;
teach me to die, that so I may
rise glorious at the aweful day.

O may my soul on thee repose,
and with sweet sleep mine eyelids close;
sleep that may me more vigorous make
to serve my God when I awake.

When in the night I sleepless lie,
my soul with heavenly thoughts supply;
let no ill dreams disturb my rest,
no powers of darkness me molest.

Praise God, from whom all blessings flow;
praise him, all creatures here below;
praise him above, ye heavenly host:
praise Father, Son, and Holy Ghost.

17 April

I've once more chosen to make use of a hymn, this time
by Frances Ridley Havergal (1836–1879). Daughter of
an Anglican clergyman, Frances wrote, alongside her
hymns, a number of poems and homilies, several
aimed especially at children. Her lovely words here
sum up what Christian trust is, or at least should be, all
about: putting our trust in God for everything in the
confidence that whatever we are called to face, he will
be with us through it.

I am trusting thee, Lord Jesus,
trusting only thee,
trusting thee for full salvation,
great and free.

I am trusting thee for pardon:
at thy feet I bow,
for thy grace and tender mercy,
trusting now.

I am trusting thee to guide me;
thou alone shalt lead,
every day and hour supplying
all my need.

I am trusting thee for power:
thine can never fail;
words which thou thyself shalt give me
must prevail.

I am trusting thee, Lord Jesus;
never let me fall:
I am trusting thee for ever,
and for all.

18 April

A common theme of praise and thanksgiving is the beauty of the natural world and grandeur of the universe, and it's just this that we see in our prayer today. Written by the American minister, theologian and pioneer of social justice Walter Rauschenbusch (1861–1918), it gratefully acknowledges the wonder of all God has made and asks for help never to overlook such simple but special blessings.

O God, I thank you for this universe;
    for its vastness and its riches,
    and for the variety of life which teems within it
    and of which I am a part.
I praise you for the sky and the winds,
    for the clouds
    and for the constellation of the heavens.
I praise you for seas and rivers,
    for mountains and trees,
    and the grass beneath my feet.
I thank you for the senses which enable me to see
    the splendour of the morning,
    to hear the song of the birds,
    and to enjoy the scents of springtime.
Open my heart, I pray,
    to all this joy and beauty,
    and save me from being so burdened by care
    or blinded by greed
    that I fail to notice when even the thorn bushes
    are aflame with your glory.
Amen.

19 April

We've already encountered the spirituality of Baha'i prayers and today we've another equally memorable example. The theme here is of faith and trust, and, in consequence, the peace of mind we can enjoy knowing that whatever we face, we have God to lead, protect, support and love us. To that, as Christians, we can only say a glad 'Amen!'

O God,
    refresh and gladden my spirit,
    purify my heart,
    illumine my powers.
I lay all my affairs in your hands.
You are my guide and my refuge.
I will no longer be sorrowful and grieved;
    I will be a happy and joyful being.
O God, I will no longer be full of anxiety,
    nor will I let trouble harass me.
I will not dwell on the unpleasant things of life.
O God, you are more friend to me than I am
    to myself.
I dedicate myself to you, O Lord.
Amen.

20 April

Our words today are taken from the so-called 'Universal Prayer' of Pope Clement XI (1649–1721). An accomplished scholar, he was equally devout, his life testifying unmistakably to the reality of his faith. This prayer, composed in 1721, covers almost every aspect of discipleship, including praise, confession, thanksgiving and petition, so I've divided it into several shorter prayers, each able to stand alone. The following extract combines a yearning for deeper faith with a heartfelt outpouring of praise.

Lord, I believe in you: increase my faith.
I trust in you: strengthen my trust.
I love you: let me love you more and more.
I am sorry for my sins: deepen my sorrow.
I worship you as my first beginning.
I long for you as my last end.
I praise you as my constant helper,
    and call on you as my loving protector.
Amen.

21 April

Prayer can be hard, can't it, when you're going through the mill, life throwing up all kinds of problems that you feel unable to cope with. It's all too easy then to let your prayer life slip, but it's precisely at such times that you need it most. 'What, though, should we pray for?' you may ask. 'How can we approach God when we're feeling tired, angry, disillusioned or frustrated?' The simple answer to that is this: be honest with God and he will hear and understand. Don't tell him what you think he *expects* to hear; share rather what *you need* to say. The following prayer-cum-poem, written by Anne Brontë (1820–1849), does just that.

Oh, I am very weary,
though tears no longer flow;
my eyes are tired of weeping,
my heart is sick of woe;
my life is very lonely,
my days pass heavily,
I'm wearying of repining,
wilt thou not come to me?
Oh, didst thou know my longings
for thee, from day to day,
my hopes, so often blighted,
thou wouldst not thus delay!
God! if this indeed be all
that Life can show to me;
if on my aching brow may fall
no freshening dew from thee –
if with no brighter light than this
the lamp of hope may glow,
and I may only dream of bliss,
and wake to weary woe;

if friendship's solace must decay,
when other joys are gone,
and love must keep so far away,
while I go wandering on –
wandering and toiling without gain,
the slave of others' will,
with constant care, and frequent pain,
despised, forgotten still;
grieving to look on vice and sin,
yet powerless to quell
the silent current from within,
the outward torrent's swell:
while all the good I would impart,
the feelings I would share,
are driven backward to my heart,
and turned to wormwood, there;
if clouds must ever keep from sight
the glories of the Sun,
and I must suffer Winter's blight,
'ere Summer is begun;
if Life must be so full of care,
then call me soon to thee;
or give me strength enough to bear
my load of misery.

22 April

We've made use in this book of words from the Psalms and the New Testament, but there are prayers also in parts of the Bible where you might not expect to find them. One such place is the book of Daniel (9:4, 5, 7a, 17, 18b, 19a), where we find the following memorable prayer of confession and plea for forgiveness. It's hard to believe it comes from the Old Testament, for we find within it the essentials of the gospel – God's mercy poured out upon us not because we deserve it but out of sheer grace.

Lord God, great and awesome,
    faithful in your covenant
    and constant in love towards those
    who love you and honour your commandments,
    we have sinned and done wrong,
    wicked and rebellious in our actions,
    turning our backs on your commandments
        and instructions.
To you, Lord, belongs righteousness,
    but to us humiliation,
    for we have sinned against you.
Listen though to your servant's prayer, O God –
    to his pleas for mercy –
    and make your face shine, Lord, on your ruined
        sanctuary,
    for your name's sake.
We plead for mercy not because we have any merit,
    but recognising your great mercy.
Hear, O Lord, and forgive.
Listen and act.

23 April

Today's prayer comes from the German theologian and pastor Dietrich Bonhoeffer (1906–1945), an example from relatively recent times of extraordinary faith and courage. Implacably opposed to the evils of Nazism, he decided, after much agonising with his conscience, that it was his duty to support active resistance, and in 1943 he became involved in a plot to assassinate Adolf Hitler. When this failed he was arrested and imprisoned, being hanged just a few days before the end of the war in Europe. Amazingly, he produced some of his most memorable work while in prison – testimony indeed to the depth of his faith. The following is one of his prayers written for the close of the day.

O Lord my God,
    thank you for bringing this day to a close.
Thank you for giving me rest in body and in soul.
Your hand has been over me
    and has guarded and preserved me.
Forgive my lack of faith,
    and any wrong that I have done today,
    and help me to forgive all who have wronged me.
Let me sleep in peace under your protection,
    and keep me from all the temptations of darkness.
Into your hands I commend my loved ones;
    I commend to you my body and soul.
O God, may your holy name be praised.
Amen.

24 April

A prayer now attributed to Feodor Romanov (1553–1633), Metropolitan Philaret of Moscow from 1619 to 1633. At one time a popular choice to accede to the Russian throne, he and his wife were forced instead, by the eventual monarch Borus Godunov, to take monastic vows under the names Philaret and Martha respectively. The fall of the Godunovs, however, saw Philaret rise swiftly within the Church, leading to his eventual elevation as patriarch. His words here exude grateful and reverent acknowledgement of all God's goodness, too wonderful for words.

O Lord, I do not know what I ought to ask of you.
You love me more than I know how to love,
   and discern my innermost needs
     even before I recognise them myself.
O Father, grant unto me, thy servant,
   all which I cannot ask.
I dare not ask for a cross or consolation;
   I can only stand in your presence with my heart
     open to you,
   awed and silenced by your will and judgements
   into which my mind cannot penetrate.
Come to me and help me for your great mercy's sake.
To you I offer myself as a sacrifice,
   having no other desire than to fulfil your will.
Teach me how to pray.
Pray yourself in me.
Amen.

25 April

We turn again today to words of Thomas à Kempis (1380–1471). They focus on the theme of love, contrasting God's awesome devotion to the pale imitation we offer in return. Which of us in prayer hasn't been conscious of the massive gulf between the two? The important question is how should we respond? We can feel overwhelmed by the contrast, convinced God can have no interest in anyone as weak and faithless as we are, or, as here, we can bring our poverty to his richness, seeking to be filled by his overflowing love. Let this wonderful prayer help you do just that.

As yet my love is weak, my heart imperfect,
    and so I have great need of your strength and comfort.
Visit me often, I pray,
    and instruct me in the way of your laws.
Set me free from all evil passions,
    and heal my heart from all immoral desires.
And thus, healed and cleansed in spirit,
    may I learn how blissful it is to plunge into the
       depths of your love.
Let your love dissolve my hard heart.
Let your love raise me above myself.
Let your love reveal to me joy beyond imagination.
Let my soul exhaust itself in singing the praises of
    your love.
Let me love you more than I love myself,
    and let me love myself only for your sake.
And let me see your love shining in the hearts of all
    people, that I may love them as I love you.
Amen.

26 April

It's good sometimes simply to acknowledge God's goodness and offer him our praise and thanksgiving. Such a response can sometimes go by the wayside, squeezed out by more pressing matters so that our prayers become more a list of personal concerns and needs. If that is true for you, take time to turn to the Psalms for, as I've said earlier in this book, these positively brim over with outpourings of worship. The following comes from Psalm 57:5, 7-11. Let it also come from *you*.

Let your name be honoured, O God,
    above the heavens,
    and your glory known across the earth!
My heart is constant, O God, resolute within me.
I will sing and make music.
Wake up, soul;
    wake up lyre and harp!
With these I will wake up dawn itself!
I will publicly give you thanks, Lord,
    and sing your praise among the nations,
        for your unfailing love reaches up to the heavens,
        and your constancy extends beyond the clouds.
Let your name be honoured, O God,
    above the heavens,
    and your glory known across the earth!

27 April

Today we've another example of the memorable prayers of St Augustine of Hippo (354–430). Once more he piles up one image upon another to express everything that God means to him, and his own overwhelming need of God. As ever, here are words that repay careful reading, for the more we understand them, the more powerfully they are able to speak both *to* and *for* us.

O Love of God, descend into my heart;
    enlighten the dark corners of this neglected
        dwelling,
    and scatter there your cheerful beams.
Dwell in the soul that longs to be your temple;
    water that barren soil overrun with weeds and
        briars
    and lost for lack of cultivating.
Make it fruitful with your dew.
Come, dear Refreshment of those who languish;
    come, Star and Guide of those who sail amidst
        tempests.
You are the Haven of the tossed and shipwrecked.
Come now, Glory and Crown of the living,
    as well as the Safeguard of the dying.
Come, Sacred Spirit;
    come, and make me fit to receive you.
Amen.

28 April

How do you picture God? Is he for you stern and forbidding or full or mercy; generous and ready to forgive
or looking over your shoulder waiting to punish?
Despite all our talk of his grace, we can find it hard to
banish a sneaking sense that God is more vengeful
than some people like to paint him, ready to come
down on us like a ton of bricks should we step out of
line. From the following prayer of Clement of Alexandria
(c. 150–c. 215) it looks as if he may have experienced
the same problem, but deep down he knew God is not
like that. He asks, then, for a better understanding of
his true nature, as revealed in Christ – a prayer I for
one can echo.

O Teacher, Jesus, be favourable to your children.
Grant that we who follow your command
    may attain the likeness of your image
    and in accord with our strength
    find in you both a good God
    and a judge who is not severe.
Amen.

29 April

I'm not quite sure where the following prayer originated, but its language reflects a Native American background, with its affinity to the natural world. Of course that's not the only place we find God, and there are aspects of creation that arguably speak as much against as for his existence, but many, myself included, experience some of their profoundest spiritual moments through contact with nature. Sadly, we can be too busy sometimes to take in the loveliness of our world, or familiarity can inure us to its wonder. These beautiful words ask for God's help in getting back in touch with his presence around us.

O great Spirit,
    teach me to think quietly,
    to speak gently
    and to hear thy voice in the whispering breeze,
    the song of birds
    and in the murmuring brook.
Amen.

30 April

Today we borrow again from Baha'i spirituality, the following prayer wonderfully capturing the contrast between God's strength and our weakness. It would be easy to view this negatively, cringing before God in abject servility, but there's no hint of that here. Rather he is approached confidently, acknowledged for who he is but recognised also as one who delights in our presence and is always ready to respond to our need.

I bear witness, O my God,
>   that you have created me to know and to worship
>   you.
>   I testify, at this moment, to my powerlessness
>   and your might,
>   to my poverty
>   and your wealth.
There is no other God but you,
>   the help in peril,
>   the self-subsisting.

MAY

1 May

I've chosen today a well-loved hymn of the clergyman Henry Francis Lyte (1793–1847). A gifted poet, he was awarded the prize for best English poem three times during his time studying at Trinity College, Dublin. His faith was profoundly deepened at the deathbed of his brother, also a clergyman, and he went on to make his mark as a preacher, minister, poet and hymn-writer. On his own deathbed, he is said to have pointed skywards with the words: 'Peace! Joy!' The hymn 'Praise, my soul, the king of heaven' is perhaps the best known of all his works, perfectly capturing the sense of awe, gratitude and joy that lies at the heart of worship. A paraphrase of Psalm 103, it was sung at the weddings of King George VI and Queen Elizabeth II.

Praise, my soul, the King of heaven!
To his feet thy tribute bring;
ransomed, healed, restored, forgiven,
who like me his praise should sing?
Praise him! Praise him!
Praise the everlasting King!

Praise him for his grace and favour
to our fathers in distress;
praise him, still the same as ever,
slow to chide and swift to bless.
Praise him! Praise him!
Glorious in his faithfulness!

Father-like he tends and spares us;
well our feeble frame he knows;
in his hands he gently bears us,
rescues us from all our foes.
Praise him! Praise him!
Widely as his mercy flows.

2 May

Are we over-presumptuous sometimes in what we expect from God? We can be, can't we, almost expecting him sometimes to pander to our every whim. Similarly, we can develop an over-inflated image of our own importance, even imagining we have every right to expect God's acquiescence, it being no more than we deserve. Contrast such an attitude with that shown by St Columba (521–597) in the following prayer. Like the Apostle Paul, he considers himself the least qualified of God's people, the most he dares ask for being the lowliest place in God's kingdom. Happily, God delights to give much more, but Columba's words help us to keep a proper sense of perspective – one we do well to cultivate.

Almighty Father, Son and Holy Ghost,
    eternal ever-blessed gracious God;
    to me the least of saints,
    to me allow that I may keep a door in paradise –
    that I may keep even the smallest door,
    the furthest, the darkest, coldest door,
    the door that is least used,
    the stiffest door.
If it be but in your house, O God,
    grant that I may see your glory even from afar,
    and hear your voice, O God,
    and know that I am with you, O God.
Amen.

3 May

We've another extract today from the great prayer of Karl Rahner (1904–1984) that we encountered earlier in this book. Here the emphasis is on renewed commitment and God's gracious acceptance of what we offer him, flawed though it may be. Rahner's lovely words capture an overwhelming faith in God's unfailing mercy and his ability to see us through every circumstance of life, whatever it may bring.

Wise, merciful, loving God,
 do not cast me from your presence.
Keep me in your service all the days of my life.
Ask of me what you will.
Only grant what you command of me.
Even if I tire in your service,
 you in your patience will not tire of me.
You will come to help,
 you will give me the strength to make a fresh start
  again and again;
 to hope against hope;
 in all my defeats to have faith in victory
 and in your triumph within me.
Amen.

4 May

The Christian life has sometimes been depicted as a battle, most particularly in hymns like 'Fight the good fight' and 'Onward, Christian soldiers'. Today we shy away from such imagery, its militaristic and triumphalist overtones striking a raw nerve. Not only does it jar with the teaching of Jesus but it smacks also of jingoism – the sort of arrogance that led to the Crusades and other such conflicts. It has to be said, however, that the idea of spiritual warfare is found even within the New Testament, the Apostle Paul, for example, speaking of putting on the armour of God and doing battle with spiritual forces in high places. One person for whom such a picture would have rung true was St Martin of Tours (c. 316–397), the writer of our prayer today. Eventually a monk, hermit and bishop, he spent time first as a soldier, being required as the son of a veteran officer to serve in the Roman cavalry himself. His words here reflect his experiences of battle, while powerfully expressing his commitment to God's cause, and in that sense at least his prayer can still speak to us today.

Lord,
> if your people still have need of my services,
> I will not avoid the toil.

Your will be done.

I have fought the good fight long enough.

Yet if you bid me continue to hold the frontline
> in defence of your camp,
> I will never beg to be excused from failing strength.

I will do the work you entrust to me.

While you command,
> I will fight beneath your banner.

Amen.

5 May

How often do we spare a thought for others? Probably less often than we should. And when we do, we probably pray chiefly for the poor, sick, hungry and so forth, more specific needs rarely receiving a mention. It's only when we have a personal point of contact with a situation that it occurs to us to bring it prayerfully before God, which perhaps explains today's prayer: that of St Cyprian of Carthage (*c.* 200–258). A bishop in the early days of the Church, he fell victim to a renewed persecution of Christians instigated by the Emperor Valerian, being imprisoned and subsequently executed for his faith. Was it those months leading up to his death that gave him a special empathy for prisoners and those who guard them? We shall never know, but his prayer helps us to remember a group in society we can all too easily forget.

Most gracious Father,
> bless with your special care all prisons and places
> of refuge.
Look with compassion on those who are housed
> there.
Guide and protect those who have returned to the
> world.
Grant all of them true contrition for past sins,
> and strengthen them in their good resolutions.
Lead them from grace to grace
> so that by the help of the Holy Spirit
> they may persevere in the ways of obedience and
>> humility,
> and in the struggle against evil thoughts and
>> desires.

Grant the Holy Spirit to those engaged in teaching
   and training them,
      that they may make wise decisions concerning
         those entrusted to them.
May they labour for love of you
   with deep humility and singleness of purpose,
   purity of heart and life,
      and true zeal for your glory and the salvation of
         souls.
Give them faith and love to sustain them in
   disappointment,
      love and patience towards those under them,
      and, in your own good time,
         crown their work with an eternal recompense.
Amen.

6 May

Prayers for the end of the day always seem to have a special feel to them and the prayer I've chosen here is no exception. It comes once more from the fourth century saint and bishop Ambrose of Milan (c. 340–397), and beautifully asks for God's protection and blessing throughout the long hours of darkness. Quite who translated these words so poetically isn't known, but, in tandem with Ambrose, they've left us with another example of evening prayer to treasure.

Before the ending of the day,
Creator of the world, we pray
that with thy wonted favour, thou
wouldst be our guard and keeper now.
From all ill dreams defend our sight,
from fears and terrors of the night;
withhold from us our ghostly foe,
that spot of sin we may not know.
Our Father, this we ask be done,
through Jesus Christ, thine only Son;
who, with the Holy Ghost and thee,
doth live and reign eternally.

7 May

Of all the prayers written on the theme of penitence, few can have been used more often or be more greatly loved than the following, taken from the *Book of Common Prayer*. It recognises that what we *don't* do is equally as important as anything we do, sins of *omission* being just as damaging as those of *commission*. If any words more beautifully express the gulf between what we long to be and what we are, I've yet to find them.

Almighty and most merciful Father;
>   we have erred, and strayed from thy ways like lost
>   sheep.

We have followed too much the devices and desires of
>   our own hearts.

We have offended against thy holy laws.

We have left undone those things which we ought to
>   have done;
>   and we have done those things which we ought not
>   to have done;
>   and there is no health in us.

But thou, O Lord, have mercy upon us, miserable
>   offenders.

Spare thou them, O God, which confess their faults.

Restore thou them that are penitent;
>   according to thy promises declared unto mankind
>   in Christ Jesu our Lord.

And grant, O most merciful Father, for his sake,
>   that we may hereafter live a godly, righteous, and
>   sober life,
>   to the glory of thy holy Name.

Amen.

8 May

Our prayer today comes from the Portuguese monk and missionary St Anthony of Padua (1195–1231). When his youthful idealistic ambition of being martyred for his faith was dashed by illness, he returned from Morocco to Europe, where he swiftly made his mark as a preacher, carrying the gospel throughout Italy and France. Noted for his compassion towards the poor, he was also reputed to have a ready smile, retentive memory and keen intellect. It's the latter that comes to the fore in his words here, which recognise that true wisdom comes from God.

O God,
    send forth your Holy Spirit into my heart
        that I may perceive,
    into my mind that I may remember,
    and into my soul that I may meditate.
Inspire me to speak with piety, holiness, tenderness
    and mercy.
Teach, guide and direct my thoughts and senses from
    beginning to end.
May your grace ever help and correct me,
    and may I be strengthened now with wisdom from
        on high,
    for the sake of your infinite mercy.
Amen.

9 May

When I was at college in Oxford I regularly visited the
Pusey Library on St Giles Parade to continue my research.
It was founded by Revd Edwin Bouverie Pusey (1800–
1882), an Anglican theologian and leader of the
Oxford Movement. Noted for his unassuming integrity,
he devoted considerable time and money to personally caring for the sick during an outbreak of cholera in
the 1860s. His love and humility shines out of the following prayer.

O most gracious and loving Jesu,
my Lord and my God,
fountain of all grace,
come into my soul with the fullness of thy grace.
Jesu most patient,
too long have I made thee wait for me,
yet come to me:
endure me as a sinner,
and make me, through thy patience, to endure all
things,
and to be patient with all.
Jesu most humble,
make me through thy humility so humble
that I may never lift up myself,
for anything against anything,
as to any one.
Jesu most loving,
come with all thy love into my soul,
that I may love thee with a burning love,
and love all and each with thine own love.
Amen.

10 May

How can we make sense of the tragedies and catastrophes that so many experience? There are no easy answers, yet we need to wrestle with the questions life throws up, and to remember those who find them an obstacle to faith. Questions of faith are nothing new. The respected English scholar and clergyman Charles John Vaughan (1816–1897) acknowledges such in the following prayer, yet prays for help in keeping faith despite all that seems to deny it.

Look in mercy, heavenly Father,
    on this troubled and divided world.
Though we cannot always trace your footsteps
    or understand your working,
    give us grace to trust you with an undoubting faith.
And when the time you have set has come, Lord,
    show us the new heaven and the new earth,
    where righteousness lives
    and where the Prince of Peace rules,
    your Son, our Saviour Jesus Christ.
Amen.

11 May

Few prayers I've come across quite capture an awareness of the wonder and majesty of God as well as that
by the celebrated German theologian Karl Rahner (1904–
1984). We've already looked at extracts from this prayer
in earlier months, but to me these opening lines are
some of the most powerful of all, conjuring up an
unforgettable sense of God's awesome presence.

Almighty, holy God, to you I come, to you I pray.
I acknowledge you, Father, Son and Holy Spirit,
    praise you, glorify you and adore you.
I give you thanks for your great glory.
What can I say to you, my God?
Shall I collect together all the words which praise your
    holy Name,
    shall I give you all the names of this world,
    you, the Unnameable?
Shall I call you God of my life,
    meaning of my existence,
    hallowing of my acts,
    my journey's end,
    you my most treasured happiness?
Shall I say: Creator, Sustainer, Pardoner,
    Near One, Distant One, Incomprehensible One,
    God both of flowers and stars,
    God of the gentle wind and of terrible battles,
    Wisdom, Power, Loyalty and Truthfulness, Eternity
        and Infinity,
    you the All-merciful,
    you the Just One,
    you Love itself?
What can I say to you, my God?

Should I consecrate myself to you?
Should I say that I belong to you with all that I have
    and am?
O my God, how can I give myself to you, unless your
    grace accepts me?
How can I devote myself to your service, unless you
    call me?
I give you thanks for having called me.
Amen.

12 May

Are you good at recognising your mistakes? I'm not. I like to think otherwise, of course, as no doubt we all do, but most of us have our blind spots, somehow being closed to our deepest weaknesses. As St Ephrem of Syria (c. 306–373) recognises in the following prayer, we need God's help to look deeper, if we are to spot the weaknesses in ourselves that we're so quick to see in others.

O Lord and Master of my life,
Grant not unto me a spirit of idleness,
    of discouragement,
    of lust for power,
    and of vain speaking.
But bestow upon me, thy servant,
    the spirit of chastity,
    of meekness,
    of patience,
    and of love.
Yea, O Lord and King,
    grant that I may perceive my own transgressions,
    and judge not my brother,
    for blessed art thou unto ages of ages.
Amen.

13 May

Most of us, myself included, are a little disconcerted by mystics, their ascetic lifestyles and emotionally charged visions so far removed from our lifestyles that they leave us feeling uneasy and a tad sceptical. Yet there's no denying that they've bequeathed to us some memorable pictures of God and profound insights into his character. Today's prayer, written by the Cistercian nun Mechtild of Magdeburg (c. 1210–c. 1285), provides a perfect example. In just a few words she manages to say so much, celebrating the beauty of God and our relationship to him.

Lord, you are my lover,
    my longing,
    my flowing stream,
    my sun,
    and I am your reflection.
Amen.

14 May

Our prayer today is attributed to the Benedictine monk, writer and teacher Rabanus Maurus Magnentius (c. 780–856), abbot of Fulda and later Archbishop of Mainz. Addressed to the Holy Spirit, it seeks growth in grace, together with God's guidance and protection.

Come, Creating Spirit,
    visit the minds of those who are yours;
    fill with the highest grace the hearts of those whom
        you have created.
You are called Comforter and Protector;
    you are God's greatest gift,
    the power of life, fire, mercy,
        and ointment for the soul.
You are the sevenfold gift,
    the right finger of the Father,
    the fulfilment of the Father's promise,
    the preaching tongue.
Kindle a light in the senses,
    fill the heart with love,
    strengthen our weak bodies with the power
    of patience.
Defend from the enemy,
    give peace with ourselves,
    lead us wisely,
    protect against all evil.
All knowing comes from you.
Give, that we may learn to know the Father,
    and the Son,
    and you as well, Spirit,
    that we may believe eternally.

Glory be to the Father and to the Son,
    who rose from the dead,
    and to you, Comforter and Protector,
    in eternity eternally.
Amen.

15 May

Some words repay quiet and reflective study, speaking with ever-increasing power the more we look at them. That's true for me of the following words of St Anselm (1033–1109), each one being carefully chosen to articulate his desire to serve God more faithfully. Consider carefully what he's saying and then attempt to make his prayer your own.

Let me believe,
    hope,
    love
    and live
    according to your purpose
    and your will.
Give me heart-piercing goodness and humility.
Amen.

16 May

No book of classic prayers would be complete without including the twenty-third Psalm. It's probably one of the only passages of the Bible most people are vaguely familiar with, but that very familiarity can prevent us from taking in what it's saying. Stop and read it more carefully and we realise afresh what a special prayer of trust and commitment it is. No wonder it has offered such comfort and inspiration across the years to so many.

The Lord's my shepherd, I want for nothing.
He causes me to lie down in fertile pastures,
    he leads me beside tranquil waters,
    and refreshes my soul.
He guides me along right paths for his name's sake.
Though I should walk through the gloomiest
    of valleys,
    I need fear no evil,
    for you are beside me,
    your rod and staff a constant source of comfort.
You prepare a table before me
    in the presence of my foes;
    you anoint my head with oil;
    my cup brims over.
Beyond doubt, blessing and mercy will follow me
    throughout my life,
    and I will dwell in the Lord's house for all my days.

17 May

Poetry, as I've already said, can be a wonderful medium for prayer, as illustrated by the following. It comes from the pen of Henry van Dyke (1852–1933), an American clergyman, academic and author. Pastor of the Brick Presbyterian Church in New York from 1883 to 1899, he went on to become professor of English literature at Princeton University for the next 24 years, during which time he also served as US minister to the Netherlands (1913-16). He is most celebrated for his lines 'Time is . . . too slow for those who wait, / too swift for those who fear, / too long for those who grieve, / too short for those who rejoice, / but for those who love, / Time is Eternity'.

From the prison of anxious thought that greed
   has builded,
from the fetters that envy has wrought,
   and pride has gilded,
from the noise of the crowded ways and the fierce
   confusion,
from the folly that wastes its days in a world of
   illusion,
(Ah, but the life is lost that frets and languishes
   there!)
I would escape and be free in the joy of the open air.

By the faith that the flowers show when they bloom
   unbidden,
by the calm of the river's flow to a goal that is hidden,
by the trust of the tree that clings to its deep
   foundation,

by the courage of wild birds' wings on the long
   migration,
(Wonderful secret of peace that abides in Nature's
   breast!)
teach me how to confide, and live my life, and rest.

18 May

Try as we might, we struggle to get our heads round the idea of grace. We've heard too often that you don't get something for nothing, so we feel we somehow have to earn God's love, despite all assurances to the contrary. Ours, though, is a God who welcomes us not for what we might become but as we are, with all our faults and weaknesses, all our failure and ugliness. The point is beautifully made by George Herbert (1593–1633) in this lovely poem-cum-prayer.

Love bade me welcome; yet my soul drew back,
guilty of dust and sin.
But quick-eyed Love, observing me grow slack
from my first entrance in,
drew nearer to me, sweetly questioning
if I lack'd anything.
'A guest,' I answer'd, 'worthy to be here':
Love said, 'You shall be he.'
'I, the unkind, ungrateful? Ah, my dear,
I cannot look on thee.'
Love took my hand, and smiling did reply,
'Who made the eyes but I?'
'Truth, Lord, but I have marr'd them: let my shame
go where it doth deserve.'
'And know you not,' says Love, 'who bore the blame?'
'My dear, then I will serve.'
'You must sit down,' says Love, 'and taste my meat':
'So I did sit and eat.'

19 May

One of the most famous prayers is the so-called
'Anima Christi', dating back to around the fourteenth
century. Nobody's quite sure who wrote it – a few
believe the author may have been Pope John XXII,
while others suggest St Ignatius of Loyola, but both
theories are almost certainly wrong. What is beyond
doubt is that the words have spoken powerfully to
countless generations, helping them to capture a greater
sense of what God has done for them in Christ and
to respond to it in turn. The following is a poeticised
version that I came across in the parish church of
Greensted, Essex.

Soul of Christ, be my sanctification.
Body of Christ, be my salvation.
Blood of Christ, fill all my veins.
Water from the side of Christ, wash out all my stains.
May Christ's passion strengthen me,
    O good Jesus, hear me.
In thy wounds I fain would hide,
    never to be parted from thy side.
Guard me when my foes assail me,
    call me when my life shall fail me.
Command me then to come to thee,
    that I for all eternity,
    with thy saints may praise thee.
Amen.

20 May

Our prayer today comes from one of the most remarkable women in the history of the Church, St Hildegarde of Bingen (1098–1179). Valued for her wise counsel by kings, bishops and popes, she was also a healer, composer, visionary and writer at a time in which society was largely dominated by men. Besides this she founded a convent and won renown as a preacher, completing her final speaking tour at the age of 73! Her words here give beautiful expression to the life-giving grace of God, nourished and nurtured through the inner presence of his Spirit.

Holy Spirit,
  giving life to all life,
  moving all creatures,
  root of all things,
  washing them clean,
  wiping out their mistakes,
  healing their wounds,
  you are our true life,
  luminous,
  wonderful,
  awakening the heart from its ancient sleep.
Amen.

21 May

Words today of the Congregational solicitor and hymn-writer George Rawson (1807–1889). A shy man, he at first wrote under the pseudonym 'A Leeds layman', only later allowing his name to become public. His words here were written as a hymn, but to me they offer a perfect prayer for use when reading or reflecting on the Bible. They remind us of the danger of closing our minds to what we'd rather not hear or of imagining we know all there is to know. The closing lines of each verse borrow from words first used by the Revd John Robinson of Leyden to members of his congregation in 1620 as they left with the Pilgrim Fathers on board the *Mayflower* to begin a new life in America.

We limit not the truth of God
to our poor reach of mind,
by notions of our day and sect,
crude, partial and confined.
No, let a new and better hope
within our hearts be stirred:
the Lord has yet more light and truth
to break forth from his word.

Who dares to bind to his dull sense
the oracles of heaven,
for all the nations, tongues, and climes,
and all the ages given?
That universe, how much unknown!
That ocean unexplored!
The Lord has yet more light and truth
to break forth from his word.

O Father, Son and Spirit, send
us increase from above;
enlarge, expand all Christian souls
to comprehend thy love:
And make us to go on to know,
with nobler powers conferred,
the Lord has yet more light and truth
to break forth from his word.

22 May

You may be surprised today by the source of our prayer. Even when I tell you it comes from the Bible, you'll probably have little inkling as to chapter and verse. The natural assumption is that it's taken from one of the Psalms or perhaps the book of Isaiah. In fact, though, it's found in 1 Kings 8:30b, 36a, 39 – a book you may tend to associate with dry and perhaps even dull history. It was first prayed by Solomon for the people of Israel at the dedication of the temple, but we can use it equally to intercede for people the world over in the mistakes they have made and will continue to make.

From your dwelling-place in heaven,
    listen to us,
    and when you hear,
    forgive.
Hear us in heaven
    and forgive the sins of your people,
    teaching them instead the true way they should
      walk.
Forgive,
    act
    and deal with all appropriately,
    for you alone know what goes on in human hearts.

23 May

Today's prayer is memorable for it's wonderful imagery. Originating in the New Hebrides, it beautifully conveys the idea of discipleship as a journey – a journey that involves sudden storms that can throw us off course or sink us altogether, yet one in which Christ is always there to guide us, lovingly looking to see us through.

O Jesus,
    be the canoe that holds me in the sea of life.
Be the steer that keeps me straight.
Be the outrigger that supports me in times of great
    temptation.
Let thy Spirit be my sail that carries me through each
    day.
Keep my body strong
    so that I can paddle steadfastly on in the long
        voyage of life.
Amen.

24 May

We've a morning prayer today, attributed to the so-called Optina Elders, a group of monks from the Optina Pustyn Hermitage, Russia, who won renown during the nineteenth century for their profound spiritual wisdom. There were fourteen in all – including such revered names in the Eastern Orthodox tradition as Leonid, Anthony, Macarius, Ambrose, Naktary, Sebastian and Barsanuphius. Together these offered counsel to a host of people from all walks of life, including Tolstoy and Dostoevsky. The tradition of the Optina Elders endured until the Bolshevik revolution, which saw the closure of the monastery and arrest of many monks, some of whom were subsequently tortured and shot. Today, however, Optina Pustyn is once again a place of pilgrimage and worship.

Grant unto me, O Lord,
    that with peace of mind I may face all that this new
        day is to bring.
Grant unto me to dedicate myself completely
    to thy holy will.
For every hour of this day, instruct and support me
    in all things.
Whatsoever tidings I may receive during the day,
    do thou teach me to accept tranquilly,
        in the firm conviction that all eventualities fulfil thy
           holy will.
Govern thou my thoughts and feelings in all I do
    and say.
When things unforeseen occur,
    let me not forget that all cometh down from thee.

Teach me to behave sincerely and rationally toward
    every member of my family,
      that I may bring confusion and sorrow to none.
Bestow upon me, my Lord,
    strength to endure the fatigue of the day,
      and to bear my part in all its passing events.
Guide thou my will and teach me to pray,
    to believe,
    to hope,
    to suffer,
    to forgive,
    and to love.
Amen.

25 May

Today we've another of the eminently practical prayers of Evelyn Underhill (1875–1941), taken once again from her book *Meditations and Prayers* (1949). Taking as her starting point symbols associated with Holy Communion, she relates these to daily life, asking for Christ's help in using ordinary things in his service. Life will be dominated by the mundane for most of us, moments of high spiritual drama being few and far between. Faith needs to find God as much in the commonplace as the unusual – perhaps there especially.

Help me to do your will in whatever work you give;
  willing to use very simple things as the instruments
    of love,
  as you did:
  the towel and the basin;
  the cup, plate, and loaf;
  willing to do the most menial duties
    for the sake of love.

26 May

Few people have given us more memorable prayers than the Apostle Paul. We've encountered a few of them already, and today we've another, this one coming from Ephesians 3:20, 21. You'll no doubt have heard it many times used in public worship but perhaps may not have realised the words come from the Bible. They unforgettably remind us of God's greatness that repeatedly goes far beyond our all-too-limited horizons.

Now to him who by his power at work within us
    is able to achieve inestimably more than anything
    we can ask or even dream of,
        to him be glory in the Church and in Christ Jesus
        in this and every generation,
        now and always.
Amen.

27 May

We dip once more today into other spiritual traditions, using here words from the seventeenth-century poet and seer Sant Tukaram (c. 1608–1649). An Indian peasant and mystic, his teaching on the importance of love in encountering the divine won him a huge following that continues to this day. To me, his beautiful prayer here is reminiscent of words of Jesus. It may come from an altogether different tradition, but God, I believe, can speak powerfully to Christians through it nonetheless.

Of what avail this restless, hurrying activity,
    this heavy weight of earthly duties?
God's purposes stand firm,
    and you, his little one,
    need only one thing:
    trust in his power
    and he will meet your need.
Your burden rests safe on him,
    and you, his little one,
    may play securely at his side.
This is the sum and substance of it all:
    God is,
    God loves you,
    God bears all your care.

28 May

Christians believe true peace is found in Christ, and St Augustine of Hippo (354–430) would have been one of the first to reinforce that conviction, our hearts being restless, he tells us, until they find God. Peace, though, should not be the same as complacency, true commitment necessarily involving an ongoing hunger and thirst for spiritual fulfilment and growth in grace. Far from resting on our laurels, we should want to progress in faith, striving towards maturity in Christ. It's this that Augustine's prayer acknowledges here, articulating a yearning that he'd want us too to share.

Late have I loved you,
  O Beauty so ancient and so new.
You called, and broke through my defences,
  and now I long for you.
You breathed your fragrance on me,
  and I drew in my breath
  and now I pant for you.
I tasted you,
  and now I hunger and thirst for you.
You touched me,
  and I burn for your peace.
Amen.

29 May

Every Christian at some time or other finds themselves wrestling with the mystery of unanswered prayer. Despite the promise of Jesus that we will receive whatever we ask for in faith, all too often our requests are not granted, and it's hard to understand why. This isn't the place to go into a full discussion of the matter, but it's worth remembering that we're not alone in finding prayer a puzzle sometimes, the Bible itself containing many outpourings of frustration at God's seeming silence. Importantly, no apology is made for such feelings. Rather they are brought openly and honestly before God, it being considered perfectly legitimate to express despair, doubt, anger and disappointment before him. Take, for example, the following words, put together from Psalms 89:46a, 83:1, 86:1, 88:2 and 102:1a. They may well speak equally for you.

How much longer, Lord?
Are you going to hide yourself away for ever?
O God, do not remain silent;
    please don't keep quiet or do nothing.
Listen and answer me, Lord,
    for I'm desperately in need.
Let my prayer reach you;
    hear my cry, I beg you.
Listen to my prayer, Lord,
    and answer me, when I call.

30 May

We've a truly ancient prayer today, coming from the Didache (meaning 'Teaching') – an ancient Christian treatise dating back to the first century. Containing guidelines for the early Church, this important document, referred to by the renowned historian Eusebius, was considered lost until it was rediscovered in 1883 by Philotheos Bryennios, the Greek Orthodox Bishop of Nicomedia. Its words here, written during a time when Christians were viciously persecuted for their faith, offer a succinct prayer of intercession for the Church.

Be mindful of your Church, O Lord.
Deliver it from all evil,
    perfect it with your love,
    sanctify it,
    and gather it together from throughout the world
    into the kingdom which you have prepared for it.
For yours is the power and the glory for ever and ever.
Amen.

31 May

How often before we pray do we carefully consider what we should pray for and whether we're suitably prepared to do so? That's the theme of today's words, coming yet again from St Augustine of Hippo (354–430). Drawn from *The Soliloquies*, they remind us that we can all too easily approach prayer casually, even complacently, forgetting who it is we are addressing. Perhaps it was his awareness of this danger that contributed to Augustine's profound spirituality, reflected in so many of his prayers. This one may be short on words, but it's long on meaning.

O God,
   Founder of the universe,
   help me that I may pray aright,
   that I may act as one worthy to be heard by you,
   and, finally, set me free.
Amen.

JUNE

1 June

It's not just the mistakes we're aware of that we need to recognise and confess; it's also those we may, intentionally or otherwise, have pushed out of our consciousness. The following prayer, written by Thomas Wilson (1663–1755), one-time Bishop of Sodor and Man, helps us do just that.

Forgive my sins, O Lord;
   the sins of my present and sins of my past,
   the sins which I have done to please myself,
   and the sins which I have done to please others.
Forgive my casual sins and my deliberate sins,
   and those which I have tried so hard to hide
   that I have hidden them even from myself.
Forgive me, O Lord, for all of them,
   for Jesus Christ's sake.
Amen.

2 June

The following 'Universal Prayer' was written by the eighteenth-century Catholic writer Alexander Pope (1688–1744). Widely regarded as the most gifted poet of his era, he had a difficult life, not just dogged by ill health but growing up at a time when Catholics faced far-reaching discrimination. His mastery of the rhyming couplet is reflected in the following lines, short but to the point.

If I am right, thy grace impart,
still in the right to stay;
if I am wrong, O teach my heart
to find that better way!

3 June

I've made no secret of my love for the *Book of Common Prayer*, and our prayer today is another illustration of why I value it so much. How many words do you know that can match the lyricism yet profundity of this simple evening collect? It's a beautiful prayer suitable not just for the end of the day but anytime, anywhere.

O God, from whom all holy desires,
    all good counsels,
    and all just works do proceed;
    give unto thy servants that peace which the world
        cannot give;
    that both our hearts may be set to obey thy
        commandments,
    and also that by you, we, being defended
        from the fear of our enemies,
    may pass our time in rest and quietness;
    through the merits of Jesus Christ our Saviour.
Amen.

4 June

Prayers have historical interest for all kinds of reasons, and today is a case in point. It comes from a hymn written by the English poet Isabella S. Stephenson (1843–1890), and was frequently sung by British families and soldiers during the dark years of the First World War. Thankfully few of us will find ourselves in their situation, but the prayer is equally applicable in praying for absent friends, separated by time and space but not forgotten.

Holy Father, in thy mercy,
hear our anxious prayer.
Keep our loved ones, now far absent,
'neath thy care.

5 June

What words should we use to praise God? All too often our attempts to worship him founder as we struggle to express ourselves, and it's at times like those that recourse to prayers of the past can be so useful. Many across the years have communicated their thoughts in ways we can scarcely begin to, capturing a breathtaking sense of God in all his wonder. Such is the case for me with the following traditional Ethiopian-Jewish prayer. It doesn't just express what I want to say; in a very real sense it carries me into the presence of God himself.

You alone are God.
You were from of old,
    and you will be until eternity, always, first and last,
    now and always for ever and ever.
Your epoch will not come to an end;
    you are the same and your kingdom will not be
        abolished.
Your power is invincible and your strength untiring.
Your magnificence will not be humbled,
    the splendour of your name not be dispelled,
    the praise of your exalted fame not be diminished,
    your light not be darkened,
    your decree not be abrogated,
    the pillar of your word not be overthrown,
    your wisdom not fall into error,
    your counsel not be concealed.
You alone are God, God of all,
    Lord of all,
    king of all,
    creator of all,
    conqueror of all,

sovereign over all,
slayer of all,
destroyer of all,
saviour of all,
life of all,
sustainer of all,
protector of all,
restorer of all,
raiser of all,
supporter of all,
helper of all,
a righteous God over all creation.
Amen.

6 June

Central to the gospel is the idea that God is slow to anger and full of love, delighting to bless rather than punish us. So does that rule out any possibility of him executing discipline? If by that we mean vindictive or petulant retribution, the answer is undoubtedly yes, but, as the following prayer recognises, chastisement can stem from a very different motive, it being necessary at times to be cruel to be kind. That's what the celebrated English writer John Donne (1572–1631) has in mind here. Far from fearing punishment, he expressly asks for it as a means towards changing his life for the better. Do we have the courage to echo his words?

O think me worth thine anger, punish me,
burn off my rusts and my deformity,
restore thine image so much, by thy grace,
that thou mayest know me, and I'll turn my face.

7 June

For our prayer today we turn to India and the words of
Rabindranath Tagore (1861–1941), playwright, composer
and novelist. A champion of Bengali culture, Tagore
became Asia's first Nobel Laureate in 1913, and from
these lines, taken from his book *Gitanjali* ('Song Offerings'), it's easy to see why. His words counsel us against
approaching prayer lightly, for if we truly seek God's
will, as we should, we may find his answer more challenging than we'd bargained on.

My debts are large,
    my failures great,
    my shame secret and heavy;
    yet when I come to ask for my good,
    I quake in fear lest my prayer be granted.

8 June

If there's one theme that has dominated prayer across history it's been the desire to know and love God better. We see just this in our prayer today, written by St Alphonsus Liguori (1696–1787), a poet, priest and painter as well as founder of the Congregation of the Most Holy Redeemer, or Redemptorists, devoted to serving the poor and destitute. Despite protestations of ill health, he was appointed Bishop of Sant'Agata dei Goti in 1772 – a position he retired from three years later. A prolific writer, he had the gift of relating faith to daily life, always emphasising the love and mercy of God in doing so.

Eternal Father,
    your Son has promised that whatever we ask in his
      name will be given to us.
In his name I pray:
    give me a burning faith,
    a joyful hope,
    a holy love for Jesus Christ.
Give me the grace of perseverance in doing your will
    in all things.
Do with me what you will.
I repent of having offended you.
Grant, O Lord, that I may love you always
    and never let me be separated from you.
Amen.

9 June

One of the great symbols at the heart of the gospel
is light. 'I am the light of the world,' declared Jesus,
'whoever follows me will not walk in darkness, but will
have the light of life.' A claim echoed in those wonderful
words near the beginning of John's Gospel (1:5): 'The
light shines in the darkness, and the darkness has
not extinguished it.' This does not, of course, simply
concern Jesus for, as he made clear, we should reflect
that light in turn: 'Let your light shine before others, so
that they may see the good deeds you do and give
glory to your Father in heaven' (Matthew 5:16). We
cannot hope to fulfil that calling on our own. As the
following prayer of St Columba (521–597) illustrates,
it depends entirely on God working within us.

O Lord, grant us that love which can never die,
  which will enkindle our lamps but not extinguish
    them,
  so that they may shine in us and bring light
    to others.
Most dear Saviour,
  enkindle our lamps that they may shine for ever in
    your temple.
May we receive unquenchable light from you
  so that our darkness will be illuminated
  and the darkness of the world will be made less.
Amen.

10 June

This is another prayer concerned with shining our light, and it comes from someone who unquestionably did just that. I'm referring to Mother Teresa (1910–1997), winner of the 1979 Nobel peace prize and legendary worker among the poor of Calcutta. Few people have made such an impact on public consciousness yet few could have been more unassuming than this amazing nun who devoted so much of her life to others. If only we could pray her words and mean them, what a difference we would make to our world today.

Dear Jesus,
　　help us to spread your fragrance everywhere we go.
Flood our souls with your spirit and life.
Penetrate and possess our whole being so utterly
　　that our lives may only be a radiance of yours.
Shine through us and be so in us
　　that every soul we come in contact with may feel
　　　　your presence in our soul.
Let them look up and see no longer us, but only Jesus.
Stay with us
　　and then we shall begin to shine as you shine,
　　so to shine as to be light to others.
The light, O Jesus, will be all from you.
None of it will be ours.
It will be you shining on others through us.
Let us thus praise you in the way you love best
　　by shining on those around us.
Let us preach you without preaching,
　　not by words, but by our example;
　　by the catching force –
　　the sympathetic influence of what we do,
　　the evident fullness of the love our hearts bear to you.
Amen.

11 June

Here we have another prayer on the theme of God's amazing grace. Written once again by Thomas à Kempis (1380–1471), it contrasts our unworthiness with God's goodness, our feeble discipleship with his constant love, our ingratitude with his willingness still to bless. Do we take that for granted? I know I do. Time and time again I forget how much I owe and how much God has done. This prayer asks for help in making a more fitting and loving response.

Although I am unworthy of every good,
    yet your greatness and infinite goodness, O God,
    never cease to bless even the ungrateful
    and those who have withdrawn from you.
Oh, convert us to you,
    so that we may be thankful, humble, and devout,
    because you are our salvation.
Amen.

12 June

Most of us will probably have heard of the Dominican Order of monks, but the name of St Dominic (c. 1170–1221) may be less familiar to us. It's to him, though, that we owe our prayer today. Founder of the Order of Preachers, he subjected himself to an abstemious lifestyle, wearing a hair shirt, fasting, sleeping on sackcloth, and walking everywhere barefoot as he carried the gospel from town to town. Through it all, however, he praised God, continuing to teach his followers about the blessedness of discipleship even as he lay dying. His commitment and trust in God's promises distinguish his words here.

May God the Father, who made us, bless us.
May God the Son send his healing among us.
May God the Holy Spirit move within us
    and give us eyes to see with,
    ears to hear with,
    and hands that his work might be done.
May we walk and preach the word of God to all.
May the angel of peace watch over us
    and lead us at last by God's grace to the kingdom.
Amen.

13 June

Once more today we turn to words of St Augustine of Hippo (354–430), and, as ever, they don't disappoint. Recognising with disarming candour the poverty of his discipleship, he asks, with corresponding eloquence, for God to make up what is so clearly lacking. Yet again, here is a prayer that is simple yet special, helping us to express what we struggle to say on our own.

Lord Jesus, my Saviour,
　　let me now come to you.
My heart is cold:
　　warm it by your selfless love.
My heart is sinful:
　　cleanse it by your precious blood.
My heart is weak:
　　strengthen it by your joyous Spirit.
My heart is empty:
　　fill it with your divine presence.
Lord Jesus, my heart is yours:
　　possess it always and only for yourself.
Amen.

14 June

The so-called Serenity Prayer will be familiar to most and loved in equal proportion. A unique blend of common sense and spirituality, it is at once wonderfully down-to-earth yet full of spiritual wisdom. Adopted by Alcoholics Anonymous in a shortened version, the words speak of gaining a proper perspective on life and, with God's help, making the most of all he's given. The prayer, written by the American theologian Reinhold Niebuhr (1892–1971), is here reproduced in full.

God,
    give us grace to accept with serenity the things that
        cannot be changed,
    courage to change the things which should be
        changed,
    and the wisdom to distinguish the one from the
        other.
Living one day at a time,
    enjoying one moment at a time,
    accepting hardship as a pathway to peace,
    taking, as Jesus did, this sinful world as it is,
    not as I would have it,
    trusting that you will make all things right
    if I surrender to your will
    so that I may be reasonably happy in this life
    and supremely happy with you for ever in the next.
Amen.

15 June

For our prayer today I've turned to a well-loved hymn – arguably one of the most popular ever written. It was written by the Oxford University lecturer John Ernest Bode (1816–1874) to celebrate the Confirmation of his daughter and two sons, every word exuding joyful faith and commitment. Few hymns or prayers can offer a more perfect way of committing our lives afresh to Christ.

O Jesus, I have promised,
to serve thee to the end;
be thou for ever near me,
my Master and my friend:
I shall not fear the battle
if thou art by my side,
nor wander from the pathway
if thou wilt be my guide.

O let me feel thee near me;
the world is ever near;
I see the sights that dazzle,
the tempting sounds I hear;
my foes are ever near me,
around me and within;
but, Jesus, draw though nearer,
and shield my soul from sin.

O let me hear thee speaking
in accents clear and still,
above the storms of passion,
the murmurs of self-will;
O speak to reassure me,
to hasten or control;
O speak and make me listen,
thou guardian of my soul.

O Jesus, thou hast promised,
to all who follow thee,
that where thou art in glory
there shall thy servant be;
and, Jesus, I have promised
to serve thee to the end:
O give me grace to follow,
my Master and my friend.

O let me see thy foot-marks,
and in them plant mine own;
my hope to follow duly
is in thy strength alone:
O guide me, call me, draw me,
uphold me to the end;
and then in heav'n receive me,
my Saviour and my friend.

16 June

The author of today's prayer may come as a surprise to you, for his name is not one we would automatically associate with the Church or spirituality. Robert Louis Stevenson (1850–1894) found fame for writing of another kind, notably classic novels such as *Kidnapped*, *The Strange Case of Dr Jekyll and Mr Hyde*, *The Master of Ballantrae* and *Treasure Island*. Alongside such books, however, Stevenson wrote other, more reflective works, one such being *Celestial Surgeon*, and there we find the following poetic plea for a greater awareness of what God has done for him and for all through the suffering and death of Christ.

Lord, thy most pointed pleasure take,
and stab my spirit broad awake;
or, Lord, if too obdurate I,
choose thou, before that spirit die,
a piercing pain, a killing sin,
and to my dead heart run them in.

17 June

Surely the most famous name associated with Assisi is
that of St Francis, but not far behind must come St Clare
of Assisi (1194–1253), founder of the Order of Poor
Ladies, or St Clares as they have come to be known. It
was hearing St Francis preaching – while she was just
18 – that inspired Clare to become a nun, although
she had long been noted for her piety and devotion to
Christ. In 1216 she became abbess of San Damiano,
where she served for the rest of her life. She may have
renounced the world and its riches, but, as the following
prayer shows, she clearly counted herself rich. Through
her words we in turn can celebrate the treasure God
grants to all who love him.

O blessed poverty,
   who bestows eternal riches on those who love and
      embrace her!
O holy poverty,
   to those who possess and desire you
      God promises the kingdom of heaven
      and offers, indeed, eternal glory and blessed life!
O God-centred poverty,
   whom the Lord Jesus Christ condescended to
      embrace before all else!
   Amen.

18 June

In the book of Deuteronomy 33:27 we find what is
surely one of the most memorable lines of Scripture:
'The eternal God is your dwelling place, and underneath are the everlasting arms' (RSV). I included that
verse at just about every funeral service I conducted,
for it communicates in a way few other passages can
even begin to the assurance of God's love supporting
us in life and in death, never letting us go. We find the
same expressed, and with equal beauty, in our prayer
today, adapted from the blessing of a sick person. It asks
God to be present in every moment of life, wherever
we are and whatever we may face. It's not that the
writer doubts this will be so; simply that she or he
needs reminding of that wonderful truth. Why not
remind yourself in turn?

Lord Jesus Christ,
    be thou beside me, to defend me;
    be thou within me, to keep me;
    be thou before me, to lead me;
    be thou behind me, to guard me;
    be thou above me, to bless me;
    that with thee and in thee I may live
        and have my being,
    for ever and ever.
Amen.

19 June

Today we've what surely is one of the most famous prayers of all, coming, predictably, from St Augustine of Hippo (354–430). Quite what it is about these words that makes them so special I'm not sure. Perhaps it's their gently flowing rhythm, perhaps their simplicity, perhaps their poetry, but most of all it's probably the evident sincerity, certain faith and wonderful promise that shines from them. If we were to pray this prayer every day it surely could not fail to change us for the better.

Lord God,
    the light of the minds that know you,
    the life of the souls that love you,
    and the strength of the wills that serve you:
    help me so to know you that I may truly love you,
    and so to love you that I may fully serve you,
    whom to serve is perfect freedom.
Amen.

20 June

Some people humble and inspire us by the quality of their living, and one such was the American Elizabeth Ann Seton (1774–1821). Active in social work from an early age, in 1797 she helped set up the Society for the Relief of Poor Widows with Small Children. Ironically, she was later to be widowed herself in 1803, and left with five children to care for. Converting to Catholicism from Anglicanism in 1805, despite huge opposition from loved ones, Ann founded what was to become the Sisters of Charity. The first American to be canonised, she is credited with having founded the United States Catholic Parochial School System. This prayer expresses her desire to serve God faithfully in all she did. May it be our prayer too.

O Father,
   the first rule of our dear Saviour's life
     was to do your will.
Let his will of the present moment be the first rule
   of our daily life and work,
     with no other desire but for its most full and
       complete accomplishment.
Help us to follow it faithfully,
   so that doing what you wish we will be pleasing
     to you.
Amen.

21 June

To live with such joy and peace of mind that others cannot help but take notice – that's an ambitious goal, isn't it, but in the following prayer it's one that Robert Louis Stevenson (1850–1894) asks might become reality. I warm to his words, for surely he puts his finger on what ought to characterise us as Christians, though it all too rarely does so. If our faith corresponds even a fraction to the claims we make for it, then we should unmistakably radiate happiness, who and what we are speaking louder than any words we might use. Is that true of you? It's not for me, and I doubt it ever will be, but I'll go on praying and working towards it, for what better testimony could there ever be?

Grant us, O Lord,
    the royalty of inward happiness
    and the serenity that comes from living close to thee.
Daily renew in us the sense of joy,
    and let thy eternal spirit dwell in our souls
        and bodies,
      filling every corner of our hearts with light
        and gladness.
So that,
    bearing about with us the infection of good courage,
    we may be diffusers of life,
    and meet all that comes,
    of good or ill,
    even death itself,
    with gallant and high-hearted happiness,
    giving thee thanks always for all things.
Amen.

22 June

We've a short American prayer today, taken from the *New England Primer* – a religious textbook used by early English settlers. First printed in 1690, it was used for well over a hundred years, religion and education being inexorably combined. To my mind there was an unhealthy emphasis on punishment and death in the *Primer*'s teaching, but stripped of that forbidding context these words offer a simple way of entrusting ourselves into God's eternal care, in this life or the next.

Now I lay me down to sleep,
I pray thee, Lord, my soul to keep;
If I should die before I wake,
I pray thee, Lord, my soul to take.

23 June

What does it profit someone, said Jesus, if they gain all the riches of this world but give away their soul? (Matthew 16:26). The answer, of course, is nothing. Some things in life are more important than money, success, possessions or comfort, nourishing not the body but the spirit, the person deep within. We can be rich, yet poor; have nothing yet possess everything. To be at peace with ourselves and, above all, at peace with God is a prize beyond words – too special, as the following words of John Donne (1572–1631) remind us, to ever be sacrificed. Use this prayer to focus on what really matters and to let go of the rest.

Eternal and most glorious God,
    suffer me not so to undervalue myself as to give
        away my soul,
    thy soul,
    thy dear and precious soul,
    for nothing;
    and all the world is nothing,
        if the soul be given for it.
Preserve therefore my soul, O Lord,
    because it belongs to thee,
    and preserve my body
    because it belongs to my soul.
Amen.

24 June

Few prayers could be simpler than the one I've chosen
for today, yet few would better repay careful thought. It
comes from the Cistercian monk, mystic and theologian
St Bernard of Clairvaux (1090–1153). Famed for his
holiness and devoted to serving others, he was one of
the most celebrated religious teachers of his time, his
life and work still being studied today. Reminiscent of
words of Jesus, he reminds us here that the kingdom of
God is within as much as anywhere. Indeed, if we cannot
find it inside us, we will never find it at all. It pays,
then, to consider who and what we are, reflecting on
how far these tally with the gospel. Take time to do
that and, like Bernard, we will realise how much in
need we are of Christ's cleansing and transforming
touch.

Come Lord Jesus,
    take away scandals from your kingdom,
    which is my soul,
    and reign there.
Amen.

25 June

Must our prayers be articulated in order to be real? I've never thought so and it is plain from the following that the Irish poet, novelist and biographer Thomas Moore (1779–1852) didn't think so either. Called by some the bard of Ireland, he wrote, among other works, 'The Last Rose of Summer' and 'The Harp That Once Through Tara's Halls'. His words here express a deep and assured confidence that God hears and responds to our innermost thoughts when we bring them quietly but sincerely to him. Words may fail us but still he listens, discerning what goes on in our hearts and always ready to answer.

As down in the sunless retreats of the ocean
sweet flowers are springing no mortal can see,
so deep in my soul the still prayer of devotion
unheard by the world, rises silent to thee.

26 June

Can God really accept us, despite all our faults and
weaknesses? Why should he have any time for flawed
and faithless people such as us? We come to him time
and again, acknowledging our faults and promising to
change but, true to form, we continue to make the same
old mistakes. Won't God lose patience eventually and
wash his hands of us? It's easy to think that, for it's
precisely what we'd do in his place, but as the following
prayer written by St John Chrysostom (c. 347–407)
reminds us, God is different, his nature being always to
have mercy. Just as Jesus mixed with those labelled
sinners throughout his ministry, so God delights to
welcome us as his children. Share, then, in these words,
and rejoice in the wonder of God's forgiveness.

O Lord, my God, I am not worthy that you should
   come into my soul,
    but I am glad that you have come to me
      because in your loving kindness
   you desire to dwell in me.
You ask me to open the door of my soul,
   which you alone have created,
    so that you may enter into it with your loving
      kindness and dispel the darkness of my mind.
I believe that you will do this
   for you did not turn away Mary Magdalene
    when she approached you in tears.
Neither did you withhold forgiveness from the tax
   collector who repented of his sins
    or from the good thief who asked to be received
      into your kingdom.

Indeed, you numbered as your friends all who came
to you with repentant hearts.
O God, you alone are blessed always, now,
and for ever.
Amen.

27 June

When you consider who wrote the following prayer, it may seem rather ordinary, for it comes from none other than John Wesley (1703–1791), the founder of Methodism and leading light of the eighteenth-century Revival. Strongly influenced by Moravian doctrine, John was committed not only to evangelism but also social justice, faith touching every part of life. We'll encounter one of his most celebrated prayers later in this book but here we have a simple expression of gratitude for all God's goodness, qualified by the recognition that whatever thanks we may offer, it can never be enough!

Eternal and merciful Father,
   I give you humble thanks
   (increase my thankfulness I beseech you)
   for all the blessings, spiritual and temporal,
   which in the riches of your mercy,
   you have poured down upon me.
Amen.

28 June

If there's one goal that should characterise Christian discipleship, it's consecrating all of life to God – everything we are and everything we do. That's precisely what the following prayer does through yet more unforgettable words of St Augustine of Hippo (354–430). Repeating the prayer is one thing but, as Augustine himself would have well understood, putting it into practice is a different thing altogether. We can only express our resolve and give of our best: we depend on God to do the rest.

Breathe in me, O Holy Spirit,
    that my thoughts may all be holy.
Act in me, O Holy Spirit,
    that my work, too, may be holy.
Draw my heart, O Holy Spirit,
    that I may love only what is holy.
Strengthen me, O Holy Spirit,
    that I may defend all that is holy.
Guard me, O Holy Spirit,
    that I myself may always be holy.
Amen.

29 June

For our prayer today we turn to a poem titled 'Thanks-giving', written by the American poet, literary critic, anthologist and editor William Stanley Braithwaite (1878–1962). Of slave descent, and left destitute after the death of his father in 1884, he worked his way up to become a leading figure in the literary world, contributing much to a revived interest in poetry within the United States. Here he offers grateful praise for the simple blessings of life – gifts we often overlook yet that speak so eloquently of God's loving hand.

My heart gives thanks for many things;
for strength to labour day by day,
for sleep that comes when darkness wings
with evening up the eastern way.
I give deep thanks that I'm at peace
with kith and kin and neighbours, too –
dear Lord, for all last year's increase,
that helped me strive and hope and do.

My heart gives thanks for many things;
I know not how to name them all.
My soul is free from frets and stings,
my mind from creed and doctrine's thrall.
For sun and stars, for flowers and streams,
for work and hope and rest and play –
for empty moments given to dreams,
for these my heart gives thanks today.

30 June

How much do you love God? That for me is the question that leaps out of the following prayer, written by St John Vianney (1786–1859); and, compared to the love expressed here I have to say that my own is found wanting. Conscripted into the army of Napoleon Bonaparte while preparing for the priesthood, Jean-Baptiste-Marie, as he is properly called, deserted and resumed his training, eventually becoming Curé of Ars in 1818, from where word of his saintly lifestyle and faith soon spread. Reading these words it's easy to see why, and though we may never quite emulate such total devotion it's an example worth aspiring to.

I love you, O my God,
    and my only desire is to love you
    until the last breath of my life.
I love you, O my infinitely lovable God,
    and I would rather die loving you,
    than live without loving you.
I love you, Lord
    and the only grace I ask is to love you eternally.
My God,
    if my tongue cannot say in every moment
        that I love you,
    I want my heart to repeat it to you as often as I
        draw breath.
Amen.

JULY

1 July

Few people have had a more enquiring mind or sharper intellect that Dr Samuel Johnson (1709–1784), so you might think that few equally would have been better qualified to wrestle with the mysteries of life, including questions of faith. I've no doubt that he did ponder many such matters, yet, as the following prayer shows, he had sufficient wisdom to realise that some things are and always will be beyond human comprehension. His words here echo the words of Job (42:2-3): 'I know that you can do anything, and that nothing is beyond you. I have spoken of mysteries I do not understand, things so wonderful they are beyond my comprehension', or of David in Psalm 131:1, 2: 'My heart, Lord, does not get above itself, nor are my eyes high and mighty. I do not fret about matters too awesome and special to understand. Rather, like an infant with its mother I am peaceful and still in my soul. That's what I'm like: a little child.' We are right to seek enlightenment, but if we can't explain something, that doesn't make it wrong. When it comes to God, we need faith as well as understanding: the two go hand in hand.

O Lord, my Maker and Protector,
    who has graciously sent me into this world
    to work out my salvation,
    enable me to drive from me all such unquiet
        and perplexing thoughts
    as may mislead or hinder me in the practice
        of those duties
    which thou hast required.

When I behold the works of thy hands
    and consider the course of thy providence,
        give me grace always to remember that thy thoughts
            are not my thoughts,
    nor thy ways my ways.
And while it shall please thee to continue me in this
    world where much is to be done
    and little to be known,
    teach me by thy Holy Spirit
    to withdraw my mind from unprofitable and
        dangerous enquiries,
    from difficulties vainly curious,
    and doubts impossible to be solved.
Let me rejoice in the light which thou hast imparted,
    let me serve thee with active zeal, and humble
        confidence,
    and wait with patient expectation for the time
    in which the soul which thou receivest,
    shall be satisfied with knowledge.
Grant this, O Lord, for Jesus Christ's sake.
Amen.

2 July

Many would have heard this prayer as they settled down in church ready for another sermon, for it was used by the preacher, poet and hymn-writer George Herbert (1593–1633). We could use it ourselves before going off to worship, listening to a recorded service or simply reading the Bible, the words asking God to speak afresh through his word and touch our life by his Spirit. Just as he's challenged countless people in years gone by, so he can speak directly to our lives, here and now.

Oh, make thy word a swift word,
    passing from the ear to the heart,
    from the heart to the life and conversation;
    that as the rain returns not empty,
    so neither may thy word,
    but accomplish that for which it is given.
Amen.

3 July

A common denominator linking many great prayers seems to be a desire to know and understand God's will better. There is no long list of requests, no asking God for this or that. Rather there's a humble acknowledgement that even prayer itself depends finally on God's inspiration if it is to be all it should be. Such is the case with the following words of St Ambrose of Milan (c. 340–397). Recognising all too well the gulf between himself and God and his inability to span the chasm, he seeks God's help and guidance in establishing a living, loving relationship. Which of us doesn't yearn for the same?

Lord, teach me to seek you,
    and reveal yourself to me as I look for you.
For I cannot seek you unless first you teach me,
    nor find you unless first you reveal yourself to me.
Amen.

4 July

It's important in our prayers to remember the needs of the world, but important also to think of those closer to home, including our nearest and dearest, for too easily we take them for granted. Many classic prayers commit friends and loved ones to God, including the following by St Anselm (1033–1109), which asks God to draw them closer into a living and loving relationship with him.

O Blessed Lord,
    who commanded us to love one another,
    grant us grace that,
        having received your undeserved bounty,
    we may love everyone in you and for you.
We implore your clemency for all;
    but especially for the friends whom your love
        has given to us.
Love them, O Fountain of love,
    and make them to love you with all their heart,
    that they may will,
    and speak,
    and do those things only which are pleasing to you.
Amen.

5 July

Our prayer today is an ancient expression of praise known as the Adoramus Te. Sung or recited for centuries within the Catholic Church, particularly during the Stations of the Cross, it has found a place today within many other traditions. Composed originally in Latin, the English version below is now more commonly used. The prayer offers simple but heartfelt worship for the redemption of the world through Christ. It takes us back to the basics of the gospel that sometimes we can too easily overlook.

We adore you, most holy Lord Jesus Christ,
　　here and in all your churches that are in the whole
　　　　world,
　　and we bless you,
　　because you have suffered for us,
　　and by your Holy Cross you have redeemed
　　the world.
Amen.

6 July

I've chosen more words today from the *Book of Common Prayer*. Intended for use at the start of the day, they ask for guidance and protection from what might lead us astray or cause us harm. Above all, the emphasis is on walking faithfully with God, living with Christ's help in a way that is pleasing to him. Join your voice with that of generations before you in committing this day to him.

O Lord our heavenly Father,
  Almighty and everlasting God,
  who hast safely brought us
    to the beginning of this day:
  defend us in the same with your mighty power;
  and grant that this day we fall into no sin,
  neither fall into any kind of danger;
  but that all our doings may be ordered
    by thy governance,
  to do always what is righteous in your sight;
  through Jesus Christ our Lord.
Amen.

7 July

One of the most famous prayers in history, and a
summary of what prayer is all about, is that of Jesus in
the Garden of Gethsemane: 'Abba, Father, you can do
anything, so spare me from drinking this cup. Yet don't
do what I want, but what you will' (Mark 14:36).
Much the same idea underlies the following prayer of
St Teresa of Avila (1515–1582), her whole concern
being to give God free reign in her life. So much is this
the case that she can speak of answered prayer as God's
punishment were he to grant anything that clashed with
his will. His wishes may be challenging and hard to
bear but she knows that ultimately they will be for her
good. What of us? We may sometimes casually throw
into conversation the expression 'God willing' but do
we go any further? Are we truly ready to seek his will in
our lives, and to obey?

Govern all by your wisdom, O Lord,
   so that my soul may always be serving you
     as you will
   and not as I choose.
Do not punish me, I beseech you,
   by granting that which I wish or ask,
   if it offend your love which would always live
     in me.
Let me die to myself that I may serve you.
Let me live to you who in yourself are the true life.
Amen.

8 July

One of the issues that dominates current affairs is the environment, and rightly so, for we've come to realise that, as a species, and particularly in the Western world, we've carelessly plundered this world's resources with no thought of tomorrow. Not only are we faced with global warming; we face equally the prospect of eco-logical disaster: every day, it is reckoned, some creature or other becoming extinct. Sadly the record of the Church in this area is an undistinguished one, too many Christians having turned their backs on this life in the hope of a better one to come. A few, though, have spoken out, emphasising that we are called to steward creation rather than abuse it. One such was St Basil of Caesarea (c. 330–379). He asks here for a deeper understanding among all humankind of our underlying unity with everything that God has made and, consequently, our responsibility towards it.

O God,
    grant us a deeper sense of fellowship
        with all living things,
    our little brothers and sisters
    to whom in common with us you have given
        this earth as home.
We recall with regret that,
    in the past,
    we have acted high-handedly and cruelly
        in exercising our domain over them.
Thus, the voice of the earth which should have risen
    to you in song
    has turned into a groan of travail.

May we realise that all these creatures
    also live for themselves and for you –
    not for us alone.
They too love the goodness of life,
    as we do,
    and serve you better in their way than we do
        in ours.
Amen.

9 July

One of the most celebrated prayers of all time is that of St Francis of Assisi (1182–1226). Not only is there something special about its wonderfully poetic language, but its concern for others coupled with a desire to grow in grace takes us to the heart of what Christian discipleship is all about. It speaks so powerfully of the needs of the world, common to every age, but also of what we are called to do in response. We may feel inadequate for the task, as indeed we are, but God can take even the smallest deed and use it beyond our imagining. It may not achieve much in the grand scheme of things, but even a small chink of light in the darkness is better than no light at all.

Lord, make me an instrument of your peace:
    where there is hatred, let me sow love,
    where there is injury, pardon,
    where there is doubt, faith,
    where there is darkness, light,
    where there is despair, hope,
    and where there is sadness, joy.

Divine Master,
    grant that I may not so much seek to be consoled
        as to console,
    to be understood as to understand,
    to be loved as to love.
For it is in giving that we receive,
    it is in pardoning that we are pardoned,
    and in dying that we are born to eternal life.
Amen.

10 July

Across the years Christian Aid has used to great effect
some wonderful slogans and prayers, the words of
which have captured the public imagination and stirred
consciences in a way almost impossible to resist. One
such prayer is the following, coming from Latin America
and expressing in a nutshell not just what Christian
Aid is all about but what the Christian faith is about as
well: love that shows itself in action; words that prove
themselves through deeds. If everyone used this prayer
every day and meant it, what a difference it would
make to our world.

O God,
   to those who have hunger,
   give bread,
   and to those who have bread,
   give the hunger for justice.
Amen.

11 July

Few hymns are better loved that the following by J. G. Whittier (1807–1892). It's so familiar that we can forget it's both a poem and a prayer, and a memorable one at that. We're probably unaware that this great hymn was originally a 17-verse poem titled 'The Brewing of Soma', written to counter the excesses of intoxication produced by an Indian drink of that name while, at the same time, taking a swipe at over-passionate Christian worship. One of the greatest of American poets, Whittier was deprecating concerning his hymn-writing abilities. 'I am not really a hymn-writer,' he declared, 'for I know nothing of music. Only a very few of my poems were written for singing. A good hymn is the best use to which poetry can be devoted but I do not claim that I have been successful writing one.' Countless generations who've sung his words would beg to differ. Here, I cite just three verses of the six most commonly used.

Dear Lord and Father of mankind,
forgive our foolish ways!
Reclothe us in our rightful mind,
in purer lives thy service find,
in deeper reverence praise,
in deeper reverence praise.

Drop thy still dews of quietness,
till all our strivings cease;
take from our souls the strain and stress,
and let our ordered lives confess
the beauty of thy peace,
the beauty of thy peace.

Breathe through the heats of our desire
thy coolness and thy balm;
let sense be dumb, let flesh retire;
speak through the earthquake, wind and fire,
O still small voice of calm!
O still small voice of calm!

12 July

We've another Celtic prayer today, coming this time from the *Carmina Gadelica*, a collection of Scottish prayers, hymns, poems and songs put together and translated by the author, antiquarian and folklorist Alexander Carmichael (1832–1912). Reminiscent of the lines 'God be in my head' from the Sarum *Book of Hours*, the language and style of this prayer is characteristic of the tradition that Carmichael worked tirelessly throughout his life to retrieve and restore. It recognises that God is present in every aspect of life, always encircling us with his love. These lovely words are not so much a request as a statement of faith – a grateful acknowledgement of the living reality that shapes everyone and everything.

God to enfold me,
God to surround me,
God in my speaking,
God in my thinking.

God in my sleeping,
God in my waking,
God in my watching,
God in my hoping.

God in my life,
God in my lips,
God in my soul,
God in my heart.

God in my sufficing,
God in my slumber,
God in my ever-living soul,
God in my eternity.

13 July

What can we offer God in response to his goodness, asks Psalm 116? According to the hymn-writer and poet Frances Ridley Havergal (1836–1879) in one of her most celebrated hymns, the answer, quite simply, is everything. Daughter of Revd W. H. Havergal, Frances composed her first hymn aged just 21, going on to write many more, including 'Master, speak! Thy servant heareth', 'Lord, speak to me' and 'I am trusting thee'. She once said, 'Writing is *praying* with me, for I never seem to write even a verse by myself and feel like a little child writing; you know a child would look up at every sentence and say, "And what shall I say next?" That is just what I do.' Clearly God answered her prayer, the following verses exemplifying total commitment to Christ.

Take my life, and let it be
consecrated, Lord, to thee;
take my moments and my days,
let them flow in ceaseless praise.

Take my hands, and let them move
at the impulse of thy love;
take my feet, and let them be
swift and beautiful for thee.

Take my will, and make of thine:
it shall be no longer mine;
take my heart: it is thine own;
it shall be thy royal throne.

Take my love; my Lord, I pour
at thy feet its treasure-store;
take myself, and I will be
ever, only, all for thee.

14 July

Our prayer today again makes use of a hymn, this time written by Godfrey Thring (1823–1903), one-time rector of Alford in Somerset and subsequently prebendary of Wells. He produced numerous hymns, his chief concern being to counter what he saw as hymnody pandering to narrow party interests. His words here were inspired by the words of Matthew 4:24, and reflect Christ's constant compassion for the sick and dying. Ill health, of course, can strike any of us at any time, in a trice turning our world upside down. For too many it's done just that and, at the very least, they need the knowledge that they're remembered in our prayers.

Thou to whom the sick and dying
ever came, nor came in vain,
still with healing words replying
to the wearied cry of pain,
hear us, Jesus, as we meet,
suppliants at thy mercy-seat.

Still the weary, sick, and dying
need a brother's, sister's care;
on thy higher help relying
may we now their burden share,
bringing all our offerings meet,
suppliants at thy mercy-seat.

15 July

Recent years have seen a resurgence in Celtic spirituality, and understandably so, for the poetry of that tradition, coupled with its anchoring in the natural world, help it to speak powerfully of God's presence in daily life. Today's prayer – more strictly a blessing – is a classic example. Drawing on aspects of creation it speaks of something beyond: the peace of God that passes understanding yet runs through all things. As you read this prayer recognise that it expresses what God desires for you and, in turn, ask such blessing on others.

Deep peace of the running wave to you.
Deep peace of the flowing air to you.
Deep peace of the quiet earth to you.
Deep peace of the shining stars to you.
Deep peace of the infinite peace to you.

16 July

Do we ask God to help in dealing with the pressures, problems and responsibilities of daily life? Undoubtedly. But do we then actually look for and follow his guidance? Probably not. We pay lip-service to faith but so often proceed to do our own thing, trusting rather in our own plans and ingenuity. Not that they're necessarily opposed, but they *can* be, the two potentially in stark contrast. The following prayer, another from Augustine of Hippo (354–430), recognises that *our* way is not always *God's* way, but God's way is always the best.

O God, from whom to be turned is to fall,
    to whom to be turned is to rise,
    and with whom to stand is to abide for ever;
    grant us in all our duties your help,
    in all our perplexities your guidance,
    in all our dangers your protection,
    and in all our sorrows your peace,
    through Jesus Christ our Lord.
Amen.

17 July

Life brings its highs and lows, doesn't it. The troughs can cause us to seek God's help, but they can also test our faith to the limit or destroy it altogether. Having as clear a sense of God's presence in the bad times as in the good is hard indeed, but this perhaps is the hallmark of true faith. We see it in the following poetic prayer of John Henry Newman (1801–1890), titled 'The soul before God', in which he almost welcomes being brought low since it casts him totally upon God, who will finally lift us up. He knows that whatever we face, even death itself, is but a stepping stone on the way to God's eternal kingdom. Popular wisdom may tell us that 'the higher we rise, the harder we fall' but, for Newman, true faith stands that saying on its head.

Take me away, and in the lowest deep
   there let me be,
   and there in hope the lone night-watches keep,
   told out for me.
There, motionless and happy in my pain,
   lone, not forlorn –
   there will I sing my sad perpetual strain,
   until the morn.
There will I sing, and soothe my stricken breast,
   which ne'er can cease
   to throb, and pine, and languish, till possess'd
   of its Sole Peace.
There will I sing my absent Lord and Love –
   take me away,
   that sooner I may rise, and go above,
   and see him in the truth of everlasting day.
Amen.

18 July

There are no easy answers to unanswered prayer or times when God seems distant, but faith must try to make sense of these moments as much as any. One possible answer is given by the Danish philosopher and theologian Søren Kierkegaard (1813–1855) who, in the following prayer, explores the possibility that God may have a higher purpose in withholding an answer, or even be speaking to us through silence.

Father in heaven,
    you speak to us in many ways.
Even when you are silent, you still speak to us,
    in order to examine us,
    to try us,
    and so that the hour of understanding
      may be more profound.
Oh, in the time of silence,
    when I remain alone and abandoned
      because I do not hear your voice,
    it seems as if the separation must last for ever,
    but, Father, it is only a moment of silence in the
      intimacy of a conversation.
Bless, then, this silence,
    and let me not forget that you are silent through
      love,
    and that you speak through love,
    so that in your silence and in your word
    you are still the same Father,
    and that you guide and instruct even by your
      silence.
Amen.

19 July

Our prayer today is one of the most ancient you could hope to find, coming from St Clement of Rome, reckoned to be the fourth pope and, according to some, though this is probably mistaken, the Clement referred to in Philippians 4:3. Whoever he was, it seems likely that he knew the Apostle Peter first-hand, so we're dealing here with one of the truly early Christians. When he was born is unknown, but he died around AD 102 – martyred according to some traditions, but dying a natural death according to others. His prayer here is a memorable prayer of intercession, committing all kinds of needs into the loving hands of God.

We beseech you, O Lord,
  to grant us your help and protection.
Deliver the afflicted,
  pity the lowly,
  raise the fallen,
  reveal yourself to the needy,
  heal the sick,
  and bring home your wandering people.
Feed the hungry,
  ransom the captive,
  support the weak,
  comfort the faint-hearted.
Let all the nations of the earth know that you alone
  are God,
  that Jesus Christ is your child
  and that we are your people and the sheep of your
    pasture.
Do not keep count of the sins of your servants,
  but purify us through the bath of your truth and
    direct our steps.

Help us to walk in holiness of heart,
   and to do what is good and pleasing in your eyes
   and in the eyes of our rulers.
Master, let your face shine on us to grant us every
   good in peace,
      protect us by your powerful hand,
      deliver us from every evil by the might of your arm.
Grant us and all who dwell on this earth
   peace and harmony, O Lord.
Amen.

20 July

Is faith something we inherit from others or must we always take it on for ourselves? According to the writer of this prayer, St Symeon the New Theologian (949–1022), there was no question about the answer, the thrust of all his works being that discipleship involves a personal experience of God. Yes, we may learn about it from others, even grow up schooled in faith, but eventually we must make it our own if it is to be real. In Hymn 27:125-32, he wrote: 'Do not say that it is impossible to receive the Spirit of God. Do not say that it is possible to be made whole without him. Do not say that one can possess him without knowing it. Do not say that God does not manifest himself to man. Do not say that men cannot perceive the divine light, or that it is impossible in this age! Never is it found to be impossible, my friends. On the contrary, it is entirely possible when one desires it.' His prayer here reflects his conviction that each of us can personally know God as a living reality in our lives.

O Light that none can name,
    for it is altogether nameless,
    O light with many names,
        for it is at work in all things,
    I give you thanks,
    for you are a light to me that knows no evening,
    a sun that never sets.
You cannot remain hidden,
    for you fill everything with your glory.
You never hide yourself from anyone,
    even though we continually hide from you,
    reluctant to come near you.

For where could you hide yourself,
    given that you have no place in which to take your
        rest?
Or why should you hide,
    given that you turn away from no one and are
        afraid of none?
Pitch your tent within me, gracious Master.
Take up your dwelling in me now
    and remain in your servant unceasingly,
    inseparably, to the end.
At my departure from this life and afterwards,
    may I be found in you and reign with you,
        who are God over all.
Stay with me, Master, do not leave me alone.
When they find you dwelling within me,
    my enemies who seek always to devour my soul,
        will be put to flight;
    they will have no more power against me
    when they see you, who are more powerful than all,
    lodging in the house of my humble soul.
You did not forget me, Master, when I was in the
    world and sunk in ignorance,
        but you chose me and separated me from the world
        and set me up in the presence of your glory.
Keep me constant and unshaken in the interior
    dwelling-place that you have made within me.
Though dead, I live when I gaze on you;
    possessing you, though poor, I am forever rich,
    more wealthy than any ruler.
Eating and drinking you,
    clothing myself in you from day to day,
    I shall be filled with blessings and delight beyond
    all telling.
For you are every blessing and all splendour and joy,
    and to you is due glory, to the holy, consubstantial
        and life-giving Trinity,

worshipped and confessed by all the faithful
and adored in Father, Son and Holy Spirit,
now and ever, and to the ages of ages.
Amen.

21 July

We've encountered prayers earlier in this book which suggest that if God were to answer our every prayer it would effectively be a curse rather than blessing, and we encounter much the same idea here in succinct but perceptive words of the poet, scholar, linguist and hymn-writer James Merrick (1720–1769). He recognises that God has to be selective sometimes in what he grants, for we all too often ask for the wrong things, believing them to be good when in fact they would prove to be the opposite. Similarly, we can be so concerned with trivia that we fail to ask for those things we truly need. If we were allowed just four lines of prayer we could do a lot worse than use this brief stanza of Merrick's: it takes us to the heart of what true prayer is all about.

Not what we wish, but what we want,
oh! let thy grace supply,
the good unask'd, in mercy grant;
the ill, though ask'd, deny.

22 July

We've another prayer today of Evelyn Underhill (1875–1941), and it reflects more than most her willingness to accept sacrifice and self-denial for the cause of Christ. Taken from her book *Meditations and Prayers* (1949), her words here, with their emphasis on letting go of all reward save faithfully offering service, carry overtones of the famous prayers of Ignatius Loyola and Francis of Assisi. Few of us will come anywhere near such unreserved dedication, but if we can echo her words and seek to make them our own, we will open the way to God working within us, taking what we are and shaping what we shall become.

Teach me to enter the life of service that alone
    is freedom,
      which accepts humiliations, hardness, poverty,
      hiddenness, sacrifice, spend-thrift love
      with a glad generosity,
      asking nothing.
Cleanse my service of all selfishness,
    spiritual or material,
    all criticism or impatience,
    all secret desire for consolation,
    recognition or reward.
Take all that I have and all that I am
    and subdue it to your service.
Amen.

23 July

Relationships can be hard, can't they? We mean well but somehow put our foot in things. We try not to argue but end up in a blazing row. We aim to think the best of others only to find ourselves listening to gossip and half believing it. And so we could go on. Despite our best intentions, we'll all experience times when friendships are strained or we hurt those we love, let alone those we find it harder to get on with. The following prayer, words of Eusebius (c. 275–339), Bishop of Caesarea and considered by some to be the father of Church history, focuses on what is often called 'the golden rule'; namely the injunction by Jesus to do to others what we'd have done to ourselves. It's a good yardstick to apply in our relationships, and a perfect inspiration for prayer on this theme.

May I be an enemy to no one
    and the friend of what abides eternally.
May I never quarrel with those nearest me,
    and be reconciled quickly if I should.
May I never plot evil against others,
    and if anyone plot evil against me,
        may I escape unharmed and without the need
            to hurt anyone else.
May I love, seek and attain only what is good.
May I desire happiness for all and harbour
    envy for none.
May I never find joy in the misfortune of one who
    has wronged me.
May I never wait for the rebuke of others,
    but always rebuke myself until I make reparation.
May I gain no victory that harms me or my opponent.

May I reconcile friends who are mad at each other.
May I, insofar as I can, give all necessary help
  to my friends and to all who are in need.
May I never fail a friend in trouble.
May I be able to soften the pain of the grief-stricken
  and give them comforting words.
May I respect myself.
May I always maintain control of my emotions.
May I habituate myself to be gentle,
    and never angry with others because of
      circumstances.
May I never discuss the wicked or what they have
  done,
    but know good people and follow in their
      footsteps.
Amen.

24 July

In many ways we're fortunate today as Christians. Unlike countless generations before us, we're not persecuted for our faith nor penalised in any way for allegiance to Christ. Yet true commitment still isn't easy. In fact, it's probably as hard as it's ever been, albeit for different reasons. Christianity today is largely marginalised, regarded as the preserve of the eccentric few. Indifference can be as hard to handle as hostility, added to which we face massive if subtle temptations to compromise, diluting our convictions until they mean little if anything. Our prayer today, from the poet and hymn-writer John Donne (1572–1631), intercedes for new Christians of a bygone age, but it's just as relevant for today, and applies not just to new believers but to all. Through these words, then, ask God's blessing on all his people, that faith may flourish despite all that conspires against it.

O most merciful Father,
    for thy most innocent Son's sake:
    and since he has spread his arms upon the cross,
    to receive the whole world,
    O Lord, shut out none of us
    (who are now fallen before the throne of thy
        majesty and thy mercy)
    from the benefit of his merits;
    but with as many of us as begin their conversion
    and newness of life in this minute,
    this minute, O God, begin thou thy account with
        them and put all that is past
    out of thy remembrance.

Accept our humble thanks for all thy mercies;
  and continue and enlarge them upon the whole
    Church.
Amen.

25 July

Across the centuries, an emphasis upon silent prayer
and reflection has characterised the Christian mystical
tradition, exemplified in those like St John of the Cross
(1542-1591). The following is one of his many prayers,
and touches upon that need for inner quietness.

O sweetest love of God, too little known,
    whoever has found you will be at rest.
Let everything change, O my God,
    that I may rest in you.
How sweet to me is your presence,
    you who are sovereign good!
I will draw near to you in silence,
    and will uncover your feet,
        that it may please you to unite me with yourself,
        making my soul your bride.
I will rejoice in nothing until I am in your arms;
    O Lord, I beseech you, leave me not for a moment.
Amen.

26 July

It's not known who wrote the following prayer, but it deserves to be remembered nonetheless. A beautiful prayer of intercession, it offers an important reminder that words alone are not enough, however sincere they may be. God needs each of us not only to catch a vision of what he desires for the world, but also to commit ourselves to doing what we can to help bring that dream to fruition. We may not be able to do much, but we can all do something.

Give me, Lord God, a vision of the world as your love
    would make it;
    a world where the weak are protected
        and none go hungry or poor;
    a world where the benefits of civilised life
        are shared
    and everyone can enjoy them;
    a world where different races, nations and cultures
    live in tolerance and mutual respect;
    a world where peace is built with justice
    and justice is guided by love;
    and give me the inspiration and courage to share
        in the task of building it,
    through Jesus Christ my Lord.
Amen.

27 July

Most of us would like to think we strive after the important things in life but in practice we tend to concern ourselves with what's far less important, dwelling on outward appearance rather than the person underneath. As Christians we're not immune from that tendency, the fact that we may look the part by no means proving our faith is real. That truth underlies this prayer, written by the English essayist, poet and humorist Charles Lamb (1775–1834) and taken from *A Birthday Thought* (written under the pseudonym Elia). Troubled by fits of depression and a severe speech impediment, Lamb nonetheless enjoyed a rich social life, mixing in the same circles as Samuel Taylor Coleridge, William Wordsworth and Percy Bysshe Shelley, but he was clearly aware that social niceties could conceal a poverty within. Simple they may be, but these few lines remind us of an important truth.

I ask and wish not to appear
more beauteous, rich or gay:
Lord, make me wiser every year,
and better every day.

28 July

We're all something of an enigma, aren't we? We're full
of good intentions but struggle to honour them, intend-
ing to do one thing but so often doing quite another.
As the old saying has it, the spirit is willing but the
flesh is weak. We need to bring both before God: our
desire to serve yet failure to do so, our fine ideals but
feeble results. In today's prayer, St Augustine of Hippo
(354–430) shows us how to do just that, seeking help
with the first and forgiveness for the second.

O Lord my God,
    I believe in you, Father, Son and Holy Spirit.
Insofar as I can,
    insofar as you have given me the power,
    I have sought you.
I became weary and I laboured.
O Lord my God,
    my sole hope,
    help me to believe and never to cease seeking you.
Grant that I may always and ardently seek out your
    countenance.
Give me the strength to seek you,
    for you help me to find you
    and you have more and more given me the hope
        of finding you.
Here I am before you with my firmness and my
    infirmity.
Preserve the first and heal the second.
Here I am before you with my strength and my
    ignorance.
Where you have opened the door to me,
    welcome me at the entrance;

where you have closed the door to me,
open to my cry;
enable me to remember you,
to understand you,
and to love you.
Amen.

29 July

Our prayer today comes from the celebrated Dutch humanist and theologian Desiderius Erasmus (1466–1536). Though he lived during a time of religious ferment which saw the burgeoning of Protestantism, he remained a Catholic throughout his life, albeit one sharply critical of what he saw to be the errors of the Catholic Church. His overriding concern though, as it should be for us all, was to stay faithful to Christ as best he could.

Lord Jesus Christ,
  you are the Way, the Truth and the Life.
Never let us stray from you, who are the Way,
  nor to distrust you, who are the Truth,
  nor to rest in anything other than you, who are the
    Life.
Teach us, by your Holy Spirit, what to believe,
  what to do,
  and how to take our rest.
Amen.

30 July

Few of us find patience easy. Life is short, so we want things now rather than later, and though we try to curb our impetuosity, time and again we succumb. What we need is an inner tranquillity of spirit, and that's what the following prayer, attributed to St John of the Cross (1542–1591), asks for.

O blessed Jesus,
  give me stillness of soul in thee.
Let thy mighty calmness reign in me;
  rule me, O King of gentleness, King of peace.
Give me control, great power of self-control,
  control over my words, thoughts and actions.
From all irritability, want of meekness,
    want of gentleness,
      dear Lord, deliver me.
By thine own deep patience, give me patience.
Make me in this and all things more and more
    like thee.
Amen.

31 July

Our greatest problem in prayer is not that we don't know what to ask for, or that we struggle to express ourselves on those rare occasions when we do. Rather, it's that our awareness of God is so limited that we have little if any sense of his presence. More often than not our hearts are closed to spiritual things, so pre-occupied with other concerns that when we make time for him we feel out of our depth. Before anything, then, our prayer needs to be simply for God to draw close to us and open our eyes, helping us to catch a greater vision of who and what he is. That's what St Augustine of Hippo (354–430) asks for in the following prayer and, as always, what memorable words they are.

O God, the Light of the heart that sees you,
    the Life of the soul that loves you,
    the Strength of the mind that seeks you:
    may I ever continue to be steadfast in your love.
For your mercies' sake, O Lord my God,
    tell me what you are to me.
Say to my soul: 'I am your salvation.'
So speak that I may hear, O Lord;
    my heart is listening;
    open it that it may hear you,
    and say to my soul: 'I am your salvation.'
After hearing this word, may I come in haste
    to take hold of you.
Hide not your face from me.
Let me see your face even if I die,
    lest I die with longing to see it.
Be the joy of my heart;
    take all of me to yourself, and abide therein.

The house of my soul is, I confess, too narrow for you.
Enlarge it that you may enter.
It is ruinous, but do repair it.
It has within it what must offend your eyes;
   I confess and know it,
     but whose help shall I seek in cleansing it
       but yours alone?
To you, O God, I cry urgently.
Cleanse me from secret faults.
Keep me from false pride and sensuality
   that they do not get dominion over me.
Amen.

AUGUST

1 August

Prayer can come from the unlikeliest of sources, and few are more unlikely than the French philosopher François-Marie Arouet, better known by his pseudonym Voltaire (1694–1778). Vehemently opposed to Christianity, he famously declared that the Bible would be defunct within a century of his death, consigned to the scrap heap of history. His surprise to find it still alive and well would probably only be surpassed by discovering one of his prayers included in this book! To my mind, though, it fully deserves inclusion, for whatever you may think about his views, Voltaire's appeal for greater tolerance in a world where religion has so often made for division is as topical as ever, and one we do well to heed.

O! thou God of all beings, of all worlds,
    and of all times,
    we pray, that the little differences in our clothes,
    in our inadequate languages,
    in our ridiculous customs,
    in our imperfect laws,
    in our illogical opinions,
    in our ranks and conditions which are so
        disproportionately important to us
    and so meaningless to you –
    that these small variations that distinguish
        those atoms that we call men,
    one from another,
    may not be signals of hatred and persecution!
Amen.

2 August

Here is a prayer from the late-Roman statesman, writer and philosopher Anicius Manlius Severinus Boethius (c. 480–524/5). Born into an influential family in Rome, he rose to become consul to the Ostrogoths in 510, but was eventually executed by King Theodoric the Great on suspicion of colluding with his enemies. Tradition has it that the real reason for his execution was his Christian faith, and though some scholars have recently disputed this, it still seems the most likely explanation. His words here ask for help and guidance to know God better, but reveal an already astonishing depth of faith and insight.

Father,
    grant the spirit power to climb to your ineffable
        dwelling place,
    the fountain of light,
    and be purified.
Break through the mists of earth that obscure your
    glory or tie us down.
Shine out in your splendour,
    you who are calm weather
    and a place of quietness and serenity for all
        who faithfully serve you.
You are the end and the beginning –
    our guide and vehicle along the way,
    the journey, and the journey's end.
Amen.

3 August

Most of us want to pray for others, but find it difficult to do so, not being sure what exactly or who we ought to pray for. It's good, then, to find words that help guide and articulate our thoughts, and few do that better than the following, written by the Scottish philosopher and writer William Angus Knight (1836–1916).

Almighty and most merciful Father,
> who has taught us not to think only of ourselves
> but also of the needs of others,
>> I remember before you all who are burdened and
>>> oppressed,
>> those whose hopes have been crushed
>> and whose plans have come to nothing.
I remember also those who are afflicted by poverty,
> or worn down by sickness and disease,
> those who are in darkness or despair,
> or who are suffering for righteousness' sake.
Help them all, O God,
> to rest in you for comfort and strength.
Amen.

4 August

Which of us hasn't gazed up at the night sky and caught a sense of God in all his greatness? We no longer, of course, believe that God is somewhere out there – literally *up* in heaven – but somehow the vastness of space puts us in touch with the infinite, speaking of something beyond us, defying human comprehension. Such was the experience centuries ago of St Hilary of Poitiers (315–367), the sight of the stars and order of the universe sparking an awareness of the divine. You might like perhaps to take a night-time stroll yourself as you pray these words, allowing not just Hilary but also the wonder of creation to speak directly to you.

When I look at your heavens,
according to my own lights,
with these weak eyes of mine,
I am certain with reservation that they are your
heavens.
The stars circle in the heavens,
reappear year after year,
each with a function and service to fulfil.
And though I do not understand them,
I know that you, O God, are in them.
Amen.

5 August

When we hear the names of great Christians from the past it's hard not to put them on a pedestal as though they are altogether different from us, their commitment unlike anything we can aspire to. Yet if we take time to look at their writings, a very different picture often emerges, these people having experienced the same difficulties in discipleship, the same doubts, the same temptations and obstacles. Take Martin Luther (1483–1546), for example, the writer of this prayer. He will always be remembered not just in the Lutheran tradition but the world over as one of the formative influences behind the Protestant Reformation, his rediscovery of the doctrine of justification by faith changing the Church for ever. Alongside his various writings he also translated the Bible and wrote several hymns – testimony surely to his inner sanctity. Yet his prayer here gives an insight into Luther the man, as human and fallible as we are. Take heart from his words, and use them to acknowledge both your need and your faith, however hesitant the latter may be.

Look, Lord,
on an empty vessel that needs to be filled.
In faith I am weak – strengthen me.
In love I am cold – warm me and make me fervent
so that my love may go out to my neighbour.
I doubt and am unable to trust you completely.
Lord, strengthen my faith and trust in you.
You are all the treasure I possess.
I am poor, you are rich,
and you came to have mercy on the poor.

I am a sinner, you are goodness.
From you I can receive goodness,
    but I can give you nothing.
Therefore I shall stay with you.
Amen.

6 August

We've a very old prayer today from the Egyptian writer and scholar St Dionysius (also called Dionysius the Great (*c.* 190–265), Bishop of Alexandria. He twice had to flee for his life during periods of Roman persecution, which perhaps explains his leniency towards those who, under similar pressure, outwardly at least abandoned their faith. His experience of persecution may also lie behind his words here in which he prays for peace in the world. He knew all too well the human cost brought about by violence and division, and longed for that day when God would establish harmony among all. Times may have changed but the underlying troubles of our world are just the same. We can echo his prayer from the heart.

O God the Father,
    good surpassing everything good
    and just surpassing everything just,
    in whom is tranquillity, peace and harmony,
    heal the divisions that divide people
        from each other,
    and bring us back to the unity of love,
    so that we bear some likeness to your divine nature.
Just as you are above all things,
    make us one in thought,
    the bond of love and ties of divine affection
        uniting us one with another
    through your peace that renders everything peaceful.
We ask it through the grace, mercy and love of your
    only Son,
    our Lord Jesus Christ.
Amen.

7 August

Few prayers have been more often repeated than that of St Ignatius Loyola (1491–1556), and it's hardly surprising, for his words are a paradigm of unreserved commitment. They reflect the way of Christ, so different from that of the world in which people give, expecting a reward, or offer as little as they can get away with. Loyola, by contrast, offers all he has and everything he is, recognising that it is only through letting go that we truly receive. I doubt many of us can pray this prayer and mean it, such unreserved devotion is a rare thing, but through these lovely words we can, if nothing else, ask God's help in more fully committing our lives to him.

Teach me, good Lord,
   to serve you as you deserve:
   to give, and not to count the cost;
   to fight, and not to heed the wounds;
   to toil, and not to seek for rest;
   to labour, and to ask for no reward,
   except that of knowing that I do your will;
   through Jesus Christ my Lord.
Amen.

8 August

There's a real poignancy about this prayer, for it was written by Mary, Queen of Scots (1542–1587), the ill-fated monarch executed during the reign of Queen Elizabeth I. A devout Catholic, if somewhat headstrong during her youth, she spent much of her life under house arrest, effectively in prison. How bitter she found that experience can be seen from her words here, as she begs God for freedom – a prayer, of course, that was never to be answered, except through the release of death. Few of us will experience imprisonment, but much else can hold us captive – fear, guilt, shyness and doubt, to name but some. Whatever it may be, use Mary's words (translated from the Latin by the Victorian poet Algernon Charles Swinburne in *Mary Stuart*) to seek the liberty that God alone can bring.

O Lord, my God,
    I have trusted in thee;
    O Jesu, my dearest One,
    now set me free.
In prison's oppression,
    in sorrow's obsession,
    I weary for thee.
With sighing and crying,
    bowed down in dying,
    I adore thee,
    I implore thee,
    set me free.
Amen.

9 August

The spirituality of the Native Americans is well known, and today we have a small example from the Chinook tribe. It reveals a characteristic affinity with nature but also a sense of something greater, a presence we experience personally yet that is also outside us, the source and sustainer of everything that is, has been and shall be. Through these words acknowledge in turn the wonder of God's creation, his love for you and his sovereignty over all.

May all I say and all I think
  be in harmony with thee,
  God within me, God beyond me,
  Maker of the trees.

10 August

What comes first in your life? There is much we understandably celebrate, all kinds of things that give
sparkle and meaning to our existence, and it's natural
to strive after these, eager to make them our own. Any
happiness they give, though, depends on whether they
become our slave or master. Value them above all else
to the extent that we invest our happiness in them, and
they can possess our soul, ultimately denying rather
than enriching life. I'm reminded of the words of Jesus
in Matthew 6: 'Do not be anxious, saying, "What shall
we eat?" or "What shall we drink?" or "What shall we
wear?" But seek first the kingdom and righteousness of
God, and you shall be given all of these in addition'
(vv. 31a, 33). The following Baha'i prayer emphasises
the need to sort out our priorities and to recognise that
true fulfilment comes from God.

O my God, O my Lord, O my Master!
I beg thee to forgive me for seeking any pleasure
    save thy love,
    or any comfort except thy nearness,
    or any delight besides thy good-pleasure,
    or any existence other than communion with thee.
Amen.

11 August

Some prayers are so simple we can overlook them or recite them parrot-fashion without taking in what they're saying. A classic example is the grace many of us were taught to repeat as children: 'For what we are about to receive may the Lord make us truly thankful.' Our prayer today is another traditional blessing over a meal, and though it may be less familiar you may well feel it's too short and twee for serious consideration. Yet you'd be wrong, for this prayer reminds us of three special things we so often take for granted: food, leisure and home. Would one of the world's starving millions, or a child labourer in a sweatshop, or a homeless family in a refugee camp make that mistake? Not likely! Make time to consider how lucky you are, and thank God for it.

For food that stays our hunger,
for rest that brings us ease,
for homes where memories linger,
we give our thanks for these.

12 August

'Human beings may plan their way, but it is the Lord who directs their steps. The human mind may formulate many ingenious plans, but the Lord's purpose will always triumph.' So says the book of Proverbs (16:9; 19:21), but do we believe such words? We may say we do, but when it comes to day-to-day decisions what heed do we pay to God in making them? I'm not suggesting he has every detail of our life mapped out for us – personally I don't believe that for a moment – but we have clear guidance as to the sort of lifestyle he wants from us and there are moments also when we're conscious of his prompting, whether to call, challenge, question or rebuke. Do we listen to his voice or surreptitiously silence it? Do we follow his wishes or prefer our own? The following prayer of Teresa of Avila (1515–1582) asks for help in faithfully responding to God's guidance, wherever it might lead.

Lord, grant that I may always allow myself to be
    guided by you,
    always follow your plans,
    and perfectly accomplish your holy will.
Grant that in all things,
    great and small,
    today and all the days of my life,
    I may do whatever you require of me.
Help me to respond to the slightest prompting
    of your grace,
    so that I may be your trustworthy instrument
      for your honour.
May your will be done in time and in eternity
    by me,
    in me,
    and through me.
Amen.

13 August

Interfaith dialogue is a contentious issue, people under-standably being afraid it will lead to a compromising of convictions, each tradition reduced to the lowest common denominator. If seeking a single creed is the aim, such fears would certainly be justified, but if the goal is greater understanding and respect despite our very real differences – much as the ecumenical move-ment has achieved among Christians – then we're talking of something altogether more laudable. Though we'd take issue with many aspects of the world's great faiths, each has produced profound insights to move and inspire, today's prayer from the Buddhist tradition being a case in point. Who can fail to be moved by its beautiful sentiments, and which could tally better with the way of Christ? Buddhist, Christian or otherwise, here are words we could happily pray together.

May I become at all times, both now and for ever,
   a protector for those without protection,
   a guide for those who have lost their way,
   a ship for those with oceans to cross,
   a bridge for those with rivers to cross,
   a sanctuary for those in danger,
   a lamp for those without light,
   a place of refuge for those who lack shelter
   and a servant to all in need.
Amen.

14 August

Earlier in the year we made use of words written by the hymn-writer J. H. B. Masterman (1867–1933), and today we're going to do the same, turning this time to a hymn that, though written close to a century ago, seems as relevant today as ever. If the world was weary of its pain in Masterman's time, it's probably all the more so now, but whereas people then still had faith that things might change for the better, nowadays people are less sure, disillusionment being the order of the day. We need to avoid cynicism, continuing to work in whatever ways possible to make things better, but equally we need to recognise that real change can only come through God transforming lives. Use these words, then, to pray for new beginnings in our bleeding broken world.

Almighty Father, who dost give
the gift of life to all who live,
look down on all earth's sin and strife,
and lift us to a nobler life.

Lift up our hearts, O King of kings,
to brighter hopes and kindlier things,
to visions of a larger good,
and holier dreams of brotherhood.

The world is weary of its pain,
of selfish greed and fruitless gain,
of tarnished honour, falsely strong,
and all its ancient deeds of wrong.

Hear thou the prayer thy servants pray,
uprising from all lands today,
and o'er the vanquished powers of sin
O bring thy great salvation in.

15 August

Here is another prayer by St Ignatius Loyola (1491–1556) and once more it expresses total surrender, unreserved commitment to Christ. On one level when I read such words I feel almost dismayed, for they represent a faith more complete than any I will ever achieve, an allegiance beside which mine pales in comparison. Yet, on another level I'm encouraged and inspired, for words like these simultaneously speak of the sort of devotion I aspire to, the loyalty I yearn to give even though I fail to do so. If sharing in great prayers of the past were dependent on measuring up to those who first prayed them or the faith they possessed, we'd soon exhaust the possibilities. Use them, though, to help voice our longing to love God better, and he will hear and answer.

Take, Lord, all my entire liberty,
　　my memory,
　　my understanding
　　and my whole will.
You have given me all that I am and all that I have,
　　and I surrender it all to you to be disposed of
　　　　according to your will.
Give me only your love and your grace;
　　with these I will be rich enough,
　　and will desire nothing more.
Amen.

16 August

Not all prayers have been written by outwardly religious people. The one I've chosen for today, for example, comes from an unlikely source indeed, being attributed to Sir Francis Drake (*c.* 1540–1596) – a bold hero to some but merciless pirate to others. His love of the sea and adventurous spirit are well in evidence here, but so too is a surprisingly deep faith in the God who calls us, in every aspect of life and faith, to explore ever new horizons.

Disturb us, Lord, when we are too well pleased with
    ourselves,
    when our dreams have come true because we have
        dreamed too little,
    when we arrived safely because we sailed too close
        to the shore.
Disturb us, Lord, when,
    with the abundance of things we possess,
    we have lost our thirst for the waters of life;
    having fallen in love with life,
    we have ceased to dream of eternity;
    and in our efforts to build a new earth,
    we have allowed our vision of the new heaven
        to dim.
Disturb us, Lord, to dare more boldly,
    to venture on wider seas
    where storms will show your mastery;
    where losing sight of land,
    we shall find the stars.
We ask you to push back the horizons of our hopes;
    and to push us into the future in strength, courage,
        hope and love.
Amen.

17 August

The following prayer reminds us once again of the insights found in other religious traditions. It's drawn from Sufism, an early form of Islam that laid heavy emphasis on loving God and serving others. God is seen as pervading all things, while ultimately being beyond them, the goal of the Sufi mystic being to let go of self and recognise the ultimate unity of all things. As a Christian these words speak powerfully to me of the God who is all in all, and in whom alone I find true wholeness.

Beloved Lord, Almighty God,
    through the rays of the sun,
    through the waves of the air,
    through the all-pervading life in space,
    purify and revivify me, and, I pray,
    heal my body, heart and soul.
Amen.

18 August

Above all else prayer is about focusing on the presence of God, opening our heart and mind to him in order to know him better. Our words today do just that. Taken from the epic prayer of Karl Rahner (1904–1984), which we've already quoted from earlier in this book, it focuses on the loving nature of God, asking that it may permeate our whole being so that he and we may become more fully one.

You who are love itself,
    give me the grace of love,
    give me yourself,
    so that all my days may finally empty
    into the one day of your eternal life.
Amen.

19 August

As the Apostle Paul reminds us in 1 Corinthians 13, in this life we know God only in part, our understanding of his love and purpose being partial at best. Yet, while this will always be so until we see him face to face in eternity, we should never stop seeking deeper insight or fuller faith. That's precisely what St Anselm (1033–1109) asks for in this prayer: daily growth in grace until that time when the full truth is revealed in all its wonder.

My God,
    I pray that I may so know you and love you
        that I may rejoice in you.
And if I may not do so fully in this life
    let me go steadily on to the day when I come
        to that fullness.
Let me receive that which you promised through your
    truth,
    that my joy may be full.
Amen.

20 August

Short prayers can say as much sometimes as longer ones, their brevity encouraging us to reflect on every word. Take the following attributed to Martin Luther (1483–1546). It's a simple prayer of consecration, suitable for grace before a meal, but it's also one we could use every day, inviting Christ to come into our life so that we might more fully appreciate his many blessings so easily taken for granted. The words are easily learnt and well worth remembering.

Come Lord Jesus,
be our guest,
and let thy gifts
to us be blessed.

21 August

The words of our prayer today were written as a hymn
by Thomas William Jex-Blake (1832–1915), who served
successively as principal of Cheltenham College, headmaster of Rugby School and Dean of Wells. He was
asked to write the hymn by Dr Cotton, headmaster of
Marlborough School, his brief being to articulate
thanksgiving from the perspective of a youngster. He
succeeds admirably in expressing the joy at the heart of
both life and faith, in two verses covering just about
everything we could think of, before going on in the
final verse to explore what gratitude should mean in
terms of response. Surprisingly, this is the only hymn
or verse that Jex-Blake is known to have written.

Lord, we thank thee for the pleasure
that our happy lifetime gives,
for the boundless worth and treasure
of a soul that ever lives;
mind that looks before and after,
lifting eyes to things above;
human tears, and human laughter,
and the depths of human love.

For the thrill, the leap, the gladness
of our pulses flowing free;
e'en for every touch of sadness
that may bring us nearer thee;
but, above all other kindness,
thine unutterable love,
which, to heal our sin and blindness
sent thy dear Son from above.

Teach us so our days to number
that we may be early wise;
dreamy mist, or cloud, or slumber,
never dull our heavenward eyes.
Hearty be our work and willing,
as to thee, and not to men:
for we know our souls' fulfilling
is in heaven, and not till then.

22 August

There was a time when night was viewed as the time when evil forces were on the prowl, witches, demons and so forth using darkness as cover for their diabolical activities. Such superstition may be a thing of the past, but night can still hold its menace, in some places people being afraid, for example, to go out after a certain hour for fear of drunken or loutish behaviour. For the Christian, light and darkness are still powerful symbols of good and evil, the threat of the latter being as real as ever in our world today. The following prayer, taken from the ancient Order of Compline, remains as relevant as it is beautiful.

Lighten our darkness, we beseech thee O Lord;
    and by thy great mercy defend us from all perils
      and dangers of this night;
    for the love of thy only Son our Saviour Jesus
      Christ.
Amen.

23 August

Typically referred to as the Covenant Prayer of John Wesley (1703–1791), our words today in fact come from a Lutheran pietist prayer adapted by Wesley for use in a watch-night dedication service. Since then it has been regularly used in the Methodist Church during annual acts of rededication. The prayer is frequently prefaced by words like the following: 'Christ has many services to be done. Some are easy, others are difficult. Some bring honour, others bring reproach. Some are suitable to our natural inclinations and temporal interests, others are contrary to both . . . Yet the power to do all these things is given to us in Christ, who strengthens us.' Whatever the time of year, here is an unforgettable resource for recommitting your life to Christ.

I am no longer my own, but yours.
Put me to what you will, rank me
    with whom you will;
    put me to doing, put me to suffering.
Let me be employed by you or laid aside by you,
    enabled for you or brought low by you.
Let me be full, let me be empty.
Let me have all things, let me have nothing.
I freely and heartily yield all things to your pleasure
    and disposal.
And now, O glorious and blessed God,
    Father, Son, and Holy Spirit,
    you are mine, and I am yours.
So be it.
And the covenant which I have made on earth,
    let it be ratified in heaven.
Amen.

24 August

We've another poem now from Gerard Manley Hopkins (1844–1889); perhaps the best-known and most loved lines he ever composed. They come from the poem 'Pied Beauty', which celebrates the beauty of creation and everything this communicates to us of God. The poem is all the more remarkable for the fact that Hopkins experienced frequent bouts of depression during his life coupled with increasingly poor health. It's clear from his words here, however, that the joy brought by his faith far outweighed such moments – a joy exemplified by what, reputedly, were his last words: 'I am so happy! I am so happy!'

Glory be to God for dappled things –
for skies of couple-colour as a brinded cow;
for rose-moles all in stipple upon trout that swim;
fresh-firecoal chestnut-falls; finches' wings;
landscape plotted and pieced – fold, fallow, and
    plough;
And all trades, their gear and tackle and trim.

All things counter, original, spare, strange;
whatever is fickle, freckled (who knows how?)
with swift, slow; sweet, sour; adazzle, dim;
he fathers-forth whose beauty is past change:
    Praise him.

25 August

How effective are you in witnessing to Christ? What if anything have you done to share the gospel with others? If you're like me, you'll be acutely aware of how difficult you find it to communicate your faith in a way that is both natural and effective. We'll never achieve that on our own, however many evangelistic techniques we might learn, but that doesn't mean we can evade our share in making Christ known. As the following prayer of Bishop William Walsham How (1823–1897) reminds us, we need God's help in living out and proclaiming the gospel. How's prayer, it seems, was more than answered, for he went on to play a key role in Christian outreach in the East End of London, as well as writing several hymns and books.

Most merciful Father,
    I confess that I have done little
        to promote your kingdom
    and advance your glory.
Pardon my shortcomings
    and give me greater enthusiasm in serving you.
Make me more ready and conscientious by my
    prayers, my giving and my example,
    to spread the knowledge of your truth
    and extend your kingdom;
    and may I do everything to your glory.
Amen.

26 August

Health problems tend to be associated with advancing
years, but, of course, illness can strike at any time of
life. Our natural impulse then is to pray for healing,
and, God willing, that prayer will be answered, but
there are times when healing doesn't come and people
have to come to terms with a lifetime of chronic disease
or the stark reality of some terminal illness. I'm not
sure how well I'd cope with such a situation, or indeed
with any other serious adversity, but words of Cardinal
John Henry Newman (1801–1890), adapted into a
prayer, suggest a way of consecrating even the most
testing of experiences to God.

My God, you have created me
    to do you some definite service.
You have committed some work to me not committed
    to another.
I have my place in your plan.
I may never know what it is in this life,
    but I will be told it in the next.
I am a link in a chain,
    a bond of connection between persons.
I will do good,
    and do your work,
    and, even while not consciously intending it,
    be an angel of peace and preacher of truth in
        whatever place you put me,
    so long as I keep your commandments.
So I will trust you in all things,
    for whatever and wherever I am,
    I will never be thrown away.
If I am sick, may my sickness serve you.

If I am worried, may my worry serve you.
If I am in sorrow, may my sorrow serve you.
If I am exhausted, may my exhaustion serve you.
If I am sleepless, may my wakefulness serve you.
You do nothing in vain,
    you know what you are about.
You may take away my friends,
    you may throw me among strangers,
    you may make me feel desolate so that my spirits
        sink,
    you may hide the future from me –
    still you know what you are doing.
Amen.

27 August

God, we are told, does not judge by appearances but looks into the heart (1 Samuel 16:7b). How about us? Do we possess the same depth of insight, or do we jump to conclusions based on first impressions? We will never, of course, see things quite as God does but that, nonetheless, should be our daily aim. The following prayer of St Thomas à Kempis (1380–1471) recognises we cannot do this alone, so asks for a spirit of discernment that we might look beneath the surface and truly see.

Grant me, Lord, to know what I ought to know,
    to love what I ought to love,
    to praise what delights you most,
    to value what is precious in your sight,
    and to hate what is offensive to you.
Let me not judge according to superficial appearances,
    nor condemn on the basis of what others say;
    but may I have the discernment to understand
      deeper realities,
    and above all things to seek your will.
Amen.

28 August

I've chosen another prayer today attributed to St Columba (521–597). Beautifully poetic, it expresses simple trust in God's guidance and protection. This doesn't mean, of course, that we are in any way exempt from life's traumas and tragedies – indeed, in Columba's time Christian commitment would have multiplied its dangers several times over – but we have the assurance that nothing finally will separate us from God's love.

Alone with none but thee, my God,
I journey on my way;
what need I fear when thou art near,
oh King of night and day?
More safe am I within thy hand
than if a host did round me stand.

29 August

Here is another poem, this time from the writer Francis Quarles (1592–1644). The father of eighteen children, his own father had spent many years in the service of Queen Elizabeth I, passing on royalist sympathies to the young Francis. During the English Civil War, Francis was exiled to Flanders, where he continued to write poetry. His work was panned by critics as cheap and vulgar, but to me there is real beauty, not to mention profound faith, in the following poem, titled 'Why dost thou shade thy lovely face?'

My light thou art; without thy glorious sight
mine eyes are darken'd with perpetual night.
My God, thou art my way, my life, my light.

Thou art my way; I wander if thou fly:
thou art my light; if hid, how blind am I!
Thou art my life; if thou withdraw, I die.

Mine eyes are blind and dark, I cannot see;
to whom or whither should my darkness flee,
but to the light? And who's that light but thee?

My path is lost, my wand'ring steps do stray;
I cannot safely go, nor safely stay;
whom should I seek but thee, my path, my way?

30 August

There are times, aren't there, when God seems wonderfully real, but there are times also when he seems remote from daily life to the point that we're scarcely conscious of him at all. How can that be? If God really is so important, how is it that we can all but lose sight of him? The answer, as St Anselm (1033–1109) recognises, is that we are totally different to God, our very ability to glimpse him at all depending on him first revealing himself to us. Even when he does do so, if we do not seek we will not find, for so much within us is closed to his presence. Prayer is about bringing to God our longing to know him better, and asking him to bridge the gap.

O Lord my God,
   teach my heart this day
   where and how to see you,
   where and how to find you.
You have made and remade me,
   and you have given to me all the good things
      I possess,
   and still I do not know you.
I have not yet done that for which I was created.
Let me seek you in my longing,
   let me long for you in my seeking.
Let me find you by loving you,
   let me love you when I find you.
Amen.

31 August

There are few better places to turn to in times of trouble than the Psalms. They brim over with pleas like the one below, taken from Psalm 86 (vv. 1, 3, 6, 7, 15) begging God for help and support in a moment of need. Once more it seems, David – the writer of this Psalm – was living as a fugitive in the desert, fleeing from Saul who was determined to destroy him. There's frustration, anguish and even a note of despair in these words, but as always with the Psalms, there's the underlying conviction that, despite everything, God will hear and answer.

Give ear to me, Lord, and answer,
    for I'm vulnerable and in need.
Deal kindly with me,
    for I call to you Lord throughout the day.
Hear my prayer;
    listen to my appeal for favour.
I know you answer me,
    so in this time of trouble I call to you,
    for you, Lord, are forgiving and gracious,
    a God who is slow to get angry
    and who overflows with unfailing and constant
        love.

SEPTEMBER

1 September

A problem shared, so the saying goes, is a problem halved, and sometimes prayer is simply a matter of opening our hearts to God and pouring out our fears and frustrations. In doing that we follow the tradition of the Psalms where, time and again, we see just that, the writer blurting out his woes and begging for help. Take, for example, the following from Psalm 6:2-4, 6. If you're going through hard times, these words may be just the thing to tell God how you feel.

Deal kindly with me, Lord,
    for my health is failing;
    heal me,
    for I'm disturbed in my bones,
    deeply agitated in spirit.
How long, Lord, until you help me?
Turn to me, and save my life,
    rescue me on account of your constant love.
I am tired of groaning, Lord.
Night after night I inundate my sickbed with my tears;
    I soak my divan with weeping.

2 September

What do you think of the following prayer? Is it senti-
mental nonsense or indicative of profound faith; an
unattainable dream or realistic ideal? I'll leave you to
make up your mind, but to me these words of St Gregory
of Nazianzus (c. 330–389), though perhaps a shade
pietistic, express a beautiful thought: the possibility of
being so in tune with God that every aspect of life is
touched by and responds to his presence.

While I sleep, O Lord,
    let my heart not cease to worship you;
    fill my sleep with your presence,
    while creation itself keeps watch,
    singing psalms with the angels,
    and taking up my soul into its paean of praise.
Amen.

3 September

Few words of St Augustine of Hippo (354–430) are more celebrated than those concerning our hearts finding rest in God, and I can well understand why, for they take us to the heart of our human condition and our hunger for a sense of purpose in the vicissitudes of life. The 'prayer' is typically reproduced in an abridged and somewhat truncated form, the original coming from the opening lines of Augustine's celebrated *Confessions* which are well worth quoting in full. As much a statement of faith as a prayer, these words remind us of where true fulfilment can be found.

Great are you, O Lord, and greatly to be praised;
    great is your power,
    and your wisdom is beyond reckoning.
And so we humans, who are a due part
    of your creation, long to praise you –
    we who carry our mortality about with us,
    carry the evidence of our sin
    and with it the proof that you thwart the proud.
Yet these humans,
    due part of your creation as they are,
    still do long to praise you.
You stir us so that praising you may bring us joy,
    because you have made us for yourself,
    and our hearts are restless until they rest in you.
Amen.

4 September

To do God's will rather than our own. It's easy to speak
of that, isn't it, but doing it is another matter. That,
however, is what the writer of this prayer, the American
nun Francesca Xavier Cabrini (1850-1917), learned
to do. Her overwhelming ambition was to serve as a
missionary in China, but instead she was sent by Pope
Leo XIII to work in New York City, where she founded
an orphanage, the first of 67 she was to set up in America
and Europe. Her tireless work was to transform the
lives of many, testament to the way God chose to use
her service. Our calling may be more simple, but are
we ready to hear and respond?

Fortify me with the grace of your Holy Spirit
    and give your peace to my soul
    that I may be free from all needless anxiety,
    solicitude and worry.
Help me to desire always that which is pleasing
    and acceptable to you
    so that your will may be my will.
Amen.

5 September

So many of our greatest Christian hymns offer ideal material also for prayer. So it is with the well-loved words of Charles Wesley (1707–1788) below. You've probably sung them many times, but how often have you paused to reflect on the words? It pays to do so, for they're a wonderful expression of Christian commitment and a perfect way to consecrate our lives afresh to Christ's service.

O thou who camest from above
the fire celestial to impart,
kindle a flame of sacred love
on the mean altar of my heart.

There let it for thy glory burn
with inextinguishable blaze,
and, trembling, to its source return
in humble prayer and fervent praise.

Jesus, confirm my heart's desire
to work and speak and think for thee;
still let me guard the holy fire
and still stir up thy gift in me.

Ready for all thy perfect will,
my acts of faith and love repeat,
till death thine endless mercies seal,
and make the sacrifice complete.

6 September

We've encountered the beauty of Celtic spirituality already in this book, and here we have another lovely example. A traditional Irish blessing, it uses natural symbols to evoke a sense of God's presence in all of life, granting his love, guidance and protection. Use these words to pray for others and to remind yourself of the blessing he seeks daily to give to you.

May the road rise up to meet you.
May the wind be always at your back.
May the sun shine warm on your face,
   the rain fall soft upon your fields,
   and, until we meet again,
   may God hold you in the palm of his hand.
Amen.

7 September

Part of the power of many ancient prayers is the fact that those who first uttered them went on to give their life for the sake of their faith. One such is St Apollonius of Rome (*d.* 186), a second-century senator and martyr. Shortly after becoming a Christian his new-found faith was reported to the authorities by one of his slaves, and with Christianity still being outlawed in the Roman Empire, Apollonius was taken for trial before the Senate. As part of his defence, he is said to have declared: '. . . if it were a delusion (as you assert) which tells us that the soul is immortal, and that there is a judgement after death and a reward of virtue at the resurrection, and that God is the Judge, we would gladly be carried away by such a lie as that, which has taught us to lead good lives awaiting the hope of the future even while suffering adversities'. Would you have shown such courage in his shoes? I doubt I would, for the result, as he must have known, was certain death. He was duly found guilty and beheaded.

O Lord Jesus Christ, grant us a measure of your Spirit.
Help us to obey your teaching,
>   soothe anger,
>   cultivate pity,
>   overcome desire,
>   increase love,
>   cast off sorrow,
>   shun vainglory,
>   renounce revenge,
>   and not be afraid of death.
Let us ever entrust our spirit to the everlasting God
>   who with you and the Holy Spirit lives and rules
>   for ever and ever.
Amen.

8 September

I spoke earlier of prayers coming from unlikely people and that's certainly true of the following words. They come from the poem 'God's World', written by the American poet Edna St Vincent Millay (1892–1950), a woman whose various love affairs with both men and women scandalised the society of her time. We too may baulk at her lifestyle, but there's no doubting the beauty of her words here as she celebrates the wonder of God's creation.

O world, I cannot hold thee close enough!
Thy winds, thy wide gray skies!
Thy mists, that roll and rise!
Thy woods, this autumn day, that ache and sag
and all but cry with color! That gaunt crag
to crush! To lift the lean of that black bluff!
World, world, I cannot get thee close enough!

Long have I known a glory in it all
but never knew I this.
Here such a passion is
as stretcheth me apart. Lord, I do fear
thou'st made the world too beautiful this year.
My soul is all but out of me – let fall
no burning leaf; prithee, let no bird call.

9 September

Is asking questions of God wrong? I don't think so for a moment. True faith is strong enough to admit to doubt, for there is much in life that it is hard to make sense of in terms of faith. Sometimes we search for answers in vain. At others times, experience and hindsight help us to make sense of what once seemed incomprehensible, as observed in lines from 'Peace after a Storm', a poem by poet and hymn-writer William Cowper (1731–1800).

When darkness long has veil'd my mind,
and smiling day once more appears,
then, my Redeemer, then I find
the folly of my doubts and fears.

Straight I upbraid my wandering heart,
and blush that I should ever be
thus prone to act so base a part,
or harbour one hard thought of thee!

Oh! let me then at length be taught
what I am still so slow to learn,
that God is love, and changes not,
nor knows the shadow of a turn.

10 September

Does God answer prayer? There are times when it seems not, especially when we seek healing for those who are sick. Sometimes that comes, sometimes it doesn't, and when it's a loved one or even ourselves whose health we're talking about, shattered hopes can be hard to bear. Faith, however, doesn't guarantee immunity from illness or suffering and, hard though it may be, sometimes we have to recognise that we're praying for the wrong thing, asking for healing when we should be looking for strength to bear infirmity. That's the message of the following prayer, coming once again not from a Christian source but the Bengali poet and writer Rabindranath Tagore (1861–1941).

Let me not pray to be sheltered from dangers
    but to be fearless in facing them.
Let me not beg for the stilling of my pain
    but for the heart to conquer it.
Let me not look for allies in life's battlefield
    but to my own strength.
Let me not crave in anxious fear to be saved
    but hope for patience to win my freedom.
Sarvamangalam!
Blessings to all!

11 September

What do we mean by success? Most of us spend our lives striving after this elusive goal, whether at work, in relationships, in sport or some other field. There's nothing wrong in that, of course, the pursuit of excellence being a worthwhile ideal, but as many have found, such success, if achieved, does not guarantee happiness. As the following prayer of J. H. Jowett (1864–1923) reminds us, the values of God's kingdom are different from ours, so often turning this world's expectations upside down.

Holy Lord, teach me the meaning of real success,
    and let me not become enslaved by the values
      of the world,
    but value holiness more than wealth.
May I aspire to what is eternal,
    and in that may I be successful!
Amen.

12 September

Many will have heard the following prayer while
attending a funeral service. It fits perfectly in such a
context, offering to those wrestling with the trauma of
bereavement the assurance that their loved one is at
peace in God's eternal presence. We needn't, though,
limit it simply to when we're confronted by death, for
these lovely words of John Henry Newman (1801–
1890) speak also of the God who supports us throughout life, giving a different perspective on this frenetic
world of ours.

May he support us all the day long,
    until the shadows lengthen
    and the evening comes,
    and the busy world is hushed,
    and the fever of life over,
    and our work is done.
Then, Lord, in your mercy,
    grant us safe lodging,
    a holy rest,
    and peace at the last.
Amen.

13 September

Do we take God's gifts for granted? Of course we do. Most of us, myself included, are good at asking for more but poor at recognising how much we already have. It's only on rare occasions that something happens to jog our memories and prompt us to count our blessings. We'll never change that – it's a fact of human nature – but that doesn't mean we should be complacent about it. The following traditional Scottish prayer asks forgiveness for the way we consistently overlook God's goodness, and asks for help to appreciate it more fully.

Lord of all mercy and goodness,
    let me not by any ingratitude or hardness of heart
    forget the wonderful benefits that you have
        bestowed upon me this and every day,
    but grant that I may be mindful,
        all the days of my life,
    of the incomparable gifts which you always give
        to me.
Amen.

14 September

Sometimes we come before God with a lot on our mind, asking him for this, that and everything else. At other times we're conscious simply of our unworthiness and dependence on God's grace, it being enough to acknowledge our weakness in the assurance that he will hear and respond. That's what Thomas à Kempis (1380–1471) does here, in a few powerful lines opening his life to God's transforming touch.

Trusting in your goodness and great mercy, Lord,
   I come:
   sick – I come to my Saviour;
   hungry and thirsty – to the well of Life;
   needy – to the King of Heaven.

15 September

Many of our great poets have felt God's presence most powerfully in the natural world, and Lord Byron (1788–1824) was no exception. The following lines, taken from *Prayer of Nature*, elevate what we can learn of God through creation above what we might learn through the words of the prophets. A moot point, you may argue, but I can understand where the poet is coming from, for which of us hasn't at some time or other experienced a compelling sense of the divine in similar fashion, whether through the grandeur of the sea, tranquillity of a meadow, splendour of sunset, song of a blackbird, beauty of wild flowers or some other natural phenomenon. The fact is, God can speak in many ways, moving us in turn to humble response.

Father! no prophet's laws I seek –
thy laws in Nature's works appear –
I own myself corrupt and weak,
yet will I pray, for thou wilt hear.

16 September

Few things are more destructive than suppressed
emotions or experiences, whether it's personal bitterness, feelings of guilt, unspoken fears or unpleasant
truths. However hard we try to bury such things, they
have a habit of pushing their way back to the surface,
often with much more devastating results than if we'd
faced up to them in the first place. Prayer can provide
the ideal way of tackling them head on, both through
opening up before God and through asking his help to
confront issues we've hidden even from ourselves.
That's what Evelyn Underhill (1875–1941) asks for in
the wonderfully honest and sensible prayer below. It's
taken from her book *Meditations and Prayers* (1949).

Penetrate those murky corners
   where we hide memories,
   and tendencies on which we do not care to look,
   but which we will not disinter and yield freely up
      to you,
   that you may purify and transmute them.
The persistent buried grudge,
   the half-acknowledged enmity, still smouldering;
   the bitterness of that loss we have not turned
      into a sacrifice,
   the private comfort we cling to,
   the secret failure that saps our initiative
      and is really inverted pride;
   the pessimism which is an insult to your joy.
Lord, we bring all these to you;
   and we review them with shame and penitence in
      your steadfast light.

17 September

Our prayer today is historic in more ways than one. It dates back not only several centuries, but also to a truly historic moment, being first uttered by Jacob Astley (1579–1652) during the English Civil War, just before the Battle of Edgehill in 1642. A royalist commander in charge of the infantry, he fought also at the battles of Newbury (1643) and Naseby (1645), finally being captured at Stow on the Wold in 1646. To his credit, he makes no attempt here to pray for victory, probably being all too aware that his roundhead opponents were equally convinced of the rightness of their cause. Rather he asks for help to glimpse God even in the horrors of war. Life will bring us very different experiences but we in turn need to recognise God's presence in whatever we may face and whatever wider events each day might bring.

Lord, help me to realise today
    that you will be speaking to me
    through the events of the day,
    through people,
    through things,
    and through all creation.
Give me ears, eyes and heart to perceive you,
    however veiled your presence may be.
Give me insight to see through the exterior of things
    to the interior truth.
Give me your Spirit of discernment.
O Lord, you know how busy I must be this day.
If I forget you, do not forget me.
Amen.

18 September

What's your first thought each morning as the alarm clock brusquely shatters your sleep? Is it to worship God or to roll over and go back to sleep? Mine is very much the latter, and just occasionally I get the chance to do just that, but more often, after a token few minutes denying the inevitable, I rouse myself from my stupor. It doesn't take long, though, to remember that the new day is God's gift, to be received with thanks and lived to the full. Reading the following words of the bishop, poet and hymn-writer Thomas Ken (1637–1711), I get the feeling he didn't enjoy waking up any more than I do, but he too recognised God's goodness in every new morning. He offers a perfect way of consecrating each one to God.

Awake my soul, and with the sun
thy daily stage of duty run;
shake off dull sloth, and joyful rise
to pay thy morning sacrifice.

Lord, I my vows to thee renew;
disperse my sins as morning dew;
guard my first springs of thought and will,
and with thyself my spirit fill.

Direct, control, suggest, this day,
all I design or do or say;
that all my powers, with all their might,
in thy sole glory may unite.

19 September

Being a Christian doesn't guarantee us exemption from pain and suffering, but it's natural nonetheless to ask God to protect us from it as far as possible. It was particularly natural for the writer of our prayer today to do so, for St Irenaeus (130–202) lived during a time when Christians suffered terribly for their faith, many experiencing truly dreadful deaths. One of the great figures of the early Church, Irenaeus would have known what it was to live each day in fear for one's life and would probably have faced danger himself on more than one occasion. While he knew God can't guarantee our safety, he knew also that our welfare is always close to his heart.

O Lamb of God,
    who takest away the sin of the world,
    look upon us and have mercy upon us;
    thou who art thyself both victim and Priest,
    thyself both Reward and Redeemer,
    keep safe from all evil those whom thou hast
        redeemed,
    O Saviour of the world.
Amen.

20 September

We've seen earlier in the year that in times of ill health our prayer sometimes has to be for strength to bear it rather than to be made well, and that's the message in the following words of the writer and rector Thomas Fuller (1608–1661). To live with chronic or terminal illness takes great courage, yet while some find their faith sorely tested, others have found it strengthened and enriched. None of us would welcome sickness but we must be able to meet it when it comes, as for many it surely will.

Lord,
    teach me the art of patience whilst I am well,
    and give me the use of it when I am sick.
In that day,
    either lighten my burden or strengthen my back.
Make me
    (who so often in my health have discovered my
        weakness, presuming on my own strength)
    be strong in my sickness when I solely rely on your
        assistance.
    Amen.

21 September

We've another prayer today of St Teresa of Avila (1515–1582). Tradition has it that these were her last words, and certainly the depth of her devotion throughout her life lends credence to that claim. Whether we'll have the chance to meet death with such equanimity who can say, but the faith that enabled her to do so is one we share in turn and in which we live each moment of every day.

My Lord, it is time to move on.
Well then, may your will be done.
O my Lord and my Spouse,
    the hour that I have longed for has come.
It is time for us to meet one another.

22 September

When it comes to praise there's no shortage of unforgettable prayers handed down across the centuries. Take, for example, the following, attributed to St Francis of Assisi (1182–1226). It piles up adjectives and superlatives in attempting to express the wonder of God, and in doing so reminds us of all we have to praise him for. Offer these words reverently and joyfully, celebrating everything God is and does.

You are holy, Lord, the only God,
    and your deeds are wonderful.
You are strong.
You are great.
You are the Most High.
You are Almighty.
You, Holy Father are King of heaven and earth.
You are Three and One, Lord God, all Good.
You are Good, all Good, supreme Good,
    Lord God, living and true.
You are love. You are wisdom.
You are humility. You are endurance.
You are rest. You are peace.
You are joy and gladness.
You are justice and moderation.
You are all our riches, and you suffice for us.
You are beauty.
You are gentleness.
You are our protector.
You are our guardian and defender.
You are our courage.
You are our haven and our hope.

You are our faith, our great consolation.
You are our eternal life, great and wonderful Lord,
    God almighty, merciful Saviour.
Amen.

23 September

If yesterday's prayer was memorable, so too are our words today, albeit for a different reason. They come from St Augustine of Hippo (354-430), and whereas St Francis attempted to express his worship through sheer weight of words, Augustine takes the opposite approach, recognising that no words can ever get near acknowledging God's greatness. We too need a similar sense of awe and wonder whenever we come before God in prayer.

O thou Supreme!
Most secret and most present,
    most beautiful and strong!
What shall I say,
    my God,
    my Life,
    my Holy Joy?
What shall anyone say when they speak of thee?

24 September

Our prayer today comes from Mother Janet Erskine Stuart (1857–1914), a Catholic nun from Cottesmore, in Rutland. Daughter of an Anglican vicar, she entered the Society of the Sacred Heart, succeeding Mabel Digby as Mother Superior in 1884. Her special gift lay in education and Mother Stuart took a hands-on role in the West Hill teacher-training college for women established in Roehampton by her predecessor. The college was later named Digby Stuart College in honour of these two women's contribution. Her words here show wonderful humility coupled with corresponding commitment.

Dear Lord and Saviour, Jesus Christ,
    I hold up all my weakness to your strength,
    my failure to your faithfulness,
    my sinfulness to your perfection,
    my loneliness to your compassion,
    my little pains to your great agony on the cross.
I pray that you will cleanse me,
    strengthen me,
    guide me,
    so that in all ways
    my life may be lived as you would have it lived,
    without cowardice
    and for you alone.
Show me how to live in true humility,
    true contrition
    and true love.
Amen.

25 September

How is it that Christians across the years have gained a reputation for dwelling on sin and punishment, almost as though they delight in the idea of a vengeful God? It always puzzles me, for what I see in the gospel is a God who is completely different, slow to anger and delighting to forgive, his nature always to have mercy. Clearly the writer of the following prayer – the Eastern Orthodox bishop and theologian St Gregory of Nyssa (died *c.* 385/6) – felt the same, his words here wonderfully celebrating God's free and full forgiveness. Use his words to give thanks in turn.

Lord, from you flows true and continual kindness.
You had cast us off and justly so,
    but in your mercy you forgave us.
You were at odds with us,
    and you reconciled us.
You had set a curse on us,
    and you blessed us.
You had banished us from the garden,
    and you called us back again.
You took away the fig leaves
    that had been an unsuitable garment,
    and you clothed us in a cloak of great value.
You flung wide the prison gates,
    and you gave the condemned a pardon.
You sprinkled clean water on us,
    and you washed away the dirt.
Amen.

26 September

Here is yet another example of the deep faith and spirituality of St Augustine of Hippo (354–430). Recognising the awesome contrast between his weakness and God's strength, he asks for help in putting God first in every aspect of life, being emptied in order to be truly filled. It's easy enough to repeat these words; much harder to grasp their full implications and harder still, having done so, to truly mean them.

Lord Jesus,
  let me know myself and know you,
  and desire nothing save only you.
Let me hate myself and love you.
Let me do everything for the sake of you.
Let me humble myself and exalt you.
Let me think of nothing except you.
Let me die to myself and live in you.
Let me accept whatever happens as from you.
Let me banish self and follow you,
  and ever desire to follow you.
Let me fly from myself and take refuge in you,
  that I may deserve to be defended by you.
Let me fear for myself, let me fear you,
  and let me be among those who are chosen by you.
Let me distrust myself and put my trust in you.
Let me be willing to obey for the sake of you.
Let me cling to nothing save only to you,
  and let me be poor because of you.
Look upon me, that I may love you.
Call me that I may see you,
  and for ever enjoy you.
Amen.

27 September

If there's one need as urgent in the world today as it's
ever been, it must surely be for peace. No sooner does
one conflict cease, it seems, than another starts, division
appearing endemic to humankind. We can despair
sometimes of things ever changing, just as the author
of this prayer would have done had he known that
three years after his death would see the start of the so-
called Great War (1914–1918). Why does God allow
war and hatred to continue? There are no easy answers
to that, but one thing is for certain: without his transforming touch there's no hope of lasting harmony
between nations. Join, then, with the one-time Bishop
of Oxford, Francis Paget (1851–1911), in expressing a
heartfelt longing for peace.

Almighty God,
    from whom all thoughts of truth and peace
        proceed:
    kindle, we pray you, in the hearts of all people
        the true love of peace;
    and guide with your pure and peaceable wisdom
    those who take counsel for the nations of the earth;
    that in tranquillity your kingdom may go forward,
    till the earth be filled with the knowledge of your
        love,
    through Jesus Christ our Lord.
Amen.

28 September

We've a prayer of intercession next which is as relevant as when it was first written. Coming from Eugène Bersier, a Swiss-born pastor who served in Paris between 1831 and 1889, it brings before God the pain and sorrow of our world in which all too many continue to carry heavy burdens. We so easily forget those, don't we, finding it hard to look beyond our own situation, but a faith concerned only with self is ultimately no faith at all. Use these words so that, reaching out in thought, you may reach out also in deed.

You are love,
> and see all the suffering and injustice that hold
> > sway in this world.

Have pity, we implore you, on the work of your hands.
Look mercifully on the poor, the oppressed,
> and all who are weighed down by error, labour
> > and sorrow.

Fill our hearts with deep compassion for those who
> suffer, and hasten the coming of your kingdom
> of justice and truth.

Amen.

29 September

For today I've chosen words of the poet Francis Quarles (1592–1644). With a touch of humour and considerable eloquence, he beautifully captures the contrast between the faithfulness of God and faithlessness of our response. We will go on confessing our mistakes to our dying day, but, like Quarles, we need to do so remembering that God's love will not fail.

My sinnes are like the haires upon my head,
and raise their Audit to as high a score:
In this they differ: these doe dayly shed;
but ah! my sinnes grow dayly more and more.
  If by my haires thou number out my sinnes;
    heaven make me bald before the day begins.

My sinnes are like the sands upon the shore;
which every ebbe layes open to the eye:
In this they differ: These are cover'd o'er
with every tide, my sinnes still open lye.
  If thou wilt make my head a sea of teares,
    O they will hide the sinnes of all my yeares.

My sinnes are like the Starres within the skies,
In view, in number, even as bright as great:
In this they differ: these doe set and rise;
but ah! my sinnes doe rise, but never set.
  Shine Son of glory, and my sinnes are gone
    Like twinkling Starres before the rising Sunne.

30 September

Can the God who brought the universe into being, the
sovereign creator who is before, above and beyond all,
really be concerned with insignificant people like you
and me? It seems preposterous, doesn't it, too ridiculous
for words, yet that's the message at the heart of the
Bible and at the heart, too, of this prayer. Written by
Augustine of Hippo (354–430), it offers a wonderful
reminder that though God is greater than we can ever
begin to grasp, he nonetheless values each one of us,
our welfare infinitely important to him.

Thanks be to you,
    O Creator and governor of the universe,
    for my well-being through the years
        since I arrived at birth.
Thanks be to you,
    my joy,
    my confidence,
    my God,
    for the gifts by which you have preserved me
    and enabled me to grow.
Amen.

OCTOBER

1 October

In many ways, prayer is about bringing to God what we are, in order that he can help create what we shall be. Our own efforts alone will never be enough to change us, as generations have found when their resolutions come to nothing. We need God's Spirit to work within us, moulding and transforming our inner nature into the likeness of Christ. It's a painfully slow process, and one which we frequently frustrate to the extent that it virtually has to begin all over again, but that is the goal we yearn to see fulfilled. Prayer is often the conduit through which God is able to work, as exemplified in the following words of Evelyn Underhill (1875–1941), taken from her book *Meditations and Prayers* (1949).

Teach me, O God, a proper reverence
    for all that unformed human nature on which your
      Holy Spirit rests,
    which you can penetrate, transform, make holy,
    and in which you show forth to us the glory
      of the Only-Begotten of the Father,
    full of grace and truth.

2 October

Christian traditions differ in their attitude towards praying for the dead. For some it is regular practice, for others anathema, but all, I think, would happily find a place for committing into God's care those who have just died. The following words of St Ignatius Loyola (1491–1556) offer a lovely way of doing just that, expressing faith in God's eternal kingdom while also seeking his blessing on those we've lost.

Lord,
   welcome into your calm and peaceful kingdom
   those who have departed out of this present life
      to be with you.
Grant them rest
   and a place with the spirits of the just;
   and give them the life that knows no age,
   the reward that passes not away,
   through Christ our Lord.
Amen.

3 October

I've said before that some of the greatest ever prayers come from the Bible, and this one is another case in point. Once again you will probably have heard these words many times without realising their source. They come in fact from the book of Hebrews 13:20, 21 and express faith in God's power to change both life and death. I've slightly adapted the words so that instead of being simply a blessing intended for this letter's original recipients, we can use them to seek God's blessing in turn.

Now may the God of peace,
    who through the blood of the eternal covenant
        brought our Lord Jesus –
    the great shepherd of the sheep –
    back from the dead,
    provide us with all good things,
    so that we may be able to do his will
    and offer service pleasing in his sight,
    through Jesus Christ,
    to whom be eternal honour.
Amen.

4 October

We may have heard the message of God's grace countless times before, but it never hurts to hear it again, for we find it hard to grasp and harder still to accept. Human nature is to be suspicious of receiving something for nothing. It just doesn't happen, we're told, so we understandably ask ourselves, 'Where's the catch?' Time and again we find ourselves slipping back into trying to earn salvation, convinced that somewhere down the line we have to do something to deserve forgiveness. Yet, as the following prayer of Søren Kierkegaard (1813–1855) makes clear, that is to deny ourselves the peace God longs to give. Use these words to celebrate again the wonderful truth of God's unfailing mercy.

O Lord Jesus Christ,
    your love covers the multitude of my sins.
So when I am fully aware of my sin,
    when before the justice of heaven only wrath
      is pronounced upon me,
    then you are the only person to whom I can escape.
If I try to cover myself against the guilt of sin and the
    wrath of heaven,
    I will be driven to madness and despair.
But if I rely on you to cover my sins,
    I shall find peace and joy.
You suffered and died on the cross to shelter us
    from our guilt,
    and take upon yourself the wrath that we deserve.
Let me rest under you,
    and may you transform me into your likeness.
Amen.

5 October

Researching this book I've been amazed by how many great names from history have cropped up – people I would never have automatically associated with prayer, let alone prayers that have stood the test of time. One such is Blaise Pascal (1623–1662), the celebrated French mathematician, physicist and philosopher. In 1654, following a mystical experience, he became a committed Christian, devoting much of his life thereafter to the study of theology. Dogged by poor health – he was to die prematurely aged just 39 – his approach to life was nonetheless wonderfully positive, as shown by his words here. It's an approach and a prayer we do well to imitate.

Teach us, Lord,
    to do the little things as though they were great
    because of the majesty of Christ,
    who does them in us and who lives our life.
Teach us to do the greatest things as though they were
    little and easy,
    because of your great power.
Amen.

6 October

Though we fail him God will not fail us – that is the message at the heart of the gospel, our faithlessness constantly contrasted to his faithfulness. That's the theme of our prayer today, written by the Swiss author, poet, musician and monk Notker of St Gall (c. 840–912). Though his speech was halting due to a speech impediment, his prose was lyrical and free flowing, joyfully celebrating God's goodness. His words here give us a glimpse into why King Ekkehard IV was able to describe Notker as 'stuttering of tongue but not of intellect, pushing boldly forward in things Divine, a vessel of the Holy Spirit without equal in his time'.

Praise to you, O faithful God!
You never fail those who trust in you,
    but you allow them to share in your glory.
You fight for us against everything that could attack
    or do us harm.
You are our shepherd,
    and you free us from the snare.
You protect us who honour you, O God,
    great is the sweetness that you give.
Amen.

7 October

Earlier in this book we used part of the celebrated prayer known to many as St Patrick's Breastplate. The opening stanzas cited there may not be as familiar as the lines below – words that have inspired numerous revisions by hymn-writers and poets, an example of which we will see later. The lines aren't a prayer in the traditional sense at all – much more a statement of faith – but I've no doubt that whenever Patrick used them he did so as a way of consecrating the whole of life to God. There can surely be few more memorable ways of doing so.

I arise today
> through God's strength to pilot me:
> God's might to uphold me,
> God's wisdom to guide me,
> God's eye to look before me,
> God's ear to hear me,
> God's word to speak for me,
> God's hand to guard me,
> God's way to lie before me,
> God's shield to protect me,
> God's host to save me.

Christ with me, Christ before me, Christ behind me,
Christ in me, Christ beneath me, Christ above me,
Christ on my right, Christ on my left,
Christ when I lie down, Christ when I sit down, Christ
> when I arise,
Christ in the heart of every man who thinks of me,
Christ in the mouth of everyone who speaks of me,
Christ in every eye that sees me,
Christ in every ear that hears me.

8 October

The source of the following prayer is unknown but it deserves recording for posterity. Too often prayers of confession can seem morbid, overly pious or couched in outdated terminology, but not this one. It speaks of failings we'll all recognise in ourselves, everyday weaknesses that may seem small yet that damage and impede relationships out of all proportion to their size. Simply but sincerely they are brought here before God, along with our need for forgiveness so that we can start again. Though it is never stated, that assurance of pardon is taken as guaranteed.

Our insensitivity to the needs of others,
    O Lord, forgive.
Our prejudice and fear that prevent us from loving,
    O Lord, forgive.
The narrowness of our vision and our shrinking
    from your demands,
    O Lord, forgive.
Our resentment against those who have hurt us,
    O Lord, forgive.
Our desire to do your work in our way,
    O Lord, forgive.
Our impatience with those who are different from us,
    O Lord, forgive.
Our failure to listen properly to other points of view,
    O Lord, forgive.
Our fear of coming out of the fortress of our own
    souls into fuller life and deeper love,
    O Lord, forgive.
Amen.

9 October

Over the years the gospel has been taken across the world, the Church being far stronger in many countries today than it is in our own. There was a time when we in the West saw ourselves as those with something to share, and, of course, we still have, every one of us having something to contribute to the wider fellowship of God's people. But it has increasingly come to be realised that we also have much to receive, the insights and spirituality of the Church in other cultures being able to lead us in turn to deeper faith, commitment and understanding of God. Today, for example, we have a prayer of the Kikuyu people, from Kenya. Its sure and simple faith is compelling.

O Father,
  your power is greater than all powers.
O Son,
  under your leadership we cannot fear anything.
O Spirit,
  under your protection there is nothing
    we cannot overcome.
Amen.

10 October

If the spirituality of other Christian traditions can
speak both to and for us, so also can that of the faith
that gave birth to Christianity. We've encountered that
already, of course, in the Psalms and other words taken
from the Old Testament, but Judaism also has a rich
liturgical tradition, from which the following ancient
Jewish prayer is taken. Used in the Jewish daily morning
service, it celebrates life now and life to come, while
simultaneously affirming faith in both God and
humankind.

O my God,
    the soul which you placed within me is pure.
You created it,
    you formed it,
    you breathed it into me,
    and you preserve it within me.
You will one day take it from me,
    but will restore it to me in the hereafter.
So long as the soul is within me,
    I will give thanks to you,
    O Lord my God and God of my fathers,
    Master of all works,
    Lord of all souls.
Blessed are you – the Lord,
    who restores the souls to the dead.
Amen.

11 October

How honest are you with God? Specifically, how far do you open up to him about your faults and weaknesses? Most of us probably want to do that, but come up against a problem. We either struggle to admit to skeletons in our cupboard or genuinely aren't aware of certain failings. As in so much, we need God's help in seeing ourselves as we really are, and such help needs to be sought in prayer. That's precisely what lies behind the following words of the nineteenth-century scholar and clergyman Charles John Vaughan (1816–1897). They offer an important reminder that God is always ready to forgive and forget so long as we are prepared to submit ourselves to his searching gaze.

O Lord God, our Father most loving,
    we would not, even if we could, conceal anything
        from you,
    but rejoice rather that you know us as we are
    and see every desire and every motive of our hearts.
Help us, Lord, to strip off every mask and veil
    when we come into your presence,
    and to spread before you every thought and every
        secret of our being,
    that they may be forgiven, purified, amended,
        and blessed by you,
    through Jesus Christ our Lord.
Amen.

12 October

Wanting to do God's will is one thing; actually doing it is quite another. However much we may commit our lives to him, truly understanding what he wants of us, let alone responding in faith, is more often than not beyond us. His ways are not our ways so we struggle to hear his voice. And when we do hear, we find his way costly, involving surrender and sacrifice or, as Jesus put it, taking up our cross. If, therefore, we would truly honour God's will, we need first to offer our disciple-ship – as the following words taken from the so-called 'Universal Prayer' of Clement XI (1649–1721) remind us – and then to ask for God's guidance and help in responding faithfully to it.

I offer you, Lord, my thoughts: to be fixed on you;
    my words: to have you for their theme;
    my actions: to reflect my love for you;
    my sufferings: to be endured for your greater glory.
I want to do what you ask of me:
    in the way that you ask,
    for as long as you ask,
    because you ask it.
Lord, enlighten my understanding,
    strengthen my will,
    purify my heart,
    and make me holy.
Amen.

13 October

Are we too familiar with God nowadays? Some think so, and I can understand where they're coming from. I wouldn't want to go back to the days when public worship was so formal that it was comparable to being lectured at school by the headmaster. Nor would I want to feel we have to approach God in fear and trepidation, as though we've no right to be in his presence. Faith, as I understand it, is about a daily relationship in which God delights to share. For all that, though, there is a danger of becoming too familiar in the sense of assuming he is simply 'one of us'. We need to retain the sense of reverence and privilege at being in God's presence that characterises the following prayer of St Anselm (1033–1109). Lose that, and instead of reaching up to God's level we'll be dragging him down to ours.

O supreme and inaccessible Light,
   O complete and blessed Truth,
   how far you are from me,
   even though I am so near to you!
How remote you are from my sight,
   even though I am present to yours!
You are everywhere in your entirety,
   and yet I do not see you;
   in you I move and have my being,
   and yet I cannot approach you.
O God, let me know you
   and love you so that I may find my joy in you;
   and if I cannot do so fully in this life,
   let me at least make some progress every day,
   until at last that knowledge, love, and joy
     come to me in all their plenitude.
Amen.

14 October

If you're like me, you'll have acknowledged your faults to God so many times that it seems like you're constantly repeating the same old thing. Classic prayers of confession can provide a way out of that. Not that they necessarily say anything different, but they put things in a way that helps us to articulate freshly what we're feeling. They offer also a reminder of God's awesome grace – something that in our darker moments we can all too easily overlook. Use, then, the words of this Latin prayer, dating back to the tenth century, to confess once more your mistakes and seek God's pardon.

Lord God,
    sovereign Father,
    creator of all,
    giving me body and soul
    and creating me in your image
        before time even began,
    I confess my faults to you,
    for I have sinned before you and heaven,
    my sins being as numerous as the sand
        on the seashore.
In your love, O God,
    do not turn your face from me
        and let me perish,
    but have mercy.
I dare to ask it not because I deserve forgiveness
    but because of your grace.
Look down on me, Lord,
    from your heavenly throne,
    and lighten the shadows of my heart
        with the radiance of your splendour.

Protect me, Lord, with the shield of truth and faith,
    so that the fiery darts of the evil one
        may not pierce me.
Saviour of the world, who lives and reigns for ever,
    have mercy upon me.
Amen.

15 October

Our prayer today is a celebrated one, known to many as St Teresa's Bookmark. The words were discovered in Teresa of Avila's breviary following her death – thus the prayer's unusual title. To appreciate it fully we need to know a little of Teresa's story. Born in 1515, she entered the Carmelite Order as a young woman and soon made an impression as a zealous reformer, but while some welcomed her enthusiasm, in others it provoked deep resentment. Her opponents at one point even accused her of heresy, yet just forty years after her death in 1582 Teresa was to be canonised by Pope Gregory XV and made one of only three women Doctors of the Church. Many consider her mystical experiences and repeated self-mortification to have bordered on religious hysteria, and few today would want to emulate them, but there can be no doubting the wisdom or profound faith underlying her words. Use them to reflect quietly on God's presence, and to hear his voice speaking to you.

Let nothing disturb you,
    nothing affright you.
All things are passing;
    God never changes.
Patient endurance attains to all things.
Whoever possesses God is wanting in nothing;
    God alone suffices.

16 October

'Deliver us from evil', says the Lord's Prayer, and that's something most of us would instinctively ask for, looking if at all possible to be protected from whatever might do us harm. I've no doubt that God desires to grant such a request so far as he is able, but, of course, prayer doesn't guarantee us exemption from life's ills, nor should we ever expect it to. Faith does not expect God to take away the trials and traumas of daily living but rather to find his strength within them, no matter how demanding they may be. The writer of the following prayer, the Bengali mystic Rabindranath Tagore (1861–1941), captures that important truth in these words.

Let me not pray to be sheltered from dangers
    but to be fearless in facing them.
Let me not beg for the stilling of my pain,
    but for the heart to conquer it.
Let me not crave in anxious fear to be saved,
    but hope for the patience to win my freedom.
Grant me that I may not be a coward,
    feeling your mercy in my success alone,
    but let me find the grasp of your hand
        in my failure.

17 October

' "Let the little children come to me," said Jesus; "do not stop them; for the kingdom of God belongs to such as these. I tell you this, whoever does not receive the kingdom of God like a little child will never enter it." And he embraced them, laid his hands on them, and blessed them' (Mark 10:14b-16). That call to childlike trust has inspired many across the years, including the celebrated poet and hymn-writer John Newton (1725–1807), who as well as writing many classics produced the following verse – a simple but special poetic prayer.

As a little child relies
on a care beyond his own;
knows he's neither strong nor wise;
fears to stir a step alone;
let me thus with thee abide,
as my Father, Guard, and Guide.

18 October

No book of prayer would seem complete without words somewhere from the Revd Martin Luther King Jr (1929–1968). His powerful preaching and extra-ordinary courage captured the imagination of his generation, perhaps doing more than anything else to advance moves towards greater civil rights for racial and oppressed minorities in the United States. Never afraid to speak his mind, despite hostility and persecution, he paid finally for his principles with his life. A mark of his integrity was his donating the prize money attached to his 1964 Nobel Peace Prize to the civil rights movement. He will always be remembered for his 'I have a dream' speech, echoes of which can be seen in the following words. Sadly we seem no nearer today to the kind of world he longed for than we were in his lifetime.

Oh God,
    help us in our lives and in all of our attitudes
    to work out this controlling force of love,
    this controlling power that can solve every problem
        that we confront in all areas.
Oh, we talk about politics;
    we talk about the problems facing our atomic
        civilisation.
Grant that all men will come together
    and discover that as we solve the crisis and solve
        these problems,
    the international problems,
    the problems of atomic energy,
    the problems of nuclear energy,
    and yes, even the race problem;

let us join together in a great fellowship of love
and bow down at the feet of Jesus.
Give us this strong determination.
In the name and spirit of this Christ, we pray.
Amen.

19 October

Few writers and theologians have been more influential within the Protestant tradition than the Frenchman John Calvin (1509–1564; actual name Jean Chauvin). A committed evangelical, he applied his training as a lawyer to the study of the Bible, resolved to proclaim what he took to be its authentic message. Many associate him with a narrow and austere concept of faith, though much of this is due to additions to and interpretations of his thoughts by those who came after him. Calvin's dual emphasis on the sovereignty yet mercy of God is clearly seen in the following words.

Now let us cast ourselves down before the majesty
   of our good God
   with acknowledgement of our faults,
   praying him so to make us feel them that it may
      draw us to true repentance
and make us to continue the same all the time
   of our life,
and that at the same time we may not cease
   to trust in him
and to offer ourselves boldly in his fight,
since our sins are blotted out by the blood
   that was shed for the washing of them,
and that we may so conform ourselves to this
   doctrine
that we may all the time of our life acknowledge
   that seeing he has purchased us at such a price,
we ought to give ourselves wholly to his service;
and since he has shown himself so good
   a Redeemer towards us,
we may not doubt that he will continue

his goodness from day to day
to the final completion of the thing he has begun,
and strengthen us in all assaults
till he has delivered us from the cruelty of Satan
and of all his supporters,
yes and clean taken us out of the world
to make us partakers of the happy blessedness
unto which he calls us.
And may it please him to grant this grace not only to us,
but also to all people and nations.
Amen.

20 October

Imagine a world without sunshine, or a universe without the moon and stars. It doesn't bear thinking about, does it? It's inconceivable, of course, for without the sun we wouldn't be here, and without the stars and planets there would neither be a universe nor anything else. The following prayer – actually an ancient Jewish mystical hymn – gives thanks for them all.

The earth is full of your goodness,
  your greatness and understanding,
  your wisdom and harmony.
How wonderful are the lights that you created.
You formed them with strength and power
  and they shine very wonderfully on the world,
  magnificent in their splendour.
They arise in radiance and go down in joy.
Reverently they fulfil your divine will.
They are tributes to your name
  as they exalt your sovereign rule in song.

21 October

There's a massive industry today dedicated to helping us deny the fact that we grow older. Eternal youth, of course, has always been a dream, Greek myth, for example, speaking of just this aspiration, but nowadays – through cosmetic surgery and advances in medicine – people seem to think it's partly attainable, if only for a few extra years. I understand the compulsion, for no one likes to think life is running out and few welcome the side effects of advancing years, but ageing is part of the fabric of life and what a sorry state things would be in if, in this world at least, we really could live for ever. As the following prayer of Dr Samuel Johnson (1709–1784) reminds us, we need help to grow old gracefully, trusting not in our eternity but God's.

Almighty God,
    by whose mercy my life has continued for another
      year,
    I pray that, as my years increase, my sins may not
      increase.
As age advances, let me become more open,
    more faithful and more trusting in you.
Let me not be distracted by lesser things from what is
    truly important.
And if I become infirm as I grow old,
    may I not be overwhelmed by self-pity or bitterness.
Continue and increase your loving kindness towards
    me so that, when you finally call me to yourself,
    I may enter into eternal happiness with you,
    through Christ our Lord.
Amen.

22 October

What gifts can you offer to God? And, more important, what gifts *do* you offer? We all have something to contribute in his service, whether it be large or small, but most of us are slow in coming forward, either through a natural reticence to thrust ourselves to the fore or a reluctance to commit ourselves too deeply. Either way, we risk frustrating God's purpose for he needs us to be his hands and feet, carrying his love out into the world. That may be daunting, but it's part of true commitment. With Archbishop Thomas Cranmer (1489–1556), one of the most influential figures in the English Reformation and the guiding hand behind the *Book of Common Prayer*, we need, then, to seek God's help in consecrating ourselves more faithfully to his service.

O Lord our God,
   give us by your Holy Spirit
   a willing heart
   and a ready hand
   to use all your gifts to your praise and glory;
   through Jesus Christ our Lord.
Amen.

23 October

Most readers will recognise the following prayer. It's traditionally known as the Doxology, although in fact it is but one doxology among many. The curious title comes from two Greek words, 'doxa' and 'logos', meaning 'glory' and 'word' respectively. The aim of this prayer, then, as with all doxologies, is simple: to speak of God's glory, responding in an outpouring of praise to his great goodness. Sadly these words tend to be repeated so often that we lose sight of their message. Reflect on them afresh today, and use them to express your heartfelt faith and worship.

Glory be to the Father,
    and to the Son
    and to the Holy Spirit.
As it was in the beginning, is now,
    and ever shall be,
      world without end.
Amen.

24 October

If there's one evil that scars our world today more than ever, it's surely that of prejudice. Despite untold attempts to combat this vice, it stubbornly refuses to give ground, simply finding new ways in which to manifest itself. The result is continuing fragmentation of society, people looking over their shoulder in fear, mistrust, hostility or hopelessness. If this is ever to end, it needs to begin with us, for prejudice can find as much a foothold in our hearts as in any. The following prayer, taken from the Catholic Liturgy of the Hours, asks for God's help in seeing beyond the labels to the people they so often hide.

Almighty God, ever-loving Father,
    your care extends beyond the boundaries of race
        and nation,
    to the hearts of all who live.
May the walls, which prejudice raises between us,
    crumble beneath the shadow of your outstretched
        arm.
We ask this through Christ our Lord.
Amen.

25 October

What would we give to be more sure of God's guidance?
Most of us would love to have a clearer idea of the
right way forward, everything spelt out for us in black
and white, but faith isn't like that any more than life is.
God expects us to make our own decisions in the light
of what we know and understand of his will, and that
frequently means living with uncertainty and taking a
leap in the dark. But though God doesn't give detailed
instructions for every aspect of life, we can at least pray
for guidance in the decisions we have to take. That's
what the English church historian and clergyman William
Bright (1824–1901) asks for in this prayer.

O God
    by whom the meek are guided in judgement,
    and light riseth up in the darkness for the godly;
    grant us, in all our doubts and uncertainties,
    the grace to ask what thou wouldst have us do;
    that the Spirit of Wisdom may save us from all false
        choices
    and that in thy light we may see light,
    and in thy straight path may not stumble,
    through Jesus Christ, our Lord.
Amen.

26 October

Articulating a proper sense of wonder in the presence of God isn't easy, most of us finding that words run dry. Someone who clearly didn't have that problem was the one-time Moderator of the Church of Scotland, Walter Chalmers Smith (1824–1908). The following hymn, based on 1 Timothy 1:17 – and probably the greatest of all his hymns – capture as few other prayers even begin to, an unforgettable sense of God's greatness and power.

Immortal, invisible, God only wise,
in light inaccessible hid from our eyes,
most blessed, most glorious, the Ancient of Days,
almighty, victorious, thy great name we praise.

Unresting, unhasting, and silent as light,
nor wanting, nor wasting, thou rulest in might;
thy justice like mountains high soaring above
thy clouds which are fountains of goodness and love.

To all life thou givest, to both great and small;
in all life thou livest, the true life of all;
we blossom and flourish as leaves on the tree,
and wither and perish, but naught changeth thee.

Great Father of glory, pure Father of light,
thine angels adore thee, all veiling their sight;
all laud we would render, O help us to see
'tis only the splendour of light hideth thee.

27 October

To encounter God is to find peace yet to be disturbed, for while, on the one hand, we find rest for our souls, on the other we find our lifestyle challenged and our preconceptions turned upside down. True discipleship can be costly, bringing both pleasure and pain, as God works his will within us. The first letter of Peter (1:7) draws an analogy between faith and gold, the latter being refined by fire so that all impurities are burnt off. We find a similar idea in the following prayer of the Spanish mystic and friar St John of the Cross (1542–1591), his words capturing a sense of what it means to experience God's transforming touch.

O living flame of love,
    that wounds my soul so tenderly in its deepest
        centre;
    since, by your grace, I can endure your touch,
    perfect your work in me according to your will.
Amen.

28 October

It would be simplistic to suggest that all unanswered prayer is down to a single reason, but we should always be open to the possibility that our expectations prevent us from hearing what God is trying to say. His answer may be very different from the one we want to hear, as the following reflection, attributed to an unknown soldier of the American Civil War, makes clear.

I asked God for strength that I might achieve;
I was made weak that I might learn humbly to obey.
I asked for health that I might do greater things;
I was given infirmity that I might do better things.
I asked for riches that I might be happy;
I was given poverty that I might be wise.
I asked for power that I might have people's praise;
I was given weakness that I might feel my need
    of God.
I asked for all things that I might enjoy life;
I was given life that I might enjoy all things.
I was given nothing that I asked for;
    but everything that I had hoped for.
Despite myself, my prayers were answered;
    I am among all people most richly blessed.

29 October

For today's prayer I've turned again to the Baha'i tradition. For me, it calls to mind the parable of the sower.
Just because seed falls on fertile ground doesn't mean,
as we can sometimes assume, that it will grow to its
full potential automatically. If it's to flourish, it needs
the right conditions, and above all that means a regular
source of water. For the Christian, as for the Baha'i,
that comes from an outpouring of God's grace and life-
giving mercy.

I am, O my God, but a tiny seed which you have sown
   in the soil of your love and caused to spring up
      by your bountiful hand.
This seed craves, then, in its inmost being,
   for the waters of your mercy
   and the living fountain of your grace.
Send down upon it,
   from the heaven of your loving-kindness,
   that which will enable it to flourish beneath your
      shadow and within the borders of your court.
You are he who waters from the overflowing stream
   of your living waters
   the hearts of all who have recognised you.
Praise be to God,
   the Lord of the worlds.
Amen.

30 October

One of the loveliest prayers of intercession I've come across is the following, from St Augustine of Hippo (354–430). Simply but sincerely it entrusts people facing all kinds of situations into God's care. Sometimes we need to pray specifically for particular needs but it's important also to recognise that many more are unknown to us, but just as important. God doesn't need reminding of that, but we do, and remembering the wider world in prayer can prompt us to respond to it in turn.

Watch, dear Lord,
    with those who wake, or watch, or weep tonight,
    and give your angels charge over those who sleep.
Tend your sick ones, O Lord Christ,
    rest your weary ones,
    bless your dying ones,
    soothe your suffering ones,
    pity your afflicted ones,
    shield your joyous ones,
    all for your love's sake.
Amen.

31 October

I don't know much about the following prayer except that it has African (Pygmy) roots. What I *do* know about it is that it wonderfully captures a sense of the otherness of God, the one who is beyond comprehension, higher than our highest thoughts, yet is constantly present and active in our world. Here are simple words that succeed in speaking of the infinite and eternal. Make them your own.

In the beginning was God,
    today is God,
    tomorrow will be God.
Who can make an image of God?
He has no body.
He is the word which comes out of your mouth.
That word!
It is no more.
It is past,
    and still it lives!
So is God.

NOVEMBER

1 November
(All Saints' Day)

When we're looking for inspiration, the life and faith of those who have gone before us can be a valuable source of help. Above all, we have the suffering, death and resurrection of Jesus, the awesome message of his life-transforming love reinforced by the example of subsequent generations of Christians. Both are picked up in the following words of Evelyn Underhill (1875–1941), taken from her book *Meditations and Prayers* (1949), which is an example, in itself, of the life of prayer.

Give us light, O Lord,
   that contemplating the love and patience of Jesus
      and his saints,
   we may be changed into love and patience.
Take from us by contemplation of their example,
   all selfishness.
Take from us all softness, cowardice and timidity,
   all self-love.
Give us a spirit of courage, of surrendered trust,
   so that we may be willing to spend ourselves
      and to be spent,
   for the sake of your children,
   in union with your self-giving love.

2 November

Here is another prayer that demonstrates the immense spiritual riches of Judaism. On one level it's poetry, on another a declaration of faith, on another still an expression of praise and thanksgiving, but perhaps above all it's a heartfelt outpouring of love. Deriving from the Hasidic tradition that originated in Eastern Europe in the eighteenth century, here are words through which we too can celebrate God's faithfulness, power and constant presence, come what may.

Wherever I go, only thou!
Wherever I stand, only thou!
Just thou!
Again thou!
Always thou!
Thou, thou, thou!
When things are good, thou!
When things are bad, thou!
Thou, thou, thou!

3 November

Our prayer today, written by St John Chrysostom (*c.* 347–407), was clearly intended for public worship, but it's no less applicable for personal devotion. It reminds us that God welcomes our prayers, but emphasises also that we should seek not our will but his, for what we consider to be for the best does not necessarily correspond to his understanding of our needs. Of course, we will always ask for help concerning issues and concerns close to our heart, but the prayer of faith will finally be happy to trust the future to God, trusting in his purpose and leaving the rest to him.

Almighty God,
    who hast given us grace at this time with one
       accord
    to make our common supplications unto thee;
    and dost promise that when two or three
       are gathered together in thy Name
    thou wilt grant their request:
    fulfil now, O Lord, the desires and petitions
       of thy servants,
    as may be most expedient for them;
    granting us in this world knowledge of thy truth;
    and in the world to come life everlasting.
Amen.

4 November

In an age of tension and extremism we need more than ever to build bridges between religious communities, not in any way diluting our convictions, still less pretending that we all believe the same thing, but recognising that we share points of common ground concerning both the nature of God and respect for others. Lose sight of that and religion will be hijacked by the few to divide rather than unite, estrange instead of enrich. The following words come from the Qur'an but there is nothing in them that we as Christians cannot share. Make them your prayer and make time as you do so to pray for members of other faiths, asking that whatever may separate us, it may never overshadow the principles of love, mercy, justice and peace that should be the goal of all.

All praise belongs to God,
  Lord of all worlds,
  the Compassionate, the Merciful,
  Ruler of Judgement Day.
It is you that we worship,
  and to you we appeal for help.
Show us the straight way,
  the way of those you have graced,
  not of those on whom is your wrath,
  nor of those who wander astray.

5 November

What do you pray for last thing at night? Perhaps you want to thank God for the past day, perhaps commit your loved ones into his care, perhaps ask for his help with a particular problem, or perhaps merely seek a better day tomorrow. Occasionally, though, it's no bad thing to focus on something much more simple: the gift of sleep. We only realise how important it is to us when we're denied it, most of the time taking it for granted like so much else in life. Sleep helps us to recharge our batteries, put the day behind us, relax and recuperate – a precious gift indeed. Join then with Lancelot Andrewes (1555–1626) in giving thanks for this most ordinary yet special of blessings.

Glory be to thee, O Lord,
  glory to thee.
Glory to thee who givest me sleep to remit
  my weakness
  and to remit the toils of this fretful flesh.
Amen.

6 November

We've more words today from Pope Clement XI (1649–1721), taken from his celebrated 'Universal Prayer'. In this section, he humbly acknowledges his faults, asking for God's help to both recognise and conquer them. Like me, you'll no doubt see many of your own weaknesses here – your own difficulty in looking beyond narrow self-interest, coupled with correspondingly flawed commitment. If so, you'll be able not simply to identify with these words but to make them your own.

Help me to repent of my past sins
    and to resist temptation in the future.
Help me to rise above my human weakness
    and to grow stronger as a Christian.
Let me love you, my Lord and my God,
    and see myself as I really am:
    a pilgrim in this world,
    a Christian called to respect and love all whose lives
        I touch,
      those in authority over me or those under my
        authority,
      my friends and my enemies.
Help me to conquer anger by gentleness,
    greed by generosity,
    apathy by fervour.
Help me to forget myself and reach out toward others.
Amen.

7 November

A prayer that will be familiar to many is the so-called General Thanksgiving. It dates back to Tudor times and reflects the genius of Thomas Cranmer (1489–1556), to whom, in large part, we owe the *Book of Common Prayer*. Cranmer, in turn, drew on Catholic monastic tradition, this prayer being a part of the ancient Order of Compline. The language may reflect a bygone age, but the sentiments are as valid today as ever, offering a perfect way for us to express gratitude to God for his many blessings.

Almighty God, Father of all mercies,
  we thine unworthy servants
    do give thee most humble and hearty thanks
      for all thy goodness and loving-kindness to us
      and to all men.
We bless thee for our creation, preservation,
  and all the blessings of this life;
    but above all for thine inestimable love
    in the redemption of the world by our Lord Jesus
      Christ,
    for the means of grace,
    and for the hope of glory.
And we beseech thee,
  give us that due sense of all thy mercies,
  that our hearts may be unfeignedly thankful,
  and that we shew forth thy praise,
    not only with our lips,
  but in our lives;
  by giving up ourselves to thy service,
  and by walking before thee in holiness and
    righteousness all our days;

through Jesus Christ our Lord,
to whom with thee and the Holy Ghost
be all honour and glory,
world without end.
Amen.

8 November

We've another prayer attributed to Sir Francis Drake (c. 1540–1596). There's no seafaring imagery here, unlike the prayer of his we used earlier in this book, but we glimpse the determination that must have helped make him the man he was. If we can show similar resolve in our faith, determined to honour our commitment come what may, we won't go far wrong in the journey of discipleship.

O Lord God,
    when thou givest to thy servants to endeavour any
        great matter,
    grant us to know that it is not the beginning,
    but the continuing of the same unto the end,
    until it be thoroughly finished,
    which yieldeth the true glory;
    through him who for the finishing of thy work
    laid down his life,
    our Redeemer, Jesus Christ.
Amen.

9 November

In times of intense grief it can be especially hard to pray, our spirit being so low that we don't feel like doing anything. Is that something to be ashamed of? Of course not. God understands our grief more than any, and recognises that we need to come to terms with our sorrow, whatever might be its cause. Rather than struggling to articulate formal prayers at such moments, why not simply pour out your feelings before God? The very act of opening up like this can be therapeutic, and we can be sure too that he will hear and listen. The following poem-cum-prayer does just that. Written by Christina Rossetti (1830–1894), one of the most influential of all English women poets, it is titled 'A Better Resurrection'. It's a powerful expression of sorrow but an equally moving statement of faith.

I have no wit, no words, no tears;
my heart within me like a stone
is numb'd too much for hopes or fears;
look right, look left, I dwell alone;
I lift mine eyes, but dimm'd with grief
no everlasting hills I see;
my life is in the falling leaf:
O Jesus, quicken me.

My life is like a faded leaf,
my harvest dwindled to a husk:
truly my life is void and brief
and tedious in the barren dusk;
my life is like a frozen thing,
no bud nor greenness can I see:
yet rise it shall – the sap of Spring;
O Jesus, rise in me.

My life is like a broken bowl,
a broken bowl that cannot hold
one drop of water for my soul
or cordial in the searching cold;
cast in the fire the perish'd thing;
melt and remould it, till it be
a royal cup for him, my King:
O Jesus, drink of me.

10 November

Mornings aren't everyone's best time for prayer. Not only may we be feeling half-asleep but there are usually 101 things to be done and not nearly enough time to do them. It's a good thing, nonetheless, to make time for God even if we can snatch only a few moments, for doing that helps us to view the rest of the day in a new light. Whatever else you may have on your mind can be as nothing compared to what the author of today's prayer must have had on his, for it was written by the German pastor and theologian Dietrich Bonhoeffer (1906–1945) while in a Nazi prison, awaiting execution for his part in an attempt on Hitler's life. His involvement in that scheme was not something he'd taken lightly, but horrified by the evils of Nazism he'd decided there was no alternative. He was to pay for his courage with his life.

O God,
    early in the morning I cry to you.
Help me to pray
    and to concentrate my thoughts on you:
    I cannot do this alone.
In me there is darkness,
    but with you there is light.
I am lonely,
    but you do not leave me;
    I am feeble in heart,
    but with you there is help;
    I am restless,
    but with you there is peace.
In me there is bitterness,
    but with you there is patience;

I do not understand your ways,
   but you know the way for me.
Restore me to liberty,
   and enable me so to live now
   that I may answer before you and before me.
Lord,
   whatever this day may bring,
   your name be praised.
Amen.

11 November

None of us wants to think about death, do we? Life is for living, we say, and so it is. Brooding on our mortality would be morbid indeed, but, of course, death will finally come to us all, and there's no knowing when. Whether we're haunted by that prospect or can face it with equanimity depends on our view of life and death. The Christian sees both as being equally in the hands of God. We do not welcome the thought of our passing any more than others, for life has so much to offer, blessings beyond measure, but, as the following words taken from the Universal Prayer of Pope Clement XI (1649–1721) remind us, we believe that when this life is over those blessings continue, greater than words can express or the human mind can conceive.

Teach me to realise that this world is passing,
    that my true future is the happiness of heaven,
    that life on earth is short,
    and the life to come eternal.
Help me to prepare for death with a proper fear
    of judgement,
    but a greater trust in your goodness.
Lead me safely through death
    to the endless joy of heaven.
Grant this through Christ our Lord.
Amen.

12 November

Why be a Christian? Is it to escape God's punishment, to earn his blessing, or perhaps to secure for ourselves life after death? I suppose it could be, but if faith is rooted in reasons such as these, then it's a pale imitation of the real thing, having more to do with self than God. For me, the following words – from an old Latin hymn translated by the Revd Edward Caswall (1814–1878), the writer of 'See, amid the winter's snow' – perfectly capture what faith should rest on: not the hope of reward or fear of retribution but simply joyful response to what God has done in Christ. When we learn to meet love with love, then we have discovered faith indeed!

My God, I love thee; not because
I hope for heaven thereby,
nor yet because who love thee not
are lost eternally.
Thou, O my Jesus, thou didst me
upon the Cross embrace;
for me didst bear the nails and spear
and manifold disgrace.

And griefs and torments numberless,
and sweat of agony;
yea, death itself – and all for me
who was thine enemy.
Then why, O blessèd Jesu Christ,
should I not love thee well?
Not for the sake of winning heaven,
nor of escaping hell.

Not from the hope of gaining aught,
not seeking a reward;
but as thyself hast loved me,
O ever-loving Lord.
So would I love thee, dearest Lord,
and in thy praise will sing;
solely because thou art my God,
and my most loving King.

13 November

In the course of this book, we've already come across night-time prayers from the Order of Compline, but today we've perhaps one of the most celebrated of all. It superbly captures the contrast between the humdrum activity of daily life, with all its pressures and demands, and the inner tranquillity to be found in God. An unchanging reference point in a restless world, he calls us to remember that whatever we have to do and how-ever important it may be, we should never forget what matters most of all: his love where alone true content-ment lies.

Be present, O merciful God,
    and protect us through the silent hours of this
       night,
    so that we who are wearied
    by the changes and chances of this fleeting world,
    may repose upon thy eternal changelessness;
    through Jesus Christ our Lord.
Amen.

14 November

Prayers for healing are a contentious issue, simply because they aren't always answered. We'll probably all have begged God to help someone we know with a chronic or terminal illness, yet seen no change in that person's condition, and it's hard then not to wonder if such prayers are worth it or if we're asking for the wrong thing. Yet, as countless people can testify, including the writer of the following Jewish prayer, God *does* bring healing, in body, mind and spirit, his love giving strength, hope, resilience, inspiration and so much more. Sometimes that means becoming well, sometimes learning to live with illness yet still celebrate life, sometimes facing up to the prospect of death with faith and confidence, inner healing involving far more than deliverance from disease. In life or death, sickness or health, ours is a God who can make us whole.

Heal us, Lord, and we shall be healed;
    save us, and we shall be saved;
        for it is you we praise.
Send relief and healing for all our diseases,
    our sufferings and our wounds,
        for you are a merciful and faithful healer.
Blessed are you, Lord,
    who heals the sick.
Amen.

15 November

However much we understand of God, there is far more we cannot grasp. Whatever praise we offer, whatever worship and adoration, it can never be enough. God is greater than we can begin to imagine – beyond comprehension, beyond words, beyond all. Yes, we must do our best to acknowledge his sovereignty but eventually we must admit defeat, recognising, like Bishop Lancelot Andrewes (1555–1626), that we have barely scratched the surface. Do that and we will have started to understand what true worship is all about.

Blessing and honour, thanksgiving and praise,
    more than I can utter,
    more than I can understand,
    be yours, O most glorious Trinity,
    Father, Son and Holy Spirit,
    by all angels, all people, all creatures,
    now and for ever.
Amen.

16 November

Read today's prayer without any introduction and you may well find yourself thoroughly confused as to who or what it's all about. Written by an anonymous Trappist monk it clearly points to someone wonderfully special, blessed beyond words. Surely, then, we feel, these lines must concern God the Father, the Son or the Holy Spirit. But no, that doesn't make sense, for the image of God acknowledged here is touched by them all, transformed by their presence and consecrated to their service. So who is the subject of this prayer? That finally becomes clear in the astonishing last line: 'This is who you are.' The words are about you and me, about everyone who confesses the name of Christ, this prayer a joyful celebration of God's loving acceptance and renewing power. Flawed and faithless though we are, God counts us of infinite worth, made in his likeness. Say these words quietly and reverently, celebrating line by line what God has done for *you*.

Image of God
    born of God's breath,
    vessel of divine Love,
    after his likeness,
    dwelling of God,
    capacity for the infinite,
    eternally known,
    chosen of God,
    home of the Infinite Majesty,
    abiding in the Son,
    called from eternity,
    life in the Lord,
    temple of the Holy Spirit,

branch of Christ,
receptacle of the Most High,
wellspring of Living Water,
heir of the kingdom,
the glory of God,
abode of the Trinity.
God sings this litany eternally in his Word.
This is who you are.

17 November

We've one of those prayers today that is easy to say but hard to mean. A traditional Catholic prayer of dedication to Jesus, it expresses the sort of commitment we long to share, but all of us will be acutely aware of the gulf between the ideal portrayed here and the reality seen in our own life. Can we, then, make these words our own? I believe so, even if it means adding a mental 'Lord, help me make this real' as we say each line. We may fall short time and again, but if we sincerely make the sentiment of this prayer our goal, committing our resolve to God, then little by little he will help us get nearer to reaching it.

Lord Jesus Christ,
    take all my freedom,
    my memory,
    my understanding,
    and my will.
All that I have and cherish you have given me.
I surrender it all to be guided by your will.
Your grace and your love and wealth are enough
    for me.
Give me these, Lord Jesus,
    and I ask for nothing more.
Amen.

18 November

Imagine what it's like living on the fringes of society: to be one of the outcasts and excluded of our world, one of the poor and hungry, homeless and refugees. Sadly we forget not only how lucky we are but also those much less fortunate than ourselves. True faith should always reach out, attempting in some way to respond to their needs. Part of that response involves prayer, and if you're looking for words to help sum up your thoughts, then there are few better than the following, based on words of J. H. Jowett (1864–1923). Not that Jowett would have seen prayer as the end of the story. For him, as it should be for us, it was a way of focusing his concern so that words would lead on to deeds, compassion to action.

Father of all,
   hear me when I pray for people of every race
      and nation.
May the light of your love break upon them,
   lightening their burdens and easing their anxieties.
Especially I pray for the marginalised and the
   neglected.
May my vision, and the vision of others, be increased
   that we become more aware of forgotten
   and unwanted people.
Help us so to order our lives and our societies
   that no one is excluded.
Amen.

19 November

It's easy, isn't it, to trust God when all is going well, but when life brings sorrow and suffering faith can be put under the microscope and found wanting. Will you still be able to trust at such times, still feel as confident of God's loving purpose? The writer of this prayer, Jane de Chantal (1572–1641), did exactly that. A mother of four, she was widowed when just 28, and endured a wretched few years afterwards when forced to live with her father-in-law. Through it all, however, her commitment was undiminished, and in 1610 she founded the Order of the Visitation of Our Lady at Annecy, in France. Whether her words here were written during the years immediately after her bereavement I'm not sure, but they express quiet assurance in God's loving purpose, no matter what testing life may bring.

O my Lord,
    I am in a barren land,
    all shrivelled and broken by the ferocity of the
       north wind
    and the chill;
    but, as you can see, I ask for nothing more;
    you will send me both dew and warmth when it
       pleases you.
Amen.

20 November

We've seen already in this book on more than one occasion how the natural world can inspire praise, speaking forcefully of God's power, purpose and presence. This is another example. Not much is known of its provenance except that it dates from between the third and sixth centuries AD, but to me it's as powerful a prayer today as it must have been when it was first written. It calls upon the whole of creation to celebrate God's greatness, acknowledging all he his and everything he has done. Not, of course, that the writer seriously expects stars, mountains or seas literally to burst into song – in his view they metaphorically do so already, giving eloquent testimony to God's creative love. The real challenge here is to you and me, and whether we too join in acknowledging the Lord of all, to whom indeed belongs power, praise, honour and glory for all time.

May none of God's wonderful works keep silence,
    night or morning.
Bright stars,
    high mountains,
    the depths of the seas,
    sources of rushing rivers:
    may all these break into song
    as we sing to the Father, Son and Holy Spirit.
May all the angels in the heavens reply:
    Amen, Amen, Amen.
Power, praise, honour, eternal glory to God,
    the only giver of grace.
Amen, Amen, Amen.

21 November

For our prayer today we turn to words of the scientist, philosopher and theologian St Albertus Magnus, usually known as St Albert the Great (*c.* 1206–1280). Revered for his wisdom and breadth of knowledge, he was one of the first to emphasise that science and faith can go hand in hand rather than any dichotomy existing between the two. This prayer reflects that conviction.

We pray to you, O Lord,
> who are the supreme Truth,
> and all truth is from you.

We beseech you, O Lord,
> who are the highest Wisdom,
> and all the wise depend on you for their wisdom.

You are the supreme Joy,
> and all who are happy owe it to you.

You are the Light of minds,
> and all receive their understanding from you.

We love you, we love you above all.

We seek you, we follow you,
> and we are ready to serve you.

We desire to dwell under your power
> for you are the King of all.

Amen.

22 November

Where do you feel closest to God? In church, or in the countryside? With your nose in a prayer- or hymn-book, or with your eyes gazing out at the stars, sea, hills and trees? The two, of course, are not mutually exclusive, but without doubt I find God as much in the natural world as anywhere. So too, it seems, did Edward King (1829–1910), Bishop of Lincoln from 1885 to 1910. His words here are a joyful celebration of the beauty that surrounds us each day, the sheer loveliness of this planet God has entrusted to our care.

Thank you, O God, for the pleasures you have given
    me through my senses.
Thank you for the glory of thunder,
    the mystery of music,
    the singing of birds
    and the laughter of children.
Thank you for the delights of colour,
    the awe of sunset,
    the wild roses in the hedgerows,
    the smile of friendship.
Thank you for the sweetness of flowers
    and the scent of hay.
Truly, O Lord, the earth is full of your riches!
Amen.

23 November

Charity, we are told, begins at home, and if that's true the same could also be said of prayer. I don't just mean praying for our nearest and dearest, though that's certainly part of it. I mean also that we should commit our homes to God, asking for a special sense of his love pervading everything that takes place within their walls. I'm reminded of a plaque once commonly seen: 'Christ is the head of this house, the unseen guest at every meal, the silent listener to every conversation.' Regularly include such a prayer as the following, taken from the Order of Compline, in your personal devotions and you'll be well on the way to making those words ring true.

Visit, we beseech thee, O Lord,
   this house and family,
   and drive far from it all the snares of the enemy.
Let thy holy angels dwell herein,
   who may keep us in peace,
   and let thy blessing be always upon us.
Through Christ our Lord.
Amen.

24 November

How far do we practise what we preach? That's a question which we, as Christians, should always be asking ourselves if we are not to be guilty of hypocrisy. It's easy enough to talk of love, much harder to actually show it. But as the words of Jesus remind us, serving him very often involves serving others – in other words, caring enough to show it – and that's the theme of the so-called Christopher Prayer.

Father, grant that I may be a bearer of Christ Jesus,
    your Son.
Allow me to warm the often cold, impersonal scene
    of modern life with your burning love.
Strengthen me by your Holy Spirit
    to carry out my mission of changing the world
    or some definite part of it for the better.
Despite my lamentable failures,
    bring home to me that my advantages are your
      blessings to be shared with others.
Make me more energetic in setting right what I find
    wrong with the world
    instead of complaining about it.
Nourish in me a practical desire to build up
    rather than tear down,
    to reconcile instead of polarise,
    to go out on a limb rather than crave security.
Never let me forget that it is far better
    to light one candle than to curse the darkness,
    and to join my light, one day, with yours.
Amen.

25 November

Like many people, I've always dreamt of writing a novel. Not any old novel, of course, but a bestseller, read the world over. The writer of our prayer today – Charles Kingsley (1819–1875) – did just that, writing not just one book but several, including *The Water Babies*, *Hereward the Wake* and *Westward Ho!* among his many publications. In his shoes, I'd have felt a touch smug about that, and perhaps Kingsley did too, but if he did he was determined to keep things in perspective, as his words here clearly show. He may have been a celebrated author (not to mention accomplished scholar as well), but first of all he was a minister of the Church and, above all, a servant of Christ.

Take away from me, O God,
    all pride and vanity,
    all boasting and forwardness,
    and give me the true courage that shows itself
        in gentleness;
    the true wisdom that shows itself by simplicity;
    and the true power that shows itself by modesty.
Amen.

26 November

We learn from an early age the importance of firm
foundations in any building project. Which child hasn't
delighted countless times over in the story of the three
little pigs, the houses of straw and bricks crashing to
the ground, but the brick-built home able to withstand
the attentions of the big bad wolf? It takes us longer,
though, to recognise the importance of spiritual foundations; indeed, many never recognise it at all, basing
their happiness on what all too easily can come
tumbling down like a pack of cards. As Jesus reminds
us in the parable of the wise and foolish builders, life
will eventually put us all to the test. The following prayer
of Bishop Thomas Wilson (1663–1755) asks for help
in building on sure foundations, so that at the moment
of truth we will not be found wanting.

Grant, O God,
    that amidst all the discouragements, difficulties,
    dangers, distress and darkness of this mortal life,
    I may depend upon your mercy
    and on this build my hopes,
        as on a sure foundation.
Let your infinite mercy in Christ Jesus deliver me
    from despair,
    both now and at the hour of death.
Amen.

27 November

The secret of many classic prayers is the beauty of their language and imagery, and that's certainly the case with the following words. They come from St Anselm (1033–1109) and take as their theme a mother's love for her children; Anselm likens this to the love God holds for us. He builds on this analogy, conjuring up a wonderful picture of God's passionate devotion, nurturing, supporting and enfolding us each day. This, without doubt, is one of those prayers that will not only speak *for* you but equally speak *to* you – a prayer you'll want to return to again and again.

Jesus, as a mother you gather your people to you:
    you are gentle with us, as a mother with her
        children;
    often you weep over our sins and our pride:
    tenderly you draw us from hatred and judgement.
You comfort us in sorrow and bind up our wounds:
    in sickness you nurse us,
    and with pure milk you feed us.
Jesus, by your dying we are born to new life:
    by your anguish and labour we come forth in joy.
Despair turns to hope through your sweet goodness:
    through your gentleness we find comfort in fear.
Your warmth gives life to the dead:
    your touch makes sinners righteous.
Lord Jesus, in your mercy heal us:
    in your love and tenderness remake us.
In your compassion bring grace and forgiveness:
    for the beauty of heaven may your love prepare us.
Amen.

28 November

The Christian life is often portrayed as a journey, and so it is with our words today. Their writer, Walter John Mathams (1853-1931), knew more about travelling than most of us, having spent his early years at sea during which time, among various adventures, he sailed to the Alaska gold fields in search of fame and fortune. He was to turn his back, however, on all that in 1874, entering Regent's Park College to train for the Baptist ministry. A gifted preacher, he was to serve in several pastorates: one was in Australia, and for three years he was chaplain to the armed forces in Egypt. Life, then, took him to many places, but the journey that mattered was the one he writes of here. Join with him in asking for God's guidance on your own pilgrimage of faith.

Christ of the upward way, my Guide divine,
where thou hast set thy feet may I place mine:
and move and march wherever thou hast trod,
keeping face forward up the hill of God.

Give me the heart to hear thy voice and will,
that without fault or fear I may fulfil
thy purpose with a glad and holy zest,
like one who would not bring less than his best.

Give me the eye to see each chance to serve,
then send me strength to rise with steady nerve,
and leap at once with kind and helpful deed
to the sure succour of a soul in need.

Give me the good stout arm to shield the right,
and wield thy sword of truth with all my might,
that, in the warfare I must wage for thee,
more than a victor I may ever be.

Christ of the upward way, my Guide divine,
where thou hast set thy feet may I place mine:
and when thy last call comes, serene and clear,
calm may my answer be, 'Lord, I am here.'

29 November

How would you sum up the nature of God? In the New Testament one description predominates, God time and again seen in terms of love, to the point that the First Letter of John bluntly tells us: 'God *is* love' (1 John 4:8). That truth underlies our prayer today, written centuries ago by St Gertrude the Great (1256–1302). Placed in the care of the Benedictine convent of Helfta, Thuringia, at the age of five, Gertrude spent the rest of her life devoting herself to a life of contemplation following a sequence of mystical experiences. She produced a book titled *Legatus Divinae Pietatis* (Herald of Divine Love) that was widely regarded as a classic and her prayer here can certainly be counted as such, reminding us of that awesome love we all too easily forget.

O sacred heart of Jesus,
    fountain of eternal life,
    your heart is a glowing furnace of love.
You are my refuge and my sanctuary.
O my adorable and loving Saviour,
    consume my heart with the burning fire with which
        yours is aflamed.
Pour down on my soul those graces which flow
    from your love.
Let my heart be united with yours.
Let my will be conformed to yours in all things.
May your will be the rule of all my desires and actions.
Amen.

30 November

It's so easy, isn't it, to take the good things of life for granted. We don't mean to – it's simply human nature – but it's often only when we're confronted by people less fortunate than ourselves that we realise how much we have to be grateful for. Suddenly we feel ashamed at having complained about our lot, and ashamed above all of having failed to thank God for his goodness. More than anything else, then, we need to pray for his help in appreciating all we have and showing our gratitude in action. Today we have words to help us do just that, taken from the *Book of Common Prayer*.

O merciful Creator,
> thy hand is open wide to satisfy the needs of every
>   living creature:
> make us, we beseech thee, ever thankful for thy
>   loving providence;
> and grant that we, remembering the account that
>   we must one day give,
> may be faithful stewards of thy good gifts;
> through Jesus Christ our Lord,
> who with thee and the Holy Spirit lives and reigns,
> one God, for ever and ever.
Amen.

DECEMBER

1 December

What do you make of the following prayer? Written by John Hoyland (1887-1957), a Quaker missionary who worked in India during the great flu pandemic there, it asks God for cleansing and deliverance from our many faults. I find some lines here unsettling, for they paint a bleak picture of human nature, yet I can't really dispute Hoyland's appraisal for, as news headlines seem daily to remind us, there are few depths to which people will not stoop. I suspect, though, that the intention here was to shock in order to bring home the awesome contrast between human weakness and divine purity, the holiness of God compared to our innumerable faults. The closer we get to God, the more we recognise the gulf between us. Thankfully this brings home also his forgiving and renewing power, which alone can save us from ourselves.

From man's unfaithfulness,
 our hearts turn longingly to you,
 O love eternal and unchanging.

From man's weak fickleness,
 our hearts turn longingly to you,
 O will inimitable.

From man's exceeding feebleness
 our hearts turn longingly to you,
 O might omnipotent.

From man's gross filth
 our hearts turn longingly to you,
 O purity divine and absolute.

From man's deformity
 our hearts turn longingly to you,
 O beauty perfect and ineffable.
Amen.

2 December

'Blessed are those who hunger and thirst for righteous-ness,' said Jesus in his Sermon on the Mount (Matthew 6:6), 'for they will be filled.' No doubt we nod our heads in agreement at such words, but how many of us actually apply them to our lives? We may pay them lip service, but how far is spiritual growth a priority for us? For St Thomas Aquinas (1225–1274) there was clearly no question as to what should come first in life, as the following prayer makes clear. Use it to refocus on what really matters, so that you may discover the blessing Jesus promised and be truly filled.

Most loving God,
> give me a steadfast heart, which no unworthy
> > thought can drag downwards;
> an unconquered heart, which no hardship can wear
> > out;
> an upright heart, which no worthless purpose can
> > ensnare.
Give me also, O Lord my God,
> understanding to know you,
> diligence to seek you,
> and a faithfulness that will finally embrace you;
> through Jesus Christ my Lord.
Amen.

3 December

Whether we're young or old – in years or in faith – we need help from others and, above all, from God: they can offer guidance, support, correction and encouragement, each so important if we are to find the right path and stick to it, for initial enthusiasm can grow cold and, having started on the right path, we can lose our way. That's true not just for us but for all, many who set out on the path of discipleship slipping up along the way. Recognising, then, the many pitfalls to faith we should make time to remember those who profess the name of Christ, asking that God may equip them to stay true to their calling. The following prayer of St Irenaeus (130–202) offers well-chosen words to help us do just that.

Father,
  give perfection to beginners,
  understanding to the little ones,
  and help to those who are running their course.
Give sorrow to the negligent,
  fervour to the lukewarm,
  and a good consummation to the perfect.
Amen.

4 December

Prayers don't have to be complicated to be profound, nor, as we have seen several times in this book, do they necessarily have to be Christian. God can speak to us through other traditions, just as we can approach him through the same. The following words, for example, are attributed by some to Abu Bakr (c. 573–634), companion and later father-in-law of the prophet Muhammad. One of the first converts to Islam, and also the first of the Muslim caliphs, he reminds us that while others see only part of the truth about us, God sees all.

I thank you, Lord, for knowing me better than I know
   myself,
     and for letting me know myself better than others
       know me.
Make me, I pray, better than they suppose,
   and forgive me for what they do not know.
Amen.

5 December

I expect you'll instantly recognise the words of our prayer today. It's actually a hymn, written by Frances van Alstyne (1820–1915), and its outpouring of praise has captured the imagination of successive generations. What most may not realise as they sing these words is that Van Alstyne lost her sight while she was still an infant. Quite how I'd have coped with that I'm not sure, but I suspect there would have been more than an element of self-pity, yet in these words there is no trace of that: only grateful worship in celebration of God's grace and mercy. Too often we focus on what we *don't* have; this hymn urges us to give thanks for what we *do*.

To God be the glory! great things he hath done;
so loved he the world that he gave us his Son;
who yielded his life an atonement for sin,
and opened the life-gate that all may go in.

Praise the Lord, praise the Lord! Let the earth hear his
    voice!
Praise the Lord, praise the Lord! Let the people rejoice!
O come to the Father, through Jesus the Son,
and give him the glory; great things he hath done.

O perfect redemption, the purchase of blood!
To every believer the promise of God;
the vilest offender who truly believes,
that moment from Jesus a pardon receives.

Praise the Lord, praise the Lord! Let the earth hear his
    voice!
Praise the Lord, praise the Lord! Let the people rejoice!
O come to the Father, through Jesus the Son,
and give him the glory; great things he hath done.

Great things he hath taught us, great things he hath
   done,
and great our rejoicing through Jesus the Son;
but purer, and higher, and greater will be
our wonder, our rapture, when Jesus we see.

Praise the Lord, praise the Lord! Let the earth hear his
   voice!
Praise the Lord, praise the Lord! Let the people rejoice!
O come to the Father, through Jesus the Son,
and give him the glory; great things he hath done.

6 December

Spiritual growth doesn't happen by itself, nor does it come through our own efforts or ingenuity. It's a gift of God, brought about by the work of his Spirit within us, teaching, challenging, inspiring, equipping – taking what we are and turning us into a new creation. We can't leave it all to God, of course. We need to hunger and seek, to spend time reading, listening, enquiring and reflecting, but finally it's God who gives growth. Above all, then, like St Augustine of Hippo (354–430) in the words below, we need to pray for the Spirit to touch our hearts and fill our lives.

Holy Spirit,
    powerful Consoler,
    sacred Bond of the Father and the Son,
    Hope of the afflicted,
    descend into my heart
    and establish in it your loving dominion.
Enkindle in my tepid soul the fire of your Love
    so that I may be wholly subject to you.
We believe that when you dwell in us,
    you also prepare a dwelling for the Father
        and the Son.
Deign, therefore, to come to me,
    Consoler of abandoned souls,
    and Protector of the needy.
Help the afflicted,
    strengthen the weak,
    and support the wavering.
Come and purify me.
Let no evil desire take possession of me.
You love the humble and resist the proud.

Come to me,
  glory of the living
  and hope of the dying.
Lead me by your grace
  that I may always be pleasing to you.
Amen.

7 December

God's strength in our weakness – it's a recurring theme in the Bible, and one that has been a source of inspiration for many, including William Cowper (1731–1800) in the following poem. Titled 'Temptation', it in fact explores far more, applying the incident of Jesus stilling the storm to his own life. Alongside a cry for help in the face of personal turmoil, there's also assurance that Christ will hear and answer, seeing us in turn safely through times of crisis even though we can't see how.

The billows swell, the winds are high,
clouds overcast my wintry sky;
out of the depths to thee I call –
my fears are great, my strength is small.

O Lord, the pilot's part perform,
and guard and guide me through the storm;
defend me from each threatening ill,
control the waves – say, 'Peace! be still.'

Amidst the roaring of the sea
my soul still hangs her hope on thee;
thy constant love, thy faithful care,
is all that saves me from despair.

8 December

Reading the Bible isn't easy, is it? Some of it seems
obscure and irrelevant, and in even the best modern
translations parts come across as archaic. Add to that the
fact that we've read or heard many passages countless
times before, and it's not perhaps surprising that we
don't turn to it as often as we might. Yet if we fail to do
so, we impoverish ourselves as a result, for God speaks
more powerfully through the Scriptures than probably
anything else. Yes, we need guidance and discernment
but, as the following words of the *Book of Common
Prayer* remind us, the Bible is God's gift, able to lead us
into a fuller understanding of truth. Pray, then, for
help in using it better.

Blessed Lord,
    who hast caused all holy Scriptures to be written
        for our learning:
    grant that we may in such wise hear them,
    read, mark, learn and inwardly digest them,
    that by patience, and comfort of thy holy Word,
    we may embrace, and ever hold fast the blessed
        hope of everlasting life,
    which thou hast given us in our Saviour Jesus
        Christ.
Amen.

9 December

It's often said that love is the most abused word in the English language, for we give it such a variety of meanings ranging from 'desire', 'like', to 'adore'. That's why the Greek language famously has four words for our one: *eros*, meaning physical or sexual love; *philia*, referring to friendship; *storge*, having to do with family relationships; and *agape*, which in the New Testament is generally reserved for the unreserved yet undeserved love of God. We're more than capable of the first three, but the last is beyond us, few of us getting anywhere near it. Our love is limited and conditional, more often than not dependent on receiving love in return, whereas God's love flows out to us day after day. The contrast is captured by St Augustine of Hippo (354–430) in the following prayer through which he asks to love God a little more as God loves him.

Give me yourself, O my God,
  give yourself to me.
Behold I love you,
  and if my love is too weak a thing,
  grant me to love you more strongly.
I cannot measure my love
  to know how much it falls short of being sufficient,
  but let my soul hasten to your embrace
  and never be turned away until it is hidden
    in the secret shelter of your presence.
This only do I know,
  that it is not good for me when you are not with me,
  when you are only outside me.
I want you in my very self.
All the plenty in the world which is not my God
  is utter want.
Amen.

10 December

You may recall the poetic writing of George Herbert (1593–1633) from earlier in this book. Today we have another lovely example of his craft. In three memorable verses he invites Christ more fully into his life, to heal, strengthen, guide and illuminate in the way only he can do. His carefully chosen words speak powerfully of all that these mean, and offer a perfect way of asking Jesus to dwell more fully in our hearts.

Come, my way, my Truth, my Life:
such a way as gives us breath;
such a truth as ends all strife;
such a life as killeth death.

Come, my Light, my Feast, my Strength:
such a light as shows a feast;
such a feast as mends in length;
such a strength as makes his guest.

Come, my Joy, my Love, my Heart:
such a joy as none can move;
such a love as none can part;
such a heart as joys in love.

11 December

We've encountered some memorable morning prayers during the course of this book, and today we have another of equal stature. It comes from Philaret, Bishop of Moscow in the nineteenth century, and asks essentially for two things: first, for a deeper understanding of God's purpose and second, for help in honouring this in our daily thoughts, words and actions. If we can echo the sentiments of this prayer every morning and mean them, what a difference it would make to life and the way we live each day.

O Lord,
    help me to greet the coming day in peace,
    and in all things to rely upon your holy will.
In every hour of the day reveal your will to me.
Bless my dealings with those who surround me,
    and teach me to treat whatever this day might bring
      with a tranquil spirit
    in the firm conviction that your will governs all.
In everything I do and say, guide my thoughts
    and feelings.
In unforeseen events, let me not forget that everything
    is sent by you.
Teach me to act firmly and wisely,
    without embittering or embarrassing others.
Strengthen me to bear the demands of the coming
    day, whatever they may be.
Direct my will,
    teach me to pray.
    and pray yourself in me.
Amen.

12 December

There's something about today's prayer that I love. I can't quite put my finger on it for, coldly analysed, it's just four short lines of text, yet it resonates deep within, saying in a sense all that needs to be said. It comes from the Order of Compline as woven into the *Book of Common Prayer*, and some might suggest that its appeal lies in wish fulfilment, the words reflecting a childlike longing for a sense of security that is hopelessly at odds with the real world. Perhaps that's true, but our faith, of course, extends beyond the real world to what as yet is unseen and unknown. In that trust we can indeed commit every hour of the day into God's keeping, confident that his love extends for all eternity.

Preserve us, O Lord, while waking,
    and guard us while sleeping,
    that awake we may watch with Christ,
    and asleep we may rest in peace.
Amen.

13 December

To live in a way pleasing to Christ, showing something of his nature in who and what we are – that, surely, is the goal of every Christian, and that effectively is what the celebrated writer Robert Louis Stevenson (1850–1894) asks for in the prayer below. Above all, he seeks help and guidance in daily relationships, asking that in the ups and downs of daily life – particularly the difficult moments it is sure to bring – he may stay loving to friend and foe alike, demonstrating the same commitment to others as Christ has shown to us.

Give us grace and strength to forbear and to persevere.
Give us courage and gaiety and the quiet mind.
Spare to us our friends,
    soften to us our enemies.
Bless us, if it may be, in all our innocent endeavours.
If it may not,
    give us the strength to encounter that which is to
      come,
    that we may be brave in peril,
    constant in tribulation,
    temperate in wrath,
    and in all changes of fortune,
    and down to the gates of death,
    loyal and loving to one another.
  Amen.

14 December

I've always found the words of Matthew 25, with their emphasis on serving God through serving others, immensely challenging. They remind us that though works need faith, faith also needs works, the two going hand in hand. Yet though I assent to this with my mind, how often does that touch my heart? How often, in other words, and in what ways, do I respond to the needs of those around me? Our prayer today comes from someone well qualified to speak on the subject – none other than Mother Teresa (1910–1997), that great servant and supporter of the poor. Taking the theme of Matthew 25 as her starting point, she asks for guidance to respond more effectively. Like her, let us pray this prayer, and mean it.

Lord,
    shake away my indifference and insensitivity
        to the plight of the poor.
When I meet you hungry, thirsty or as a stranger,
    show me how I can give you food,
    quench your thirst,
    or receive you in my home –
    and in my heart.
Show me how I can serve you in the least of your
    brothers and sisters.
Amen.

15 December

There are two vital truths of faith that we can some-times lose sight of. One is that we worship a *personal* God rather than some remote and detached deity. The other is that God values each of us as *individuals*, instead of seeing us as merely people in general. I'm reminded of the song 'If I were the only girl in the world and you were the only boy'. In a sense with God we *are* the only girl or boy, for God places infinite worth on every one of us, treasuring us as something precious and unique. That's the wonderful truth captured in the following words of St Augustine of Hippo (354–430) – a beautiful expression of praise and thanksgiving.

O God, who so cares for every one of us
    as if you cared for each one alone;
    and so for all, as if all were but as one,
    you are the Life of our lives,
    you are constant through all change.
Blessed are all who love you.
Amen.

16 December

Do you struggle to make sense of faith? I do, day after day, and the older I get, the harder it becomes to reconcile Christian convictions with what we see and experience of the world. There are times when I question – many times – belief seeming to fly in the face of facts, yet always I come back to that inner joy, peace, love and hope that, like generations before me, has changed my life. For now we must live with tension between what is and what is yet to come, God's purpose daily being obscured and obstructed. We need to hold on to that conviction, and, like the prophet Habakkuk in the words below (1:2-4a; 2:1), feel able to pour out our confusion, confident that God not only hears and understands but shares our frustration.

O Lord,
    how long must I cry to you for help before you will listen?
How long must I cry, 'Violence!' before you will save?
Why do you let me witness wrongdoing and endure trouble?
Destruction and aggression are all around me;
    conflict and disputes spring up everywhere.
The law is watered down such that justice has no chance of winning through.
I will stand at my sentry post,
    and position myself on the battlements.
I will keep watch to see what he will say to me,
    how he will answer my grievance.

17 December

Few, if any hymns, are as popular as the Revd Henry Lyte's classic 'Abide with me' known by Christians and non-Christians alike. Quite why it resonates with so many people I'm not sure. Partly, no doubt, it's the tune that appeals, which is ironic given that an early publication indicated it was meant to be spoken rather than sung. The words though are equally powerful, speaking not, as some assume, of the end of the day but about the end of life, and the Christian assurance of life after death. Lyte (1793–1847) had good reason to choose this theme for, having suffered poor health throughout his life, he was a desperately sick man as he wrote these words, reportedly having to crawl into the pulpit in order to deliver his final sermon in September 1847, just two months before he died. Physical frailty, however, had not stopped him working tirelessly throughout his ministry; it was Lyte, apparently, who coined the phrase 'It is better to wear out than to rust out'. The words of this hymn have stood the test of time, offering inspiration to generations in times of grief and difficulty.

Abide with me; fast falls the eventide;
the darkness deepens; Lord, with me abide;
when other helpers fail, and comforts flee,
help of the helpless, O abide with me.

Swift to its close ebbs out life's little day.
Earth's joys grow dim; its glories pass away.
Change and decay in all around I see;
O thou, who changest not, abide with me.

I need thy presence every passing hour.
What but thy grace can foil the tempter's power?
Who, like thyself, my guide and stay can be?
Through cloud and sunshine, Lord, abide with me.

I fear no foe, with thee at hand to bless;
ills have no weight, and tears no bitterness.
Where is death's sting? Where, grave, thy victory?
I triumph still, if thou abide with me.

Hold thou thy cross before my closing eyes;
shine through the gloom and point me to the skies.
Heaven's morning breaks, and earth's vain shadows
    flee!
In life, in death, O Lord, abide with me.

18 December

To know and love God better – we can't ask for that often enough, can we? But how to do so, that's the problem. Somehow, saying the same old thing time after time just doesn't feel right. It too easily becomes habit, a going through the motions so familiar to us that it no longer comes from the heart. Fresh words may say nothing different in themselves, but they can speak with a new immediacy, thus helping to express what's innermost in our heart. For me the following prayer does just that. It comes from St Thomas Aquinas (1225–1274), and in a few well-chosen lines it articulates what we ourselves so often struggle to find words for.

Grant me, O Lord my God,
    a mind to know you,
    a heart to seek you,
    wisdom to find you,
    conduct pleasing to you,
    faithful perseverance in waiting for you,
    and a hope of finally embracing you.
Amen.

19 December

Do we come to faith through working things out, only making an act of commitment when we've discovered the answer to every question? No. So is faith about blind belief, accepting as true what we cannot make sense of? Again, the answer is no. The fact is that each is important: faith *and* understanding – we need a bit of both. We'll never be able to reconcile all the objections that can be raised against Christianity, but we must be able to offer genuine reasons for our convictions, and some substance to back them up. The point is made in the following words of St Anselm (1033–1109), taken from the Preface to his *Proslogium*. He asks for greater insight even while recognising his horizons will always be limited, the human mind unable to grasp every truth. Faith needs understanding, but understanding also needs faith.

I acknowledge, Lord, and I give thanks
    that you have created your image in me,
    so that I may remember you,
    think of you,
    love you.
But this image is so obliterated and worn away by
    wickedness,
    it is so obscured by the smoke of sins,
    that it cannot do what it was created to do,
    unless you renew and reform it.
I am not attempting, O Lord,
    to penetrate your loftiness,
    for I cannot begin to match my understanding with it,
    but I desire in some measure to understand your truth,
    which my heart believes and loves.

For I do not seek to understand in order that I may
   believe,
   but I believe in order to understand.
For this too I believe,
   that 'unless I believe, I shall not understand'.
Amen.

20 December

Is it possible to be a Christian in our modern-day world, in light of everything that's been discovered about the history of our universe and workings of our world? Many sceptics suggest not, but interestingly a disproportionately large number of scientists lay claim to a very strong Christian faith. Certainly naive fundamentalism is hard to maintain, but, properly understood, science and religion are by no means mutually exclusive. Indeed, learning more of the natural world and miracle of life can open our eyes all the more to the wonder of God. That's the theme of the following prayer, written by the celebrated German mathematician, astronomer and scientist Johann Kepler (1571–1630), who saw God's hand at work in the order and grandeur of the universe.

O thou who through the light of nature
    hast aroused in us a longing for the light of grace,
    so that we may be raised in the light of thy majesty,
    to thee, I give thanks, Creator and Lord,
    that thou allowest me to rejoice in thy works.
Praise the Lord, ye heavenly harmonies,
    and ye who know the revealed harmonies.
For from him, through him and in him, all is,
    which is perceptible as well as spiritual;
    that which we know and that which we do not
        know,
    for there is still so much to learn.
Amen.

21 December

Today is the winter equinox, the darkest day of the year. Many, though, face darkness of a different kind, life bringing testing that can be hard to bear. What does faith have to say about such moments? Should we expect swift deliverance, a ray of hope swiftly breaking through? I don't think so. Faith nowhere promises us an easy ride, protected from everyday trials and traumas. What it *does* promise is strength to get through these, peace even in the fiercest storm, light shining *in* the darkness. That's an apposite message for this Advent season, and one that lies behind today's prayer, written by Love Maria Willis (1824–1908) and more commonly encountered as a hymn. Taking Psalm 23 as her starting point, she helps us understand that life is not all green pastures and still waters – at least not in the sense of some fanciful idyll.

Father, hear the prayer we offer:
not for ease that prayer shall be,
but for strength, that we may ever
live our lives courageously.

Not for ever in green pastures
do we ask our way to be;
but the steep and rugged pathway
may we tread rejoicingly.

Not for ever by still waters
would we idly rest and stay;
but would smite the living fountains
from the rocks along our way.

Be our strength in hours of weakness,
in our wanderings be our guide;
through endeavour, failure, danger,
Father, be thou at our side.

22 December

If you were to take a poll of all-time favourite Bible readings I'm sure you'd find our words today somewhere in the top ten. They come from the magnificent Psalm 139 (vv. 1, 2, 6-10), and they've spoken powerfully to generations across the centuries, communicating an unforgettable sense of God's constant presence and unfailing love. In these memorable verses we have, on the one hand, exquisite poetry and, on the other, the profoundest of prayers. Use them to acknowledge the awesomeness of God before which we can only kneel in homage and gasp in wonder.

O Lord, you have searched me and known me.
You know when I sit down and when I rise up;
   you discern my thoughts from far away.
Such knowledge is too wonderful for me;
   it is so high that I cannot attain it.
Where can I evade your spirit?
Where can I flee from your presence?
If I soar up to heaven, you are there.
If I make my bed in Sheol, you are there.
If I sail on the wings of the morning
   and settle at the uttermost limits of the sea,
   even there your hand will lead me,
   your right hand holding me firm.
If I say, 'Surely darkness will steal over me,
   night will envelop me',
   darkness is not dark to you;
   the night is as bright as day;
   for you both dark and light are the same.

23 December

We tend to see God in terms of opposites, don't we: light and darkness, good and evil, joy and sorrow, life and death. It's natural enough, for we relish the first but not the second, and on the whole we see God's hand at work in the positives rather than negatives. We're quite right to do so, but we should beware of concluding that certain parts of life are outside of God's reach, as though he is Lord of some aspects rather than the whole. I don't believe for a moment God wills any of our sorrow and suffering, but I *do* believe he is able to take even the bleakest of experiences and work within them. Christmas reminds us that the light shines in the darkness. The gospel proclaims death as the gateway to life. And at the cross we see evil turned to good. As the following prayer of Bishop Lancelot Andrewes (1555–1626) makes clear, nothing we face is outside the scope of God's redeeming love and transforming grace.

O Lord, the day is yours, and the night is yours;
　　you have prepared the light and the sun;
　　　　they continue this day according to your ordinance,
　　for all things serve you.
Blessed are you, O Lord,
　　for you turn the shadow of death into morning,
　　and renew the face of the earth.
Amen.

Christmas Eve

Our prayer today may be short and simple but it takes us to the very heart of the Christmas season with its wonderful message of God's Word taking flesh. Based on the Wisdom of Solomon 18:14, the prayer comes from the Christmas Vespers of the Orthodox liturgy, and it beautifully captures a sense of that night long ago when shepherds first heard the good news and hurried to Bethlehem to see for themselves the newborn King. With them, we today can celebrate the glorious truth that the sovereign God entered our world, sharing our humanity so that we might enter his kingdom and share his eternal life.

While all things were in quiet silence,
    and night was in the midst of her swift course,
    thine Almighty Word, O Lord,
    leaped down out of thy royal throne.
Alleluia!
Amen.

Christmas Day

During the course of this book one name has cropped up more than any other, that of St Augustine of Hippo (354–430); so it seems fitting to turn to him at this great Christian season. His words here focus on a single theme – joy – this being a time for heartfelt celebration at what God has done for us through the gift of his Son. Whoever we are, whatever our situation, we are called to give thanks, for in Christ is the answer to our deepest needs, the one who brings hope, justice, love, life and freedom. Join, then, in these words of old, acknowledging with Augustine the joy not just of Christmas but of life itself.

Let the just rejoice, for their Justifict is born.
Let the sick and infirm rejoice, for their Saviour is
    born.
Let the captives rejoice, for their Redeemer is born.
Let slaves rejoice, for their Master is born.
Let free people rejoice, for their Liberator is born.
Let all Christians rejoice, for Jesus Christ is born.
Amen.

26 December

Christmas Day is over, or at least it is for those of us in the West, but for those in the Eastern Orthodox tradition it is yet to come, the birth of Christ being celebrated on 7 January. There is, I think, a lesson we can draw from that: the fact that the message Christmas proclaims is not tied to a particular place and time but goes on being true for all people in all places, day after day. The following prayer comes fittingly from the Eastern Orthodox Church, and captures a sense of the awesome significance of God sharing our humanity and walking our earth, the Word made flesh. It is not just shepherds and magi that give thanks but all creation, and that poses an all-important question to you and me: in what way have we responded to this most precious of gifts?

What shall we offer thee, O Christ,
    who for our sakes hast appeared on earth as Man?
Every creature made by thee offers thee thanks.
The angels offer thee a hymn;
    the heavens a star;
    the magi, gifts;
    the shepherds, their wonder;
    the earth, its cave;
    the wilderness, the manger:
    and we offer thee a Virgin Mother.
O God from everlasting,
    have mercy upon us.
Amen.

27 December

Our prayer today comes from a classic Christmas carol: 'O little town of Bethlehem', written by the Revd Phillips Brooks (1835–1893) of Philadelphia. He wrote the carol in 1868, after having been on a pilgrimage to the Holy Land, the views of Bethlehem he saw there inspiring his celebrated words. His church organist Lewis Redner (1831–1908) wrote the melody – that this carol was originally sung to – for his Sunday school children's choir. The carol has delighted generations since, every line possessing a special beauty, but for me the final verse speaks most powerfully of all, joyfully responding to God's gift of Christ.

O holy Child of Bethlehem,
descend to us, we pray;
cast out our sin and enter in,
be born in us today.
We hear the Christmas angels
the great glad tidings tell:
O come to us, abide with us,
our Lord Emmanuel.

28 December

Our love of God will always be imperfect and our discipleship constantly flawed. We can live with that most of the time, but occasionally it causes us to lose heart. What's the use of pretending, we ask ourselves? How can God have time for us when we fail and fail again? Such self-knowledge can cause faith to grow cold or it can stir us to greater resolve. Our prayer today – yet another classic from St Augustine of Hippo (354–430) – exemplifies the latter response. He recognises as much as any how far he falls short, but asks that, if only by the tiniest degree, he may grow a little nearer to God. In other words, rather than dwelling on our faults or setting impossible goals, we should focus on God's grace and all he continues to do.

Dear God, I seek to know you,
   to love you,
   to rejoice in you.
If I cannot do these perfectly,
   may I at least advance to higher degrees each day
   until I come more nearly to approach perfection.
God of truth, may my knowledge of you increase;
   may my love of you grow every day more and more;
   may my joy in you become full.
Amen.

29 December

The prayer I've chosen for today comes from the writings of the Danish theologian and philosopher Søren Kierkegaard (1813–1855). It concerns inner peace or tranquillity of spirit, the secret of which lies in a trusting relationship with God. Knowing this in theory is one thing; putting it into practice quite another. As Kierkegaard recognises, we need God's help each day in letting go of our fears and putting ourselves in his hands. 'O God, teach me to breathe deeply in faith', he once wrote, and that simple prayer is fleshed out more fully in the following.

O Lord,
    calm the waves of this heart;
    calm its tempests.
Calm thyself, O my soul,
    so that God is able to repose in thee,
    so that his peace may cover thee.
Yes, Father in heaven,
    often have we found that the world cannot give us
      peace,
    O but make us feel that thou art able to give peace;
    let us know the truth of thy promises:
    that the whole world may not be able to take away
      thy peace.
Amen.

30 December

This is a strange season, isn't it? On one hand, it's full of promise as another year beckons; on the other, it brings regrets as we look back on missed targets, un-realised hopes and wasted opportunities over the past twelve months. Alongside pleasure there is pain, and as well as delight, disappointment. The older we get, the more we realise how important it is to make the most of life, but the more we realise also how illusory are many of the dreams and goals we set ourselves. We begin to glimpse that true fulfilment lies in something deeper, and that's the message of today's prayer, taken from Psalm 90:1-4, 10, 12. It calls us to think in terms of God's timing rather than our own, and to seek his kingdom, so that we will make the most of life not just now but always.

Lord, you have been our home across the centuries.
Before the mountains were formed
    and before you fashioned this world we live in,
    from eternity to eternity you are God.
You return us to dust, saying,
    'Back to what you once were, you mortals!'
A thousand years are like a passing day in your sight,
    as short-lived as the night-watch.
Our fleeting span is seventy years,
    perhaps eighty if we are strong;
    throughout they are filled with struggle and sorrow,
    here today and gone tomorrow.
Teach us to make the most of our days
    and so to discover the secret of inner wisdom.

31 December

Another year is drawing to a close, and if you're anything like me you'll be finding that hard to believe. Where has all the time gone, we ask ourselves? It's a good question, but a better one is posed by lines found above an old clock in Chester Cathedral. It asks effectively what we do with the time we're given, however fast it seems to go.

When as a child I laughed and wept,
    time crept.
When as a youth I waxed more bold,
    time *strolled*.
When I became a full-grown man,
    time RAN.
When older still I daily grew,
    time FLEW.
Soon I shall find, in passing on,
    time GONE.
O Christ! wilt thou have saved me then?
Amen.

SEASONAL
SUPPLEMENT

Mother's Day

Few relationships are more intense than that between a mother and her newborn child. On the one hand there is passionate and protective love; on the other, total dependence. And though gradually the child learns to stand on its own two feet as it grows towards maturity, something of that special bond usually continues for life. The image is beautifully picked up on in Psalm 131, where the opening two verses offer a perfect prayer for Mother's Day. For all our modern-day sophistication, they remind us, we are still finally dependent on God, he the one who brings us life and nurtures and sustains it. Join, then, in this unforgettable expression of trust in the God who is not only our Father but also our Mother.

Lord, my heart does not get above itself
    nor do I lift my eyes higher than I can hope to see.
I do not dwell on matters beyond my comprehension,
    too wonderful for me to fathom.
No, I see myself instead as a weaned child,
    as one whose mother has set my soul at rest.
That's what my soul's like:
    a child gently soothed by a mother's love.

Shrove Tuesday

One of the great Lenten prayers is that of St Ephrem of Syria (c. 306–373), used regularly within both the Catholic and Orthodox liturgies throughout this season. Indeed, the faithful are urged to recite it when they first awake, at midday, and last thing at night. You may not want to go that far, but Ephrem's words provide an ideal way to prepare for our celebration of Lent.

Lord Jesus Christ, King of kings,
  you have power over life and death.
You know what is secret and hidden,
  and neither our thoughts nor our feelings
    are concealed from you.
Cure me of duplicity; I have done evil before you.
Now my life declines from day to day and my sins
  increase.
O Lord, God of souls and bodies,
  you know the extreme frailty of my soul
    and my flesh.
Grant me strength in my weakness, O Lord,
  and sustain me in my misery.
Give me a grateful soul
  that I may never cease to recall your benefits,
  O Lord most bountiful.
Be not mindful of my many sins,
  but forgive me all my misdeeds.
O Lord, disdain not my prayer –
  the prayer of a wretched sinner;
  sustain me with your grace until the end,
  that it may protect me as in the past.
It is your grace which has taught me wisdom;
  blessed are they who follow her ways,

for they shall receive the crown of glory.
In spite of my unworthiness,
   I praise you and I glorify you, O Lord,
   for your mercy to me is without limit.
You have been my help and my protection.
May the name of your majesty be praised for ever.
To you, our God, be glory.
Amen.

Ash Wednesday

Repenting through wearing sackcloth and ashes isn't the done thing nowadays, but in medieval times it was a common and very public way of showing remorse for wrongdoing. Derived from an ancient Hebrew practice, it demonstrated not only contrition but also a desire to make amends, turning away from one's faults and starting again. That, of course, is precisely what Ash Wednesday is all about. It calls us to examine ourselves, honestly and openly facing up to our mistakes and seeking pardon and renewal. And today's words, taken from the *Book of Common Prayer*, help us do just that, acknowledging our weakness and seeking renewal through God's grace. Use them to consecrate this season of Lent and all of life to his service.

Almighty and everlasting God,
    you hate nothing that you have made
    and forgive the sins of all who are penitent:
    create and make in us new and contrite hearts
    that we, worthily lamenting our sins
    and acknowledging our wickedness,
    may receive from you, the God of all mercy,
    perfect remission and forgiveness;
    through Jesus Christ our Lord.
Amen.

Passion Sunday

What can we offer to Christ in response to his sacrifice on the cross and gift of eternal life? We can give him our commitment and service, but whatever we bring will never be enough to express our gratitude let alone repay his love. Finally we must simply kneel in wonder, giving glory to him for the sheer magnitude of his grace. Today's prayer, another from St Ephrem of Syria (c. 306–373), does just that, responding in awed worship to the suffering servant and risen Saviour, our Lord Jesus Christ.

I give you glory, O Christ,
    because you, the only-begotten, the Lord of all,
      underwent the death of the Cross to free my sinful
        soul from the bonds of sin.
What shall I give to you, O Lord,
    in return for all this kindness?
Glory to you, O Lord, for your love,
    for your mercy,
    for your patience.
Glory to you, for forgiving us all our sins,
    for coming to save our souls,
    for your incarnation in the Virgin's womb.
Glory to you, for your bonds,
    for receiving the cut of the lash,
    for accepting mockery.
Glory to you, for your crucifixion,
    for your burial,
    for your resurrection.
Glory to you, for your exaltation,
    for being preached to men,
    for being taken up to heaven.

Glory to you who sit at the Father's right hand
and will return in glory.
Glory to you for willing that the sinner be saved
through your great mercy and compassion.
Amen.

Palm Sunday

What does it mean to acknowledge Christ as King? It's not enough just to say the words or to offer our Sunday worship. After all, many on that first Palm Sunday acclaimed Jesus with open arms, only for their professions of faith to evaporate when put to the test. Genuine homage to Christ means offering him our allegiance, accepting his authority in our life and serving where he wills. The hymn-writer George Herbert (1593–1633) memorably captures that truth in today's prayer, reminding us that commitment involves not just part of life but all: seven-days-a-week discipleship.

King of glory, King of peace,
I will love thee;
and, that love may never cease,
I will move thee.
Thou hast granted my appeal,
thou hast heard me;
thou didst note my ardent zeal,
thou hast spared me.

Wherefore with my utmost art,
I will sing thee,
and the cream of all my heart
I will bring thee.
Though my sins against me cried,
thou didst clear me,
and alone, when they replied,
thou didst hear me.

Seven whole days, not one in seven,
I will praise thee;
in my heart, though not in heaven,
I can raise thee.

Small it is, in this poor sort
to enrol thee:
e'en eternity's too short
to extol thee.

Monday of Holy Week

The cross is the key symbol of the Christian faith, but it's something we can occasionally romanticise, forgetting the awful suffering it represents. Some even wear a crucifix as an ornament these days, but there was nothing ornamental about what Jesus went through as he writhed in agony, the life ebbing from his broken body. We need to remember the costliness of the sacrifice, both to appreciate what God has done for us and to understand how he is able to work even in the most appalling evil and suffering. Today's prayer, one of 15 written for Holy Week by St Bridget (*c.* 450–525) – known to some as 'Mary of the Irish' – graphically recalls Christ's sacrifice and asks for help in making a fitting response to such awesome love.

O Jesus!
I remember the multitude of wounds
    which afflicted you from head to foot,
       torn and reddened by the spilling of your precious
          blood.
O great and universal pain which you suffered in your
    flesh for love of us!
What is there you could have done for us which you
    have not done?
May the fruit of your sufferings be renewed in my soul
    by the faithful remembrance of your passion
    and may your love increase in my heart each day
    until I see you in eternity,
       you who are the treasury of every real good and joy,
       which I beg you to grant me in heaven.
Amen.

Tuesday of Holy Week

Sorting through prayers suitable for Holy Week, the following caught my eye. It's a short Gaelic prayer, hailing from Ireland, and in a few words it succeeds in relating the passion of Christ to life today in a highly practical way. So often we open our mouths without thinking, sometimes with far-reaching consequences. We need God's help sometimes to curb our tongue.

O Jesus, Son of God,
   who was silent before Pilate,
   do not let us wag our tongues
   without thinking of what we are to say
   and how to say it.
Amen.

Wednesday of Holy Week

This season speaks of many things, not least the humility of Christ. Betrayed with a kiss, he refused to seek revenge; falsely accused, he offered no defence; set upon and insulted, he made no protest; flogged and nailed to a cross, he prayed for his persecutors. Pursuing an agenda so very different from that of the world, he put others first and self second, meeting hatred with love and evil with good. Try as we might, such selflessness is beyond us. Like St Gregory the Great (c. 540–604) in the following prayer, we can only acclaim the one who in death, as in life, reveals the Way, the Truth and the Life.

O Lord,
  you received affronts without number from your
    blasphemers,
  yet each day you free captive souls from the grip
    of the ancient enemy.
You did not avert your face from the spittle of perfidy,
  yet you wash souls in saving waters.
You accepted your scourging without murmur,
  yet through your mediation you deliver us from
    endless chastisements.
You endured ill-treatment of all kinds,
  yet you want to give us a share in the choirs of
    angels in glory everlasting.
You did not refuse to be crowned with thorns,
  yet you save us from the wounds of sin.
In your thirst you accepted the bitterness of gall,
  yet you prepare yourself to fill us with eternal
    delights.
You kept silent under the derisive homage
  rendered you by your executioners,

yet you petition the Father for us although you are
    his equal in divinity.
You came to taste death,
    yet you were the Life and had come to bring it to
      the dead.
Amen.

Maundy Thursday

In its way Maundy Thursday is as astonishing as any day in the Christian calendar, for it speaks of truly breathtaking grace. At its heart, of course, is the Last Supper, that final meal shared by Jesus with his disciples; but to appreciate what that means we have to remind ourselves of the context in which it took place. This was no occasion for the perfect, holy or faithful – reserved for pillars of Christian commitment, the like of which we can never hope to emulate – it was for frail flawed believers, those who understood just a fraction of what it meant and whose commitment would waver and crumble when put to the test. That's who Jesus died for: people like you and me – undeserving yet offered all. We know well enough that we are just as likely to abandon, deny or even betray Jesus as those first disciples. Our only hope of staying true to Christ, as Padre Pio (St Pio of Pietrelcina, 1887–1968) observes in the following prayer, is for *him* to stay close to us.

Stay with me, Lord,
    for it is necessary to have you present so that I
        do not forget you.
You know how easily I abandon you.
Stay with me, Lord,
    because I am weak and I need your strength,
    that I may not fall so often.
Stay with me, Lord,
    for you are my life and without you I am without
        fervour.
Stay with me, Lord,
    for you are my light and without you
        I am in darkness.

Stay with me, Lord, to show me your will.

Stay with me, Lord, so that I hear your voice and
follow you.

Stay with me, Lord,
for I desire to love you very much and always to be
in your company.

Stay with me, Lord, if you wish me to be faithful to
you.

Stay with me, Lord,
as poor as my soul is I want it to be a place of
consolation for you,
a nest of Love.

Stay with me, Jesus,
for it is getting late and the day is coming to a close
and life passes,
death, judgement and eternity approaches.

It is necessary to renew my strength,
so that I will not stop along the way and for that,
I need you.

It is getting late and death approaches,
I fear the darkness, the temptations, the dryness,
the cross, the sorrows.

O how I need you, my Jesus, in this night of exile!

Stay with me tonight, Jesus,
in life with all its dangers, I need you.

Let me recognise you as your disciples
did at the breaking of the bread,
so that the Eucharist be the Light which disperses
the darkness,
the force which sustains me, the unique joy
of my heart.

Stay with me, Lord, because at the hour of my death,
I want to remain united to you,
if not by Communion, at least by grace and love.

Stay with me, Lord, for it is you alone I look for,
  your Love, your Grace, your Will, your Heart,
    your Spirit,
  because I love you and ask no other reward but to
    love you more and more.
With a firm love, I will love you with all my heart
  while on earth
  and continue to love you perfectly during all
    eternity.
Amen.

Good Friday

'Do something amazing', ran the poster: 'give blood'. It's a good line that has done much to recruit blood donors, but, if we're honest, giving blood doesn't really involve much at all – a moment's discomfort at worse. Good Friday reminds us of something *truly* amazing: the one who gave his blood for us all. The imagery can seem stark, even shocking, but that's what Jesus did on the cross. His body was broken, his blood shed to make us whole, offered freely out of love. Today's prayer, written by St Catherine of Siena (1347–1380), takes that awesome truth as its starting point.

Precious Blood,
ocean of divine mercy:
flow upon us!

Precious Blood,
most pure offering:
procure us every grace!

Precious Blood,
hope and refuge of sinners:
atone for us!

Precious Blood,
delight of holy souls:
draw us!

Amen.

Easter Eve

To me, Easter Eve has the feel of a poor relation. On one side stands Good Friday with its powerful remembrance of the suffering and death of Christ. On the other is Easter, marked by its jubilant celebration of his resurrection, and corresponding triumph over hatred and evil. What does Easter Eve have to commend itself in comparison? It seems to be caught in limbo, almost as though it's a dead time between two momentous events. Yet that is precisely the point, this day is all about a dead time literally after Jesus was laid in the tomb. There was no pretence in that, no sleight of hand: he had *really* died – been cut down lifeless from the cross and a spear thrust into his side to ensure the job was done. As Jesus himself declared, 'It is finished!' Today calls us, then, to face up to our shared mortality, but it speaks also of looking forward in the confidence that death is not the end. The following prayer of Elizabeth Ann Seton (1774–1821) reminds us that though this life will be over sooner than we'd like, *true* life endures for ever.

Lord Jesus,
> who was born for us in a stable,
> lived for us a life of pain and sorrow,
> and died for us upon a cross;
> say for us in the hour of death,
> 'Father, forgive,'
> and to your Mother,
> 'Behold your child.'
Say to us,
> 'This day you shall be with me in paradise.'

Dear Saviour, leave us not,
    forsake us not.
We thirst for you, fountain of living water.
Our days pass quickly along,
    soon all will be consummated for us.
To your hands we commend our spirits,
    now and for ever.
Amen.

Easter Sunday

Take away today from the Christian calendar and we have no faith, no gospel, no hope; this life is all we've got – to be lived out in a world where the innocent suffer, injustice flourishes and evil goes unpunished. But this is a day that changes everything, standing such an assessment on its head, since good conquered evil, love overcame hatred, and life vanquished death. The grave became an empty tomb, the crucified Christ the risen Saviour – a life-giving message celebrated by the Church across the centuries. Join, then, with Gregory of Nazianzus (c. 330–389) in acknowledging what God has done in Christ, and rejoice in the wonder of this day.

Today we rejoice in the salvation of the world.
Christ is risen;
    let us arise in him!
Christ enters new life;
    let us live in him!
Christ has come forth from the tomb;
    let us shake off the fetters of evil!
The gates of hell are open,
    the powers of evil are overcome!
In Christ a new creation is coming to birth.
Alleluia!
Lord, make us new.
Alleluia!

Easter Monday

Few contrasts are as great as that between the lives of the Apostles before and after the resurrection. One moment they were scared, confused, sorrowful and broken, but the next they were overwhelmed with joy, certain of their calling, filled with power from on high. In short, they were Easter people, the context of life having changed for ever. Is that true of us? It should be. Yes, we will still wrestle with life's traumas and tragedies. Yes, like anyone else we will continue to experience our fair share of hurt and heartache. But though these may overshadow the light, they will not extinguish it, for, as words of the Victorian clergyman and hymn-writer William Bright (1824–1901) remind us, we can look beyond the clouds to where the sun still shines, to where the *Son* reigns for ever, giving life to all.

Most loving Father,
    preserve us from faithless fears and worldly
        anxieties
    and grant that no clouds of this mortal life
        may hide from us the light of that love
        which is immortal
    and which you have manifested unto us
        in your Son,
    Jesus Christ our Lord.
Amen.

Easter Tuesday

For our prayer today I've chosen what for me is a truly great Easter hymn. It was written by Baptist minister Edmond Budry (1875–1932) who, after training at Regent's Park College, served in Vevey, Switzerland, and Kingston upon Thames among his various pastorates and also spent three years as a professor at the Western Theological Seminary in the United States. His words here, written for the YMCA – of which Budry was a committed supporter – celebrate the wonder of Christ's resurrection and our own faith in life to come.

Thine be the glory, risen, conquering Son;
endless is the victory, thou o'er death hast won;
angels in bright raiment rolled the stone away,
kept the folded grave-clothes where thy body lay.
Thine be the glory, risen conquering Son,
endless is the victory, thou o'er death hast won.

No more we doubt thee, glorious Prince of life;
life is naught without thee; aid us in our strife;
make us more than conquerors, through thy deathless
    love:
bring us safe through Jordan to thy home above.
Thine be the glory, risen conquering Son,
endless is the victory, thou o'er death hast won.

Easter Wednesday

Resurrection is not just about life to come, it's also about life now and the new beginnings God makes possible in Christ. For St Gregory the Great (c. 540–604) one new beginning stands out in particular in this prayer, for it goes on being enacted day after day in countless human lives. He's referring, of course, to the forgiveness God daily offers, cleansing us from our sins and helping us to make a fresh start, his love never exhausted, his mercy without end. Celebrate again then the awesome truth that, through God's grace, you can put the past behind you, today truly being the first day of the rest of your life.

It is only right, with all the powers of our heart and
    mind,
        to praise you Father and your only-begotten Son,
        our Lord Jesus Christ.
Dear Father, by your wondrous condescension
    of loving-kindness toward us, your servants,
    you gave up your Son.
Dear Jesus, you paid the debt of Adam for us
    to the eternal Father
    by your blood poured forth in loving-kindness.
You cleared away the darkness of sin by your
    magnificent and radiant resurrection.
You broke the bonds of death and rose from the grave
    as a conqueror.
You reconciled heaven and earth.
Our life had no hope of eternal happiness before you
    redeemed us.
Your resurrection has washed away our sins,
    restored our innocence and brought us joy.

How inestimable is the tenderness of your love!
We pray you, Lord,
    to preserve your servants in the peaceful enjoyment
        of this Easter happiness.
We ask this through Jesus Christ our Lord,
    who lives and reigns with God the Father,
    in the unity of the Holy Spirit,
        for ever and ever.
Amen.

Easter Thursday

Easter reminds us that our faith finally is in things unseen. While it touches life now, bringing joy and hope to each day, it rests in the future God has in store, the riches of his eternal kingdom. What form that will take or how and when it will come about is beyond us, for it transcends human intellect and experience; but if we cannot grasp the whole we can at least understand a little, glimpsing in part now what we will one day see in full. That's the theme of today's prayer, dating back to the third-century theologian Origen of Alexandria. Join with him in seeking greater insight into the things of God.

May the Lord Jesus place his hands on our eyes
  that we may begin to catch sight of the things
    that are not seen
  more than the things that are seen.
May he open our eyes
  that they will alight on the things to come
  more than on the things of this age.
May he unveil the vision of our heart
  that it may contemplate God in spirit.
We ask this through our Lord Jesus Christ
  to whom belongs glory and power for ever.
Amen.

Easter Friday

We tend to associate carols with Christmas but in fact
many have also been written for Easter, including the
words I've chosen for today's prayer. They come from a
classic German carol from the seventeenth century titled
Hilariter – a term I've paraphrased as 'with laughing
cheer' – and they beautifully capture the joy of this
season, a joy seen as pervading the whole world, all
creation joining in glad thanksgiving. Add your voice
to that chorus of praise.

The whole bright world rejoices now,
with laughing cheer, with laughing cheer;
the birds do sing on every bough –
Alleluia! Alleluia!

Then shout beneath the racing skies,
with laughing cheer, with laughing cheer,
to him who rose that we might rise –
Alleluia! Alleluia!

And all you living things make praise,
with laughing cheer, with laughing cheer;
he guideth you in all your ways –
Alleluia! Alleluia!

God – Father, Son, and Holy Ghost –
with laughing cheer, with laughing cheer,
are God most high, our joy and boast –
Alleluia! Alleluia!

Easter Saturday

'What will heaven be like?' I've often been asked. And I've never been able to give a satisfactory answer. It stands to reason that I'm flummoxed, for however hard anyone tries they will never be able to sum up the nature of God's kingdom, nor indeed get anywhere near it. Could we do so, then heaven would literally be brought down to earth, tied to our limited human horizons rather than truly of God. What his future holds will always be a mystery, but it's one full of promise, filling us with hope and anticipation. The following prayer of John Donne (1572–1631) succeeds more than any I've come across in capturing at least a sense of the joys God holds in store, emphasising their otherness from human logic and understanding.

Bring us, O Lord God,
    at our last awakening
    into the house and gate of heaven;
    to enter into that gate and dwell in that house,
    where there shall be no darkness nor dazzling,
    but one equal light;
    no noise nor silence,
    but one equal music;
    no fears nor hopes,
    but one equal possession;
    no ends nor beginning,
    but one equal eternity;
    in the habitations of thy glory and dominion,
    world without end.
Amen.

The Sunday after Easter

The Sunday after Easter is often referred to as Low Sunday, and that somehow seems fitting, for after the spiritual crescendo starting with Lent and running through Holy Week up to Easter Sunday, it can all feel like a bit of an anticlimax in the days afterwards, bringing us back down to earth with a bump. Understandable such a feeling may be, but it's entirely wrong, for, as the Christian calendar reminds us, the truth of Easter goes on being applicable day after day after day. The following prayer, taken from the Liturgy of the Hours, brings home the simple message that what we celebrate at Easter should always be evident in who and what we are.

Ever-living God,
    help us to celebrate our joy in the resurrection
        of the Lord
    and to express in our lives the love we celebrate.
Grant this through our Lord Jesus Christ, your Son,
    who lives and reigns with you and the Holy Spirit,
    one God, for ever and ever.
Amen.

Ascension Day

Very little is known of the author of today's prayer. It's attributed to St Melito (d. *c.* 180), who was probably Bishop of Sardis in Turkey during the second century and, according to some, died as a martyr. What we do know of him is that his numerous writings were enormously influential for many years, continuing to be widely respected well into the Middle Ages. From his words here we can well understand why, for as well as an ascription of glory they offer a succinct declaration of faith in Christ, the one who, as the ascended Lord, is all in all.

Born as a son,
    led forth as a lamb,
    sacrificed as a sheep,
    buried as a man,
    he rose from the dead as a God,
    for he was by nature God and man.

He is all things:
    he judges, and so he is Law;
    he teaches, and so he is Wisdom;
    he saves, and so he is Grace;
    he begets, and so he is Father;
    he is begotten, and so he is Son;
    he suffers, and so he is Sacrifice;
    he is buried, and so he is man;
    he rises again, and so he is God.
This is Jesus Christ,
    to whom belongs glory for all ages.
Amen.

Pentecost

Today's prayer, celebrating gifts of the Holy Spirit, comes from St Bonaventura (1217–1274). Born Giovanni di Fidanza in Italy, he became a Franciscan monk in 1244, going on to become Minister General of the Order before being made a Cardinal in 1273. Hugely respected at the time for his contributions to theology, his spiritual writing was to give inspiration over many years, prayers such as the following still used today. It's easy to understand why, for his words are not only supremely applicable to Pentecost but speak also of God's life-changing power, able to transform your life and mine, now and always.

Lord Jesus,
    as God's Spirit came down and rested upon you,
      may the same Spirit rest upon us, bestowing his
        sevenfold gifts.
First, grant us the gift of understanding,
    by which your precepts may enlighten our minds.
Second, grant us counsel,
    by which we may follow in your footsteps
      on the path of righteousness.
Third, grant us courage, by which we may ward off
    the Enemy's attacks.
Fourth, grant us knowledge, by which we can
    distinguish good from evil.
Fifth, grant us piety, by which we may acquire
    compassionate hearts.
Sixth, grant us fear, by which we may draw back
    from evil and submit to what is good.
Seventh, grant us wisdom,
    that we may taste fully the life-giving sweetness
      of your love.
Amen.

Trinity Sunday

Today's prayer comes from the Revd Reginald Heber (1783–1826), his wonderful words, based on Revelation 4:8-11, having been sung in countless churches across the years. His great hymn was a favourite of Alfred Lord Tennyson, being sung at the Poet Laureate's funeral. A brilliant scholar during his time at Oxford, Heber went on to become Bishop of Calcutta in 1823, having twice previously declined the post. The Indian climate, coupled with the massive distances Heber had to cover in fulfilment of his duties, took their toll on the bishop's health and he died of a stroke after just three years in post.

Holy, holy, holy! Lord God almighty!
Early in the morning our song shall rise to thee.
Holy, holy, holy! Merciful and mighty!
God in three persons, blessèd Trinity!

Holy, holy, holy! Though the darkness hide thee,
though the eye of sinful man thy glory may not see,
only thou art holy, there is none beside thee,
perfect in power, in love, and purity.

Holy, holy, holy! Lord God almighty!
All thy works shall praise thy name,
    in earth, and sky, and sea.
Holy, holy, holy! Merciful and mighty!
God in three persons, blessèd Trinity.

Father's Day

There are so many prayers referring to God as Father that I could have included one for every day of the year twice over and still not have exhausted them. That's hardly surprising, given that the Bible uses the same terminology, just as Jesus did in the prayer he taught his disciples. The designation reminds us that God is not remote in heaven but values us as his children, caring passionately about our welfare and, when we go astray, waiting like the father of the prodigal son to welcome us home. Something of that wonderful truth comes across in words of the hymn-writer and eminent London architect James Edmeston (1791–1867) – the first verse of one of the two thousand hymns he wrote during his lifetime! They speak of the guidance, protection, provision and blessing God delights to show, if only we will trust in his fatherly love.

Lead us, heavenly Father, lead us
o'er the world's tempestuous sea;
guard us, guide us, keep us, feed us,
for we have no help but thee;
yet possessing every blessing
if our God our Father be.

29 February

Many prayers in this book have recognised the impossibility of ever giving God the worship he deserves, language simply not being up to the job. I'm quite sure that Pierre Teilhard de Chardin (1881–1955), the author of today's prayer (taken from his 1978 book *The Heart of Matter*), would have fully agreed with that, but it didn't stop him from doing his best nonetheless to describe God's greatness. Partly that's because he understood we glimpse this a little more fully in Christ, the God beyond having taken on human flesh to make known his love and purpose to all. Partly also it's because he couldn't contain the gratitude welling up within him, worship seeming the only natural response. So, in a string of pronouncements piled on top of each other, he gives us a truly memorable acknowledgement of God in all his majesty.

Glorious Lord Christ:
    the divine influence secretly diffused
    and active in the depths of matter,
    and the dazzling centre where all the innumerable
       fibres of the manifold meet;
    power as implacable as the world, as warm as life;
    you whose forehead is of the whiteness of snow,
    whose eyes are of fire,
    and whose feet are brighter than molten gold;
    you whose hands imprison the stars;
    you who are the first and the last,
    the living and the dead and the risen again . . .
    it is you to whom my being cries out with a desire
       as vast as the universe:
    'In truth you are my Lord and my God.'

Index of authors/sources

Index of biblical sources

Acknowledgements

The publishers wish to thank all those who have given their permission to reproduce copyright material in this publication.

1. 10 January: Evelyn Underhill, *Meditations and Prayers* (Longman, Green & Co, 1994).
   Also at 14 February, 28 March, 25 May, 22 July, 16 September, 1 October, 1 November

2. 15 January: Thomas Curtis Clark, *Where Restless Crowds Are Thronging*, © Hymn Society in America/Hope Publishing Company. Administered by CopyCare Ltd, PO Box 77, Hailsham, East Sussex, BN27 3EF, UK. music@copycare.com

3. 29 January: Thomas O. Chisholm, *Great Is Thy Faithfulness*, © 1923, renewal 1951, Hope Publishing Company. Administered by CopyCare Ltd, PO Box 77, Hailsham, East Sussex, BN27 3EF, UK. music@copycare.com

4. 5 April: The Grail Society, © The Grail (England) Ltd, The Grail Centre, 115 Waxwell Lane, Pinner, Middlesex, HA5 3ER, UK

5. 13 April and 29 February (page 471): © Teilhard de Chardin: *The Heart of the Matter*. Translated by René Hague and published by Collins, London, 1978

6. 6 May: © Hymns Ancient and Modern Ltd, St Mary's Works, St Mary's Plain, Norwich, NR3 3BH

7. 10 September and 16 October: © Rabindranath Tagore

8. Easter Tuesday (page 460): Edmond Louis Budry. Translated by Richard B. Hoyle (1875-1939) Copyright control

Every effort has been made to trace the owners of copyright material and we hope that no copyright has been infringed. If the contrary be the case a correction will be made in any reprint of this book.